A guide to the South Downs Way

official South Downs Way

------- unofficial routes

WINCHESTER

A 31

A 272

Petersfield

Petworth

A 283

HAMPSHIRE

A 3

Rowlands
Castle

A 286

A 285

ARUN

Chichester

Arundel

A 27

0   5   10
|--|--|--|--|--|--|--|--|--|--| miles
|----|----|----|
8   16 km

E N G L I S H

A guide to

the South Downs Way

Miles Jebb

Constable London

First published in Great Britain 1984
by Constable and Company Limited
10 Orange Street London WC2H 7EG
Copyright © 1984 by Miles Jebb
ISBN 0 09 464620 1
Set in Times New Roman 9pt
by Inforum Ltd Portsmouth
Printed in Great Britain by
The Pitman Press Bath

British Library CIP data

Jebb, Miles
A guide to the South Downs Way
1. South Downs Way (England) – Guide-books
I. Title
914.22′6   DA670.S98

The Weald is good, the Downs are best –
I'll give you the run of 'em, East to West.
Beachy Head and Winddoor Hill,
They were once and they are still.
Firle, Mount Caburn and Mount Harry
Go back as far as sums'll carry.
Ditchling Beacon and Chanctonbury Ring,
They have looked on many a thing;
And what those two have missed between 'em
I reckon Truleigh Hill has seen 'em.
Highden, Bignor and Duncton Down
Knew Old England before the Crown.
Linch Down, Treyford and Sunwood
Knew Old England before the flood.
And when you end on the Hampshire side –
Butser's old as Time and Tide
        The Downs are sheep, the Weald is corn,
        You be glad you are Sussex born!

Rudyard Kipling
'The Run of the Downs'

Acknowledgements

The lines from *The Definitive Version of Rudyard Kipling's Verse* on pages 5, 25 and 42 are reprinted by permission of the National Trust and Macmillan London Ltd; the extract from Edmund Blunden's *Poems 1914 to 1930* on page 109 is reprinted by permission of A.D. Peters & Co; the lines taken from Vita Sackville-West's *The Land* on page 53 are reprinted by permission of William Heinemann Ltd; and the extracts from Hilaire Belloc's *Complete Verse* on pages 131 and 148 are reprinted by permission of Gerald Duckworth & Co.

Contents

(The official South Downs Way is from a point in Stage 1
to a point in Stage 11, plus Stage 15)

Illustrations

All the photographs were taken by the author. **The maps** were drawn by Patrick Leeson and Brian Herrick, and appear between pages 296 and 317.

Introduction

The Weald is good, the Downs are best

The South Downs provide a prime example of the truth that in
scenery and landscape, as indeed in life and art, size is less important
than scale, and monotony less effective than variety. Their puny
dimensions may seem ridiculous to those who know the Scottish
Highlands or the hills of Wales (let alone the grandeurs of Europe),
but the fact is that their perspectives can be just as impressive and
their beauty just as moving. Where they really do differ from those
larger geological features is that they are covered with a man-made
clothing and not in a state of nature. For the most part enclosed,
ploughed and planted, we only see them in their pastoral purity in
certain places, especially along their straight northern ridge. But this
difference by no means implies that the South Downs are less
attractive now than before the advent of man; for when they were
covered with woods and scrub they would have been far less
discernible. It is their bare slopes and contours that affect us most, a
shaving process of centuries of sheep and plough. Besides, the
record of humanity on these downs is to modern eyes an
enhancement of their beauty. The clumps of beeches, the burial
mounds, the hill-forts, the cross-dykes, the chalk figures, these mute
testimonies of mankind appear almost as part of the natural scene.

The South Downs' most distinctive feature is their curvaceous
shape: only where the sea encroaches are they precipitous. In the
deep subconscious of man there lurks a dreamworld associated with
mountains and hills, and none have more feminine charms than the
South Downs. We refer to the feet, breasts, shoulders, necks, noses,
faces and brows of hills because they are suggestive of the human
figure; and these ones give an extraordinary impression, as W.H.
Hudson put it, of the 'solemn slope of mighty limbs asleep'. This
flowing gentleness is very appealing to those who live and work in
harsh blocks of brick or concrete and move around in urban
canyons.

Fortunately, this frightening modern world has left the South

Downs relatively unscathed. They were not needed by industrialists and were ignored by those who flocked to the seaside: although scarred, they were not raped. So in many ways we see them as they were in the pre-industrial age, and in particular at their feet we find the well-conserved villages where for over a thousand years agriculture was practised by societies that did not have the ability to alter their environment as drastically as do we: such attractive old flint cottages, such wonderful Norman church architecture, such picturesque pubs, such lovely gardens, and such large country houses stocked with works of art – all these add to the charms of the South Downs. There are well over fifty churches on, or within two miles of, my route, at least one in each stage. Each church dedication speaks of a continuing worship; and each place-name tells a story. Even the word 'downs' reminds us of the Celtic era of rule, since *dun* is a Celtic word meaning hill or fort: as for the 'weald', it is Old English for wood or forest, and it was the Anglo-Saxon settlers who notably hacked away at it.

The downs are best: but they are under constant threat. The pressures of the late twentieth century in southern England are such that their designation as an Area of Outstanding Natural Beauty, though it has preserved them from gross housing development, is not enough to prevent more insidious encroachments. Already we have to accept that for nearly half a century mechanized agriculture has torn up most of the age-old sheep pasture in an uncontrolled and sometimes shameful manner (a process that would have been mitigated had the South Downs been designated as a National Park). Today, while it is true that arable is preferable to unchecked scrub reversion, there are still some farmers who clear scrub or hedges indiscriminately. Highways have cut great swathes, the Brighton-bypass proposal being the latest threat. Forms of leisure activity compete intensely for small areas of space – car-parks, golf-courses, riding schools, hang-gliding, dry ski-runs, model aircraft, clay-pigeon shooting, and scrambling. A new spectre has now appeared: the threat of oil exploitation. Exploratory drilling has already started at Horndean and Graffham, and application has been made for it at Ditchling. Those who care for the downs and for their walks and rides should join the Society of Sussex Downsmen

and the Ramblers' Association in their constant battles on our
behalf, or help press for action by the appropriate authorities.

No one, however intelligent, who goes and inspects the South
Downs by car can really experience them. And no one, however
energetic, who simply walks over them can by that action
understand them. For full appreciation it is necessary to walk or ride
long distances and also to read long sentences. Whatever your
personal interests, you need to learn a bit about geology, history,
architecture, botany, etc; and it is best to do so in conjunction with a
walk. For this reason I have incorporated aspects of all these
subjects into my descriptions rather than attempting to summarise
them in this introduction, and I hope that each stage will provide its
own distinctive experience and offer by example some aspects of the
downland which apply generally. Just one geographical point that I
should make here is that the South Downs, like Gaul, fall into three
basic parts. From the east as far as the Arun they are a narrow range
sloping to the coast, largely bare of trees and predominantly arable,
with much exposed chalk. In the central part they are broader and
support large plantations and natural woods, with thicker topsoil
and areas of clay: a plain separates them from the coast. From
Butser Hill westwards they are again mostly bare, but with rather
more pasture and less arable than in the east, fanned out and
without a pronounced ridge. (The effect of these variations on the
main route is that in Stages 1–7 you are confined mainly by fences,
in Stages 8–14 mainly by hedges.) Each area has its attractions and
only together do we see their full entity.

One of the great advantages of the English climate is that you can
go long-distance walking throughout the year. The main hazard in
winter is mud (and certainly the weald must be horribly sticky when
wet); but up on the chalk there is far less of it than elsewhere.
Therefore the South Downs, so accessible and gentle, are available
to us at any time, and the pleasure they offer is equally great in any
season. Of course the charms of summer are more obvious – the
warmth, the flowers, the birdsong, the waving fields of corn. But we
should look beyond the obvious to the subtleties of the changing
year as well as the challenges of rough weather. Already in March
the larks are venturing higher, the lambs are in the fields, the

blackthorn is in bloom and daisies are plentiful; and if we are walking in a strong wind, the trees and bushes are in exciting movement. As late as November the autumnal colours are still brilliant, with russet leaves and red berries against the browns of plough or greens of winter wheat; and this is the best time for ending a walk in the twilight when the rabbits and deer come out to feed and the owl starts to hoot. In January, when a light sheet of snow covers the sleeping downs, one walks on a frosty day in a brilliant white and blue world with nature hidden, birdless except for cruising crows and pairs of whirring partridges. At any season the weather can change suddenly, with sea mists coming up without warning and visibility down to zero, or with rain alternating with bright intervals, the weald brooding in gloom and the Channel gilded in sun. These are the excitements and moods of the downs, to be welcomed provided one is properly equipped and prepared.

'I'll give you the run of 'em, East to West'

The run of the downs east to west comes from the South Downs Way, an ancient route along the ridge. In 1972 all the Sussex part of this ridgeway, plus the Seven Sisters coastal walk, was designated an official long-distance route by the Countryside Commission, with the effect that the county authorities are responsible for its upkeep and receive grants for that purpose. But the South Downs do not recognise county boundaries and run on into Hampshire, so in this guide I have extended the main route to Winchester by means of public rights of way. Also, because the downs are more than just a ridgeway, I have added my loops and spurs to add depth to the run of the downs, though of course these are merely an arbitrary selection from an extensive network of footpaths and bridleways. The Lewes loop provides an alternative route across the Ouse and goes through the Caburn hills. The Arundel loop goes out along the Arun and returns through field and forest. The Petworth spur strikes into the weald. The Lavant loop swoops around a valley with the full variety of downland, and the Stansted spur is principally an experience of forests. All these are less frequented than the official

Way; and each of them adds to our understanding of the downs, whether by seeing old town centres, great houses, museums, parks, plants, rivers or wildlife. Finally (or initially) I start my route at Eastbourne Pier with a mile and a half of promenade, as I couldn't accept the poky corner off Paradise Drive as a worthy start to such a splendid experience as the South Downs Way. The outcome is a total of 156 miles of walking. Of the twenty stages, sixteen are bridle routes (including the whole official South Downs Way apart from the Seven Sisters).

The entire route is of superb quality, virtually all traffic-free, on firm ground, easy to find and well established. The official route is particularly well maintained and signed. In East Sussex the signs are on concrete plinths, in West Sussex on wooden posts: the posts are clearer but more prone to destruction. Either way, the route can really be found without the aid of a guide-book (with a bit of trial and error, and in clear weather). Off the official route we rely on the wooden footpath or bridleway signs, which are generally also clear but sometimes missing. There is nowhere really steep or rough, except patches in Stages 12 and 17. Of the main route of 100 miles, twelve are on surfaced public roads, but these are either through villages or on very small lanes, the only main roads being half a mile in both Stages 3 and 8. There are also a further seven surfaced miles on the loops and spurs, none of them being main roads. Some further unsurfaced mileage of the main route (none on the loops or spurs) is at present designated as byways (or RUPPs) on which you may possibly encounter motorcyclists: but only in Stages 7, 9, 10 and 11 are there such sections of any length.

The text is strictly divided between facts and descriptions: the descriptions are not to be used for route-finding. The route is written in both directions and supplemented by the maps, which are all 1:55,000, so there should be no need for Ordnance Survey maps. Signposts are generally not mentioned because of their destructibility, nor are compass bearings, and only very occasionally are grid references given, because there are so many distinctive features. Gates or stiles are only mentioned when of special significance, but are marked on the maps and indicated in the summaries. On the main route there are about eighty-five gates to

open (and close, of course), but nearly half are in Stages 1–4.
Longer distances are given in miles, shorter ones and heights in
metres. In the route headings miles and kilometers are both shown,
rounded to the nearest halves. 'Cumulative ascent' means the sum of
all the 'ups' within the Stage.

All British Rail stations within about two miles of the route are
indicated, plus regular year-round bus services at points by the
route, with an indication of their frequency. Regarding taxis and
refreshments I have been selective, but give at least one pub at each
place, which can be useful for a rendezvous. 'Real ale' means that
the pub is listed in the current CAMRA guides as selling beer that has
not been pressurised. No point on my route is more than two and a
half miles from a pub. On accommodation I have likewise been
selective, but demonstrating that the entire route can be walked or
ridden without any transport. All the hotels and guest houses are as
they appear in the 1984 English Tourist Board's *Where to stay*
(except the Langrish Hotel), and using their categories of
bedrooms/services/meals: 1 is lowest, 6 is highest. Youth hostels are
well provided in the east but not in the west. With all these forms of
accommodation it is desirable to plan ahead and book to prevent
disappointment. Camping is a problem: there are hardly any
substantial camping-sites along the route. However, individual
backpackers can often get local camping permission in the villages
along the way; camping along the route itself also needs permission,
and is anyway not easy owing to absence of water. Apart from a few
public taps, drinking water is only available from pubs or houses; for
horses, cattle-troughs can be used. For further information about
accommodation or camping, consult the tourist boards or the county
councils.

I have written of my 156 miles as they appear at present, but as
every year goes by my text will become outdated. So far as the route
is concerned, I believe that changes can only be slight because it is
so well established; but there could be variances if ever the official
route were extended into Hampshire. The descriptions are more
susceptible to change. Even in an Area of Outstanding Natural
Beauty trees and hedges, fields and roads, farm-buildings and
communications equipment are all in organic condition, and flowers

are in constant change. So my text can only be a record of the South
Downs as they actually appear in 1984, not a vision of the future.

This guide is meant to be for everyone, from families out for a
three-mile walk to striders covering twenty-five miles or more. For
all, the great thing is to try to arrange to walk from A to B and not
have to retrace steps, thus doubling the ground-coverage. Two cars
is the easiest way of doing this, but public transport or taxis can do it
too. My loops provide four great circle-routes of fifteen to twenty
miles, two of them bridle. But best of all is to walk the main route
from end to end whether camping, bed and breakfasting, hotelling
or ferrying to and from your own home. If you do the hundred
miles, you will encounter a splendid cross-section of long-distancers,
ranging from the thinly disguised soldiers on their endurance
marches, through the bearded bare-backed striders, to the elderly
couples, the quartets of scouts, and all the ages in between, most
with heavy backpacks: they merit your greeting, not your cold
shoulder. Once every few years (next time in May 1986) a special
event is organised by the Long Distance Walkers' Association: the
Downsman Hundred, all along our main route. Last time (May
1980) it was completed by 185 people, thirteen of them women,
and the first two did it – running – in 16 hours 13 minutes, an
average of more than six miles an hour. Henry Bridge, aged
seventy, did it in 34 hours 4 minutes, an average of three miles an
hour. The equivalent equestrian event is the Endurance Horse and
Pony Society's Summer Solstice Ride, from Plumpton Racecourse
to the Queen Elizabeth Park and back; also a hundred miles.

After all this talk about doing the route from end to end, I'd
better admit that I haven't done the Downsman Hundred or carried
a heavy backpack with my bedding. But I have walked it all in one
go east to west, as well as riding most of it west to east. I walked
from Eastbourne to Winchester in July, starting during the last day
of a heat-wave. When I got to Alfriston I was severely dehydrated
(stupidly I didn't carry a water bottle and the Mr Wimpey cornet at
Exceat Farm only made things worse) and consumed three pints of
ginger beer before continuing as far as Firle. The weather changed
next day, so my walk to Plumpton was without any views at all but
blissfully cool. Then on to Steyning under balmy skies, and next day

to Arundel. From here my longest day was to Harting, and during it I didn't meet a single person: the South Downs Way is still a lonely trail except at summer weekends. Then to Droxford, and the last day to Winchester in company with a Wykehamist who led me through the inner sanctum of the College. I had managed to walk the hundred miles without getting into any car or transport, so I arrived at the Cathedral from the pier, as it were. Glorious seas of corn just before harvest characterised this walk, some golden, some emerald green, and some of the barley a deep olive colour. And the low tide along the Seven Sisters, with the shore platform fully extended, gave the impression that the real sea was drying up in that tremendous heat.

The ride was from HMS *Mercury* to Beachy Head, and was more logistically demanding. Months ahead we had to start making arrangements for grazing or stabling, but it worked like a charm. My companions were Alice, Brodie and Achnacarry. Alice and I had the easier time of it – comfortable billets and kind friends who ferried us. Brodie and Achnacarry had the harder time, for they were the Highland ponies who carried us from start to finish. These two amiable creatures soon adapted themselves to the new experience of a long-distance ride: sudden spurts, inclinations to gallop, and tugging at the reins were soon ruled out as superfluous and a steady plod soon adopted for most of the time, with occasional trots and canters. A freak spell of hot September weather with scarcely a breath of wind for the whole week cast a dreamlike quality on the expedition. Under the unrelenting sun we wandered eastwards, and towards the end of each afternoon our tall shadows preceded us. The heat-haze denied us distant views across the weald, but then, it also served to obscure Worthing, Shoreham, Hove, and Brighton. At times, when we passed across humps of arable downland with 100-acre fields striped brown and black from stubble burning, we might for all the world have been in Andalusia. But then the fresh green pasture and luxuriant hedgerows would soon remind us that we were in the heart of England. We were keen observers of all we saw, Alice and I concentrating on plant-identification or route-orientation, while Brodie and Achnacarry watched out for surprise shapes, flutters, barks, and bangs: though Achnacarry displayed a truly Caledonian calm when he had to have two front hoofs shod by Frank Dean, the farrier at Rodmell. At the end of this six-day journey, when we dismounted at Beachy Head feeling justifiably proud, up came a breezy brassy family and asked how much we charged for pony rides!

No remarkable incidents in either of these journeys, I admit. But it doesn't need convenient little adventures of the sort that often seem to happen to travel-writers to make the run of the downs, east to west or west to east, memorable for those who do it. The effort and the achievement, the sensory experience, the physical satisfaction – these are enough, and ultimately they are inexpressible. If this book encourages anyone, young or old, to walk twice as far as they thought they could, it will have served its primary purpose. To all those who feel really exhausted after a long walk on the South Downs, it is duly dedicated.

Stage 1
Eastbourne to Alfriston 9 miles

SPECIFICS

Stage 1 begins with 2 miles on pavement mostly along the sea-front
of Eastbourne, before coming to the official South Downs Way. It
then goes over two sections of the downs, broken by the dry valley
at Jevington: all this is chalk or flint track, except for 1½ miles on
grass and a quarter-mile on surfaced road. Mostly shrub and
pasture, with some arable and wood. Only about four gates to open.
Westbound, cumulative ascent 292 m, descent 287 m. Bridle-route
throughout (except on sea-front promenade). See maps 22 and 21.

Route westbound

From Eastbourne Pier to Alfriston Market Cross 9 miles (14.5 km)

(a) *From Eastbourne Pier to official South Downs Way bridleway
start* 2 miles (3 km)
From Eastbourne Pier go along the lower promenade: after the
Wish Tower continue (up steps) along an upper promenade
confined between wall and plants. At a circular seat emplacement,
turn right and cross King Edward's Parade. (Here turn left for start
of Stage 15. From here Stage 1 is a bridle-route.) Go up
Chesterfield Road. At end, bear right into Milnthorpe Road, then
across Meads Road into Gaudick Road. At end, half left into
Paradise Drive. Just after the junction with Link Road, take the
bridleway at the official start.

(b) *From official South Downs Way bridleway start to Jevington
Church* 3½ miles (5.5 km)
Go up the hill on grass, keeping close to the wood on the right.
Follow the track signed for Jevington and Willingdon which
continues uphill, ignoring paths to the left, to gain the crest: then

ahead to cross the A259. The way continues northwards along the
ridge, at first through the Downs golf-course and then with a
parallel grass ride, which converges to the summit of Willingdon
Hill. Here are crossing bridleways and tracks, but we maintain
direction ahead downhill, first by parallel tracks then by a sunken
lane into Jevington. At a road, turn right for a few metres, then left
up to the church.

(c) *From Jevington Church to Alfriston Market Cross* 3½ miles (6
km)
Continue up a path along a hedge between fields and follow up to
the right among bushes. At a track go left and up through a wood.
At the top, turn right through a gate along the edge of the wood to a
second gate. Then ahead on grass through a large pasture,
contouring gradually leftwards and aiming for a gateway on the
small saddle before Windover Hill. The Way now circles round to
the left of the hilltop, becoming a chalk track which later curves
leftwards around the top of a combe: then down through gates to
cross a small road. Ahead downhill by a sunken lane to a road
junction. Turn left along the road for a quarter-mile. At Plonk Barn
(junction with Stage 15) turn right on to a confined path to a
wooden footbridge over the Cuckmere. The marked route now
leads right and shortly left up a narrow lane to the Market Cross in
Alfriston High Street.

Route eastbound

From Alfriston Market Cross to **Eastbourne Pier** 9 miles (14.5 km)

(a) *From Alfriston Market Cross to Jevington Church* 3½ miles (6
km)
From the Market Cross enter the High Street and immediately go
left down a narrow lane, then right by the river. Cross the wooden
footbridge and go along a confined path to a road by Plonk Barn
(junction with Stage 15). Turn left along the road for a
quarter-mile: then, where it bears left, turn right up a sunken lane.

Cross a small road and go through a gate up a chalk track which mounts around the head of a grassy combe, then curving rightwards of the summit of Windover Hill. At the saddle beyond, go through a gate into a large pasture. The Way now contours ahead to the right of a long gorse hedge, then eases rightwards across the pasture. We come to a gate leading to a confined path at the top of a wood. At a second gate, by a bridleway junction, go left down through the wood on a track. Then leave the track to go right on a path through bushes and then down the line of a hedge between fields to Jevington Church.

(b) *From Jevington Church to official South Downs Way bridleway start* 3½ miles (5.5 km)
Go down the lane to a road. Turn right for a few metres, then left up a sunken lane which later converts to parallel tracks to the summit of Willingdon Hill. Here are crossing tracks and bridleways, but we maintain direction across the crest, going gently down and bearing right, with a fence on our right. The track continues with a parallel grass ride, then ahead through the Downs golf-course and across the A259. Go ahead on a grass track and left at a fork. Then descend through scrub keeping close to the wood on our left, and down to a road.

(c) *From the official South Downs Way bridleway start to Eastbourne Pier* 2 miles (3 km)
Go ahead down Paradise Drive. At a junction take the unmarked street (Gaudick Road) half right. At end, cross Meads Road into Milnthorpe Road, then bear left into Chesterfield Road to King Edward's Parade. (From here the route is not bridleway. Here also turn right for start of Stage 15). Cross King Edward's Parade down to a circular seat emplacement, then left along a promenade confined between wall and plants. At the Wish Tower take steps down to the lower promenade and continue on to Eastbourne Pier.

Approach by car

At start: Eastbourne is at the end of the A22; parking is restricted in
the centre (multi-storey car-park in Trinity Place) but is possible
around the South Downs Way start. *At end*: Alfriston is 1 mile off
the A27 between Eastbourne and Lewes (car-park at approach to
the village). *Also* at Jevington, 2½ miles off the A22 at Polegate.

Approach by other transport

Train: British Rail at Eastbourne (a ½ mile from start of stage) and
Berwick (2 miles from end of stage). *Local buses*: Southdown
services at Eastbourne to many places; at Alfriston to Seaford and
Eastbourne (two-hourly); at Berwick to Eastbourne, Lewes and
Brighton (two-hourly, not on Sundays). *Taxis*: Eastbourne, Town
and Country (0323–27766); Alfriston, Berwick Taxi
(0323–870239).

Refreshment

Pubs: Eastbourne, Bertie's Bar on Grand Parade (real ale);
Jevington, Eight Bells (meals); Alfriston, Star Inn (real ale, meals).
Restaurants: Eastbourne, many; Jevington, the Hungry Monk;
Alfriston, Star Inn.

Accommodation

Hotels or guest houses: Cavendish Hotel, Grand Parade, Eastbourne
BN21 4DH (Cat 6/5/5; 0323–27401); Chatsworth Hotel, Grand
Parade, Eastbourne BN21 3YR (Cat 5/5/4; 0323–30327); Kenway
Guesthouse, 56 Royal Parade, Eastbourne BN22 7AQ (Cat 2/3/2;
0323–29895); Crossways Hotel, Wilmington BN26 5SG (Cat
3/3/1; 03212–2455). *Other*: Beachy Head Youth Hostel, East
Dean Road, Eastbourne BN20 8ES (0323–20284).

Admission

Eastbourne Pier, daily: Lullington Heath (Nature Conservancy
Council), partially open daily: Wilmington Priory (Sussex
Archaeological Trust), mid-March to mid-October, weekdays and
Sunday afternoons.

Stage 1
Eastbourne to Alfriston

DESCRIPTION

I will go out against the sun
   Where the rolled scarp retires,
And the Long Man of Wilmington
   Looks naked towards the shires;
And east till doubling Rother crawls
   To find the fickle tide,
By dry and sea-forgotten walls,
   Our ports of stranded pride.

Rudyard Kipling (1865–1936)
from 'Sussex'

A blue-and-white pleasure palace projecting over the murky waters, Eastbourne pier is a worthy counterpart to Winchester Cathedral 100 miles away at the other end of our route along the South Downs. Although the pier's attractions are now largely confined to sweets and slot-machines, and the wooden planking is replaced by concrete slabs, the Victorian structures evoke past glories, such as when an orchestra played in the concert hall, and from a cupola the camera obscura captured the image of the coast from Hastings to Beachy Head and reflected it into the domed pavilion. As we start our walk along the promenade we see the façades of the principal hotels along Grand Parade whose names – Cavendish, Chatsworth, Burlington – bear witness that Eastbourne was largely developed by the estate of the Dukes of Devonshire, whose arms of three bucks' heads are displayed on the Burlington Hotel: though the older

Eastbourne Pier

history of the town is testified by the medieval arches in St Mary's church.

The promenade is paved with pink and mauve, and enlivened by rock-gardens and beds of tulips and iris. It takes us through the Band Arena, in whose gaudy classicality a Roman emperor would have felt entirely at home, and then around the Wish Tower. This is in fact Martello Tower Number 73, one of a series built on the coasts of Kent and Sussex at intervals of a few miles by the Royal Engineers during the Napoleonic wars when French invasion seemed imminent. Their name is taken from the Torre della Martello in Corsica, and they were built of brick 2 m thick, circular, and with the door well above ground level. Today it is known as the Wish Tower and instead of French invaders surf-riders skim towards it, tumbling as the waves break. After it the upper promenade is bordered with escallonia and the sandy beach below stretches on towards the chalk cliffs, its smooth expanse disfigured by the wooden groynes. Bright and cheerful streets with rosy surfaces, red-brick pavements, red tiled houses, and evergreen privet hedges lead us to the white barrier and notice of the official South Downs Way.

Going up Pashley Down, the wood of beech and ilex on our right disguises a dome-covered reservoir. Later, where we pass through scrub of hazel, thorn and gorse, a flint wall is the base of a former windmill. At the top of the rise comes our last close view of the sea, and to our right we can see the Pevensey levels fringed by the Kentish hills, on clear days glistening with water in the dykes between the pastures. In the levels – just beyond Eastbourne and along the line of a railway – is Pevensey (Pefen's river), once a port but now silted; and sharp eyes can pick out the walls of the castle, the great Norman fortress which controlled the Rape of Pevensey. These walls are built on the foundations of the Roman fort of Anderida, whose capture by Aella and his son Cissa and their Saxons at the end of the fifth century dealt a death blow to Romano–British rule. All this is what Kipling had in mind in 'dry and sea-forgotten walls, our ports of stranded pride'. The ridge heads northwards and our grass track comes towards the South Downs golf-course. The wooden palisades made to prevent shots at

the eighteenth hole from overshooting into the 'nineteenth' look
like prehistoric fortifications, but instead of tribal warriors there are
only golfers wielding clubs. After the course for nearly a mile there
is a parallel grass track on the right which passes between gorse and
thorn directly past three round barrows: but the humps on the
skyline to our left are not barrows but defence bunkers of the last
war, and the big mound on the summit of Willingdon Hill is the
foundation of a windmill.

Once over the brow of Willingdon Hill we enter the downland
and put the plain behind us. As if to denote this boundary into an
antique land, two curious stones point the way on to Jevington and
back to Eastbourne. Although at this point we are in fact on the old
Eastbourne road (before the turnpike, now the A27, was first built),
these two markers are recent, taken from the bombed ruins of
Barclays Bank in Eastbourne. We now see ahead to Firle Beacon
and Caburn, and our legs are getting into their stride. But before
descending we should pause for a moment because here are not
only the downs but the ghosts of the downs, 'marks that show and
fade like shadows on the downs'. If we look closely at the shoulder
of the hill half a mile ahead we can see amid the gorse thickets dark
lines in parallelograms. These are the traces of lynchets (also
misleadingly known as 'Celtic fields'), preserved in this way because
of the outward shift of the earth after centuries of ploughing. The
fields were in rough rectangles of 1–2 acres, modified by the lie of
the land: these ones are thought to be as much as 3,000 years old.
Then if we look further up and towards the right we see on the grass
on Combe Hill the very faint outline of a semi-circular bank, only a
foot or so high. This is one of only twelve known camps of the new
stone age in Britain. They are called 'camps' because it is evident
that the pastoralists never established permanent settlements but
were constantly on the move. Here on Combe Hill was one of their
vantage points, though the precise purposes of their camps are not
fully understood, whether practical (for corralling or bartering of
cattle) or ritualistic (for slaughter burial). Combe Hill also shows
two round barrows on its crest, and in one of them four flanged
bronze axes have been found.

Now we descend to Jevington, the downland village in this little

streamless 'dry' valley. The chalk track still has its grassy
alternative, till it enters a sunken lane between elder and hazel. The
small houses are of brick or flint, the most memorable the
flint-walled building now the Hungry Monk restaurant. But it is at
the church that we can best appreciate Jevington, the settlement of
Geofa and his original band of Saxons. The church tower is also of
the Saxon period (though four centuries later) and gives a
tremendous impression of age and strength. Age, because it is
constructed in a rough way with unshaped blocks of limestone set
amid the uncut flint, and some Roman bricks incorporated.
Strength, because it was built as a refuge against the Viking raiders.
Within, St Andrew's church contains examples of all the main
medieval styles, and is protected by a fine Tudor wagon-roof with
massive key posts and hammer-beams alternating. There is also an
elegant marble plaque to Charles Rochester, whose wife Leonora is
carved in ghostly base-relief beside him. At the far end of the
churchyard is a rare pintle gate, balanced on a central pivot.

   The South Downs Way leads ahead uphill and over to Alfriston.
But in this section it is possible to go instead on paths around the
base of the downs, and this lower route is rich in small-scale charms.
This alternative leads through the pintle gate along the road to the
Five Bells: 300 m later, left into a bridleway which soon forks right.
The path goes between hedges all the way to Folkington (the
farmstead of Folca's people, and pronounced 'Fooington'). Here is
the small church of St Peter, thirteenth-century and with a cheerful
interior, whitewashed and box-pewed. Then on, at the lower edge of
a wood, and at a fork on a brow, with Wilmington now in sight, left
and below the Long Man to rejoin the South Downs Way by a
covered reservoir.

   Back at Jevington our route proceeds along a hedge between
paddocks fenced expensively with cleft chestnut and now in
disrepair. We see the Georgian windows of Jevington Place, the
home of the family that owns the land hereabouts. Then up into
Jevington Holt, where horse-chestnuts soon give way to ash, with
undergrowth of hazel. Just up to the right is the sad sight of an

The track to Jevington, with lynchet lines

isolated patch of grass preserved from the surrounding plough only by the steepness of the hill. At the top of the wood we come to the edge of Lullington Heath. This is of special interest as an area of downland where the chalk is mixed with sandy soil and so where, for instance, wild thyme and harebells mingle happily with ling and bell heather. Our route soon leaves the upper edge of the wood and emerges into a wide field. Here, for the first time liberated from guiding fences and on top of the hill, we can savour the true downland. Under the waving sea of tall brome grass lie thyme, rockrose, horseshoe vetch, birdsfoot trefoil, dropwort, and Bee and Fragrant orchids, with Marbled White butterflies fluttering around them in July and August. Above us soar the larks, and whitethroats and yellowhammers weave about. To our right the derelict walls of Hill Barn recall the flocks of sheep that would have gathered in its yard. A line of gorse divides us from the arable and, where the gorse ends, a deviation right, over the brow of Wilmington Hill, would lead to Hunter's Burgh, a well preserved and prominent long barrow. At the end of this expanse we gaze down to our left at Deep Dene, a completely unspoilt combe studded with thorn trees.

By a neck of the downs collared with a fence we come on to Windover (windy bank) Hill. On its small summit is concentrated a collection of earthworks that make it one of the prime archaeological sites of the South Downs. At the highest point is a fine bowl barrow, surrounded by a ditch. Another smaller and less pronounced barrow is back on the neck by the fence. Just by the bowl barrow is a recent chalk quarry, and beyond that is a long barrow. A series of humps mark the refuse pits of Stone Age flint mines. All these sites are bounded to the south by the sunken cart-track used by the South Downs Way, and to the north by a straight path inclining downhill, possibly of Roman times. Finally on the western side a steep terraced road (a way between two banks) leads directly back to the summit and would seem to have ceremonial connotations, perhaps Romano–British or even earlier.

Standing on the bowl barrow, built here explicitly for prominence, we look down at the weald – the afforestation around Caneheath and the Arlington reservoir. But closer below is Wilmington (Wilma's farmstead) and at the nearer end of it is what remains of a medieval priory, its gatehouse and south wall of a great hall. If we go down and visit the priory (which was originally an apanage of the Benedictine abbey of Grestain in Normandy), we will see the sites of other buildings and an impressive crypt with four bays of rib-vaulting. Also the church of St Mary and St Peter which, as the priory church, is unusually large for a small village, with a substantial chancel in which the monks would have chanted the offices while the villagers listened in the nave. The churchyard has a giant yew tree, 7 m in girth. Back at the priory, the gatehouse now contains a museum of agricultural implements, including thought-provokers such a mudfly, an owl rake, a whimble, a haystack needle, a dibber, and a thistlepuller: and two enormous horse-shoes indicate the size of the Suffolk Punches that pulled the carts.

Just below as we look at Wilmington is the Long Man, out of sight unless we scramble down across the boundary path to inspect him, though even this is unsatisfactory since his whole effect is best from a distance and below. Close up he is merely an elongated etching, a meaningless maze of whitewashed concrete blocks (770 of them) set in the grass in 1969 to replace the whitewashed bricks of 1874. But from Wilmington he is the Long Man, the greatest 'chalk' figure in England, looking 'naked towards the shires' – or almost so, for his genitals are certainly hidden. The best thing about him is that despite the efforts of many learned men, and articles about the supposed original position of his left foot, and air photographs analysed in minute detail down to the incidence of the number of tufts and molehills – despite all this, his origin is still completely uncertain, since the first reference to him was made only 200 years ago. If he is indeed really old (which supposes that he was given a good clean and brush up fairly regularly through the centuries) then he might be the representation of some powerful god, whether Wotan or Mithras or even a Bronze Age sun god. But let his mystery remain and let us not stretch too far unprovable theories about lines of alignment and astronomical ritual in prehistoric societies.

Now we descend into the valley of the Cuckmere, though valley is perhaps not the right word for the curious phenomenon of the

passage of these little Sussex rivers through the downs – 'cutting'
would be more appropriate – since they lack an upper end and the
rivers flow from the apparent plain through to the sea along the
furrow where through the ages the great chalk dome was slowly
washed away. By a chalk track bordered with ragwort and scabious
we come round the head of Ewe Dean (model-aircraft flying area)
and pass a covered reservoir. In the gorse and thorns on the south
slopes of Windover Hill are more lynchets, though out of our sight.
At a small surfaced road, a deviation left for half a mile leads to the
tiny chancel at Lullington (the farmstead of Lulla's people, and
pronounced 'Lingken'), its white weatherboarded belfry peeping
from between a clump of trees. After a sunken lane between
sycamore we come to a road, and pass under the trees that were so
common in England but are now so rare – elms. Dutch elm disease,
accidentally imported from North America in the 1960s, has
completely changed the landscape in several counties. The fungus is
carried by tiny free-flying beetles that penetrate the trunks to make
their nursery galleries, and it deprives the trees of the ability to suck
water from the earth. For over a quarter of a mile the elms line our
route, and we do not see the like of them again. The fact that they
are here at all is probably thanks to the draconian measures ordered
by the East Sussex County Council, to destroy and burn all affected
trees.

   Plonk Barn is not a place for storing cheap wine but derives its
name from the planks of the original building. From it our route
goes between hedges to the white wooden footbridge over the
Cuckmere, and there before us is Alfriston.

The Long Man of Wilmington

Stage 2
Alfriston to **Southease** 7 miles

SPECIFICS

The route is along the ridge of the bare downs from the Cuckmere
to the Ouse. One mile is surfaced, 2 are chalk or flint track, but all
the rest is on grass or earth, with the way largely unconfined and
with arable to one side. There are at least fourteen gates to open.
Westbound, cumulative ascent 258 m, descent 260 m. Bridle-route
throughout. See maps 21, 20, and 19.

Route westbound

From Alfriston Market Cross to **Southease Church** 7 Miles (11.5
km)

(a) *From Alfriston Market Cross to Firle access road* 4 miles (6.5
km)
From the Market Cross go along the High Street, then turn right
into Star Lane, then ahead up King's Ride. Where the surfacing
ends, continue on the track uphill, later following it around to the
right. At a junction of paths, go ahead and slightly left uphill beside
arable, and with the ridge to the right. After a double gate keep
ahead on to the ridge on grass to find a flint track over Bostal Hill
and down to a car-park and bridle-gates. Then ahead up on grass
over Firle Beacon, with fencing to our left; then on and down
through gates to the car-park at Firle access road.

(b) *From Firle access road to Southease Church* 3 miles (5 km)
The way continues across the road and through gates across a field
on grass. It then picks up a track through arable and past the radio
masts on Beddingham Hill to the head of another small road
(junction with Stage 16). Then gently down the crest of the hill as a
track on grass, and through gates. Where it becomes unconfined, go

ahead on the grass to pick up a track which loops first left and then right down the face of Itford Hill to the A26 and Itford Farm (short-cut down can be used). Through the farm on a surfaced road and across the railway line and the river, to Southease Church.

Route eastbound

From Southease Church to **Alfriston Market Cross** 7 miles (11.5 km)

(a) *From Southease Church to Firle access road* 3 miles (5 km)
From Southease Church go along the small road across the river and railway line to the A26 at Itford Farm. Then 100 m right find a track left up the hill. After a gate the track curves right but later loops back, always uphill (short-cut up can be used). Heading for the highest ground, we come to a gate and a track up the ridge beside a fence. On Beddingham Hill at gates we pass the head of a small road (junction with Stage 16). Then along the track through arable past the radio masts. Where the track turns right go ahead through gates across a grass field to the car-park at Firle access road.

(b) *From Firle access road to Alfriston Market Cross* 4 miles (6.5 km)
From the road go through a gate to the left of the car-park, then keep to the top of the ridge on grass, with fencing to our right. Up the track to Firle Beacon then on down to the gates and car-park before Bostal Hill. Over Bostal Hill: where the track and fence draw away to the right, maintain direction on grass to a double gate. From here the way continues as a firm track beside arable, with the ridge to our left. At a junction of paths keep ahead and slightly right. Follow the track where it bears left and down on to the surfaced King's Drive and Star Lane to Alfriston High Street, and left to the Market Cross.

Approach by car

At start: Alfriston is 1 mile off the A27 between Eastbourne and
Lewes (car-park at approach to the village). *At end*: Southease is 3
miles south of Lewes on the secondary road past Kingston to
Newhaven. *Also*: up a small road off the A27 past West Firle up to
the ridge; and on the A26 between Lewes and Newhaven by Itford
Farm.

Approach by other transport

Train: British Rail at Berwick (2 miles from start of stage) and
Southease (at end of stage). *Local buses*: Southdown services at
Alfriston to Seaford and Eastbourne (two-hourly); at Berwick and
Firle Lane to Eastbourne, Lewes and Brighton (two-hourly, not on
Sundays); at Southease to Newhaven and Lewes (about two-hourly,
not on Sundays). *Taxis*: Alfriston, Berwick Taxi (0323–870239);
Lewes, S&G Taxis (07916–6116); Newhaven, Link Taxis
(0273–513511).

Refreshment

Pubs: Alfriston, Star Inn (real ale, meals); Firle, Ram (real ale).
Restaurant: Alfriston, Star Inn.

Accommodation

Hotels and guest houses: Star Inn, Alfriston, BN26 5TA (Cat
5/4/4; 0323–870495); Potters Wheel, High Street, Alfriston BN26
5TD (Cat 4/1/4; 0323–870276). *Other*: Alfriston Youth Hostel,
Frog Firle, Alfriston BN26 5TT (0323–870423): grazing, stabling,
camping, Pleasant Rise Farm, Alfriston BN26 5TN
(0323–870545).

Admission

Alfriston Clergy House (National Trust), daily April to October:
Charleston (Charleston Trust), intend opening: Firle Place
(Viscount Gage), June to September, Monday, Wednesday and
Sunday afternoons.

Stage 2
Alfriston to **Southease**

DESCRIPTION

Broad and bare to the skies,
The great Down country lies,
Green in the glance of the sun,
Fresh with the clean, salt air:
Screaming the gulls rise from the fresh-turned mould,
Where the round bosom of the wind-swept wold
Slopes to the valley fair.

Rosamund Watson (1860–1920)
from 'On the downs'

On the Tye, the village green at Alfriston (Aelfrice's farmstead and
pronounced 'Orlfriston'), the houses line one side and on the other
is the church whose position, size, and purity of style earn it the
name 'Cathedral of the South Downs'. It rests on a prehistoric
mound, protected by limes and beeches, and behind it are the
water-meadows of the Cuckmere and the hump of Windover Hill.
St Andrew's church was built around 1360, the materials being local
flints, with greensand quoins and facings. The flints are knapped, or
cut, to present an even surface made up of tiny dots of many shades
of white, grey, or black. The greensand is carved to construct great
windows whose tracery resembles the branches of trees. The tower
is built over the crossing of nave, chancel and transepts (for St
Andrew's is a cruciform church, in the shape of a cross), and is
capped with a graceful shingled broach spire. The interior is grand
and unadorned, with a satisfying sense of space, and with bell-ropes
suspended from the central tower. At a corner of the church mound,

Alfriston church

low down by the water-meadows, is a small thatched and timber-framed house with heavy diagonal braces. This is the Clergy House, of roughly the same date as the church and the oldest domestic building along our entire route. This is how even priests (relatively important local residents) lived 600 years ago – no chimneys, no flooring, no glazing – whilst all that building effort went into the church. Still, by the standards of the day their house was well built, with carved wooden arches and moulded beams, a central hall and accommodation for a housekeeper: until the Reformation, priests were celibate. The Clergy House was derelict until the newly formed National Trust was persuaded to acquire it in 1896 for £10.

Our second viewpoint for Alfriston is at the Market Cross: this is in fact merely the shaft and knob of a cross which was smashed by the Protestants, a missing extension which is compensated for by a fine chestnut tree. Looking up the High Street, the weatherboard building immediately on our right is Market Cross House, known as the 'smugglers' inn' because once inhabited by Stanton Collins, a local baddie who was deported in 1831: it is now occupied by Mr Phillips' excellent grocery. A short distance ahead are two ancient inns, both basically of the fifteenth century. On the left the George offers sustenance behind its closely studded wooden beams. On the right the Star disguises a fully-fledged hotel behind its medieval frontage – one of the best in Sussex – where, picked out with paint, St Michael attacks a basilisk, St Giles and St Julian a lion, St George a dragon, and on the corner a ferocious lion, the bowsprit of a captured Dutch man-of-war, threatens us as we turn up Star Lane.

Just a tactical bound from the sea, and on a route leading inland, Alfriston had a reputation as a centre for smuggling, though actually its overt commercial activity was glove-making. In the eighteenth century, indeed up to 1840, the protectionist policy of the British government forced heavy taxes on luxury imports, especially wines, tobacco, tea, and silks. But the excisemen could never effectively control the coastline and smuggling became a major industry, connived at by the gentry to secure their luxuries. The smuggling

Alfriston High Street

gangs exercised a vicious control through intimidation and thwarted the central authorities, much as the Mafia does in Sicily today. The brutality of the Collins gang and the miseries of many ordinary people are not in doubt, and the romanticisation of smuggling is ridiculous. But Kipling captures best for us the drama of a place such as Alfriston 200 years ago, when the clatter of hoofs broke the silence of the High Street:

> Five-and-twenty ponies
> Trotting through the dark –
> Brandy for the Parson
> 'Baccy for the Clerk;
> Laces for a lady; letters for a spy,
> And watch the wall, my darling, while the Gentlemen go by!

The old road along the foot of the scarp (noted from Jevington to Alfriston in Stage 1) continues as far as Firle as a bridleway, so I will describe it briefly. This alternative route leads from the Market Cross along West Street for nearly half a mile: then where the road turns sharp right keep ahead on to the bridleway; then basically follow it all the way to Firle. It passes close by two exquisite villages – Berwick and Alciston.

The church of St Michael and All Angels at Berwick (meaning barley farm and pronounced 'Bur-wick') is, like Alfriston church, built on a mound and so its 'Sussex cap' or shingled broach spire can be seen from afar. Its most remarkable feature is a series of paintings executed during the Second World War by Vanessa Bell, Duncan Grant, and Quentin Bell, at the instigation of George Bell, Bishop of Chichester (a courageous man who spoke up against the terror-bombing of German cities). He wanted to revive the ancient Sussex tradition of wall-paintings: but rather than emulating the sombre figures that we shall see at Clayton, the artists have here created a little corner of Italy, though tempered to the Sussex scene. Here is Christ in Glory attended by wafting angels in the style of Tiepolo, and the Annunciation as if to a Florentine maiden; but the kneeling figures below are actual local servicemen and priests with the line of the downs behind them, whilst the Nativity is set in Tilton

barn with Firle Beacon in the background. The Old Rectory, whose
pretty gables and pleasant frontage hide behind a screen of elms,
was built for Edward Ellman who was rector for sixty years and
curate for six years before that, thus spanning the entire reign of
Queen Victoria.

Alciston (Aelfsige's farmstead) is another shrunken village.
Thanks to an almost continuous series of bailiffs' accounts, Alciston
provides a fascinating example of Sussex agriculture in the later
Middle Ages. Situated at the scarp-foot springs (called the West
Wells and the Hardwell) and on the greensand belt, the village had
three large common arable fields, known as the West Leyne, Middle
Leyne and East Leyne. These were split into over 400 separate
allotments, of which most were held by tenants of the manor but
some by peasant proprietors. Wheat was the largest crop, but was
low in yield: for instance, in 1432 a sown area of 131 acres required
51 quarters of seed and yielded only 172 quarters. Barley yielded
better than wheat but its value was lower, and during the fifteenth
century, which was an age of recession, it was barley that declined
most in production. Although the church (dedication unknown) has
medieval features, the architectural glory of Alciston is its great
fourteenth-century barn, at 56 m one of the longest in the county
and the enduring monument to that medieval agriculture. From the
outside it resembles a hill, the vast tiled roof undulating and sloping
down on to low walls. If there is a chance to look inside, the effect is
as of the upturned hull of a wooden ship, the support beams flowing
in curves into the darkened extremities. After crossing a small road
at Bo Peep Farm (so called because the toll-gate keeper would peep
out of his small window), the bridleway continues towards Firle past
Charleston (preserved as a memorial to the same artists who
decorated Berwick church), and all the way it passes below what are
the least wooded hills of the South Downs, with the elephant's head
of Firle Beacon at the prow.

Back at Alfriston the South Downs Way proceeds uphill out of
the town past a screen of ilexes. Behind them is White Court,
named after an old 'white way' southwards. Until the white way was
made into a road it was haunted by an unusual ghost. Solitary
walkers at nightfall found they were being accompanied by a small

white terrier; at a certain point the little dog bounded into the bank
and disappeared; this was the spot where its master's murdered
body had been buried. For us, death certainly haunts our way up to
Firle Beacon. Where we leave the hedges we pass a long barrow
hidden in the bushes. Near it is where a Saxon cemetery was
recently unearthed, yielding some fine conical drinking-horns.
Further up towards Bostal Hill there is a rash of round barrows, and
then at the top Firle Beacon is dotted with more, and crowned by
another long barrow.

What are we to make of these prehistorical graves as we stride
along the ridge? We have to see them as clues to vanished societies
and as links with a time when a warrior class lorded over slaves and
gloried in heroic tales sung to them by bards in melodic
incantations: when the death of a tribal leader symbolised the death
of all the members of the tribe and required an elaborate ritual to
ensure his safe passage through death to the world of the shades. A
glimpse of this ritual is preserved for us in the concluding lines of
the great Anglo-Saxon poem *Beowulf*. These describe how, when
the hero Beowulf died, the people prepared a funeral pyre hung
about with helmets, shields and coats of mail, and placed his body
on it. The warriors then lit the fire and soon the black woodsmoke
was whirling over the conflagration, and the roar of the flames
mingled with the sound of wailing. The people then began to build
an enormous barrow high on the hill, taking ten days to dig it.
Beowulf's ashes, together with ornaments and treasure were set
inside a chamber within the barrow. Finally twelve leading warriors
circled the grave on horseback in their full regalia, chanting laments
for their lost leader and extolling his virtues. Thus was a chieftain
laid to rest, his mound – white on the downs at first – a constant
reminder of his power and fame.

But through the years death has turned to life, for on the original
mound with the ashes or the corpse within, the annual cycle of
downland flowers has bloomed two or three thousand times. All the
way from the point on Bostal Hill where both bridle-gate for riders
and kissing-gate for walkers are provided, to the car-park at Firle

Alciston Barn

access road, we are on downland grass and can look over the ridge
to the north without restrictive fences. First the cowslips, dangling
their heads against the wind, then the scabious and rampion, carpet
patches of the turf; and along the heads of the fields the vipers
bugloss, chicory, scarlet pimpernel and poppies grow. On Bostal
Hill are also found the Common Spotted and Early Purple orchids.

Bostal Hill is named from the bostal (or ancient farm-track up the
hillside) just beyond it, where are now a road and car-park. The
road was widened in the 1930s when used for car rallies – Bentleys
tested their acceleration up the steep slope. To the south a fine
sweep of dip slope wheels back towards the Cuckmere, and on it is a
prominent barrow called Five Lords Burgh because it was on the
boundary of five estates. But the best view is from Firle Beacon. To
the south the coastline is still less than four miles off, and the rolling
hills of Heighton and Blackcap run down towards it. To the
north-west is Mount Caburn and Cliffe Hill beyond. To the north is
the weald, divided from us by the lines of road and railway. Just
beyond the railway is an area of land around the village of Ripe
which is of interest for a very unusual reason. It bears the traces of
an estate of Roman times known as 'centuriation' because based on
units of 100 *jugera*. With a bit of imagination we may feel we can
pick out the rectangular layout of the hedges and fields where the
estate was cultivated by a mixture of freeholders and bonded
labourers.

Just after the first gate beyond Firle Beacon a bridleway eases off
the ridge, then goes straight down the side of a wood. This joins the
bridle-path from Alfriston and comes to the village of West Firle
(pronounced 'Furl' and meaning oakland). Firle is even more
attractive than Berwick or Alciston because it is more substantial
and compact, with a little street. Within living memory it possessed
a blacksmith, a miller, a tailor, a bootmaker, a butcher, a baker, and
a harness-maker. St Peter's church is also substantial, with a
buttressed tower, aisles flanking the nave, and beside the chancel a
chapel in which rests the alabaster tomb of Sir John Gage and his
wife Philippa. At one end of the village is Firle Place. This is the

The ridge from Firle Beacon to Beddingham Hill

most charming of the great houses along the South Downs Way, partly because of its elegant eighteenth-century style and the soft effect of its grey stone façade, but specially because of its situation right below the downs. Indeed it is so much tucked into the scarp that it cannot be seen from the way but is hidden by an overhanging wood: instead we merely see an ornamental tower above the wood and the church below it. Firle reminds us of the close links between Sussex and France, for besides being largely built of stones from the quarries of Caen, the whole effect of house, park, towering beechwood and downs above is as if from a landscape by Claude Lorraine in which minute figures in classical clothes are dwarfed by romantic vistas.

Firle is the ancestral home of the Gage family, of whom the two who emerged into national history were Sir John Gage, the trusted councillor and friend of Henry VIII, Edward VI, and Mary I, and, as Constable of the Tower of London, friend as well as gaoler to the Princess Elizabeth and Lady Jane Grey (quite an achievement to have got on with all those Tudors, especially since he and his family remained steadfast Roman Catholics throughout the period): and General Sir Thomas Gage, Governor of Massachusetts at the outbreak of the War of Independence (and loser of the battle of Bunkers Hill). But perhaps we should rather think of the lesser-known Gages who through the centuries have lived at Firle and cultivated their estates, leading private lives where 'joy and woe are woven fine'. They included Sir William Gage who acquired a plant from America and in his kitchen garden produced that succulent round green plum, the greengage.

After Firle Beacon it is down to the car-park and then gently up to Beddingham Hill with its twin radio masts and ploughed summit. There are more round barrows here, including one just by us called Males Burgh, after Godfrey le Merle who owned the land in the fourteenth century, and the sites of two settlements on the dip slope. The first is by Firle Beacon on Charleston (or Tilton) Brow, where traces of an Iron Age village have been found. The second is just past Beddingham Hill where an earlier late-Bronze Age settlement, comprising eleven small embanked enclosures, each containing a circular hut, have been extensively excavated. It is thought that four of these were dwellings and the others outbuildings or workshops: a post fence surrounded the entire group. As with many other prehistoric sites on the downs, it seems that this group was inhabited only for quite a short time, though the lynchets near it would have been cultivated for many centuries.

From Beddingham Hill (the hill above the water-meadows of Beada's people) we start our descent to the valley of the Ouse, now set out before us, with Lewes and its castle in the distance to the north, and to the south the derricks of Newhaven, perhaps with the Dieppe ferry pitching into the Channel. After a wide grass track and passing two dew-ponds – White Lion Pond and Red Lion Pond – we come onto Itford Hill, another area of downland turf and flowers, whose lower slopes are thick with orchids, thyme, and yellow vetches, with groups of gorse and hawthorn. So steeply down to Itford Farm and the noisy road, taking either the looping track or straight short-cut: then across the railway and the Ouse to Southease. We have covered a distinct and separate part of the South Downs, from Cuckmere to Ouse, 'broad and bare to the skies' and 'fresh with the clean salt air'.

Stage 3
Southease to **Lewes** 6 miles

SPECIFICS

This stage takes a rather circuitous course over the hills from the
valley of the Ouse to the gap in the downs between Lewes and
Brighton. There is a half-mile along a busy road (the earth verge can
be used), a quarter-mile on a surfaced lane, and 1 mile on a concrete
farm-track through arable land. The rest is mostly grass and
unconfined. About nine gates to open. Westbound, cumulative
ascent 190 m, descent 152 m. Bridle-route throughout. See maps 19
and 18.

Route westbound

From Southease Church to the **Newmarket Inn** 6 miles (9.5 km)

From Southease Church go up to the main road. Turn right along
the road for half a mile to Rodmell, using the verge if possible. At
Rodmell by the Holly Inn turn left up Mill Lane to its extremity. At
the top turn right along a path between hedges and on at the side of
a field. Where a farm road crosses, we maintain direction uphill
through gates and along the line of a fence. Then ahead up a
concrete farm-road through arable for nearly a mile. Where this
road bears left at the top, turn off to the right at a fence: then
immediately left through a gate. Now follow along the ridge on a
track through grass. At a gate by a saddle with crossing paths, keep
ahead on the grass to the highest point, passing to the left of a
dew-pond, then heading down towards another. Here turn left
between gateposts into another field, keeping towards the upper
side of it by a fence. At end through a gate, then immediately right
and through another gate and downhill by a path. We pass to the
right of Newmarket Plantation, first on grass then beside arable,
and so down and under the railway to the Newmarket Inn and A27.

Route eastbound

From the Newmarket Inn to **Southease Church** 6 miles (9.5 km)

From the Newmarket Inn go up the lane under the railway arch, then right up a track at the edge of fields and through gates. The track passes on grass to the left of Newmarket Plantation. Then through a gate leftwards and straight uphill to another gate at the crest. Here turn left through a further gate into a grass field, keeping to the upper side by a fence but later heading towards the far lower corner to a pond and wooden gateposts. Then half right, still on grass and seeking the highest ground and passing to the right of another dew-pond. At a saddle with crossing paths, go ahead through a gate on a track along the ridge, with a fence to the right. Later, where this comes to an end at a gate, go up right for a few metres to find a concrete farm-road. Turn left down this road for nearly 1 mile. Then ahead downhill on a path along the line of a fence beside arable. After a crosssing farm-road the path maintains direction through gates, then rises to go between hedges by a copse. Then left and down Mill Lane into Rodmell. Turn right along the main road for half a mile, using the verge where possible, then left to Southease Church.

Approach by car

At start: Southease is 3 miles south of Lewes on the secondary road past Kingston to Newhaven. *At end*: the Newmarket Inn is on the A27 between Lewes and Brighton, 1 mile from Lewes. *Also*: at Rodmell.

Approach by other transport

Train: British Rail at Southease (at start of stage), and at Lewes and Falmer (respectively $2\frac{1}{2}$ and 2 miles from end of stage). *Local buses*: Southdown services at Southease and Rodmell to Newhaven and Lewes (about two-hourly, not on Sundays); also at Lewes, many buses. *Taxis*: Lewes, S&G Taxis (07916–6166); Newhaven, Link Taxis (0273–513511).

Refreshment

Pubs: Rodmell, Holly (real ale, meals); Newmarket Inn. *Drinking water*: by Newmarket Inn.

Accommodation

Hotels or guest houses: The Forge House, Rodmell, Lewes BN7 3HS (Cat 1/1/1; 07916–4740). *Other*: Telscombe Youth Hostel, Bank Cottages, Telscombe, Lewes BN7 3HZ (0273–37077).

Admission

Monks House, Rodmell (National Trust), April to October, Wednesday and Saturday afternoons.

Stage 3
Southease to Lewes

Only the shepherd watching by his flock
Sees the moon wax and wane; endures the time
When frost is sharpest; hears the steeple chime
Each hour neglected; hears the rutting brock
Scream in the night; the prowling dog-fox bark;
Snared rabbit cry, small tragedy of dark.
The shepherd watching by his ewes and theaves
All night in loneliness, each cry knows well,
Whether the early lambing on the Downs
Rob him of Christmas, or on slopes of fell
March keep him crouching, shawled against the sleet.

Vita Sackville-West (1892–1962)
from 'The Land'

Southease (meaning south thicket) is a village with a thousand years
of recorded history, on the right bank of the flat water-meadows
through which the Ouse nowadays flows between stout banks. But
in the past the river – formerly called the Midwynd – meandered
erratically along its bed and a great part of the present meadows
were flooded. Southease was then a thriving fishing village, and
Domesday Book says 'the villeins are assessed for 38,500 herrings
and at £4 for porpoises'. The boats would have come right up to the
village and beached by the green. Today the green is the picture of
repose (no pub and no shops) and is bounded by a group of
attractive houses and the flint wall of the churchyard. Southease
church (dedication unknown) is distinctive for its round tower: in all
Sussex there are only three medieval round towers – the other two
close by at Lewes and Piddinghoe – all others being square and with

stone quoins. The reason for these three exceptions is uncertain; maybe they were cheaper without the square corners, maybe they were used as beacons or for defence. But I like to think that they were built by masons from East Anglia, where round towers are plentiful. The other notable feature of Southease church is the fragments of wall-paintings; with difficulty we can detect Christ in Majesty within a star-strewn mandorla, with the eagle of St John and the ox of St Luke on either side. Ordinary parish affairs recorded in the parish register include the marginal comment, in Latin, by the rector in 1604 on a widower's second marriage: 'A shipwrecked sailor seeks a second shipwreck.'

Despite proposals for an alternative official route, we have to get to Rodmell by the verge of a busy road for nearly half a mile, subjected to the rush of traffic. Rodmell (red soil) is a long straggling village which, like Southease, leads down to the level of the flat meadows, the houses mostly of recent date but in traditional style with thatch and tiles and long flint walls. The Old Rectory has knapped flint and latticed wooden windowpanes. Beyond it is Monks House, where Leonard and Virginia Woolf lived. Overcome by mental illness she drowned herself in the Ouse. But we should remember her not for her tragic end but as a master of descriptive style: 'Oh, it's so lovely on the downs now – a dew-pond like a silver plate in the hollow; and all the hills, not distinct as in summer, but vast, smooth, shaven, serene; and I lie on the ground and look; and then the bells tinkle and then the horses plough.' Virginia Woolf the author is closely associated with Vita Sackville-West the poet, the 'Orlando' of her romantic fancy, whose poem 'The Land' evokes so well the old agricultural ways of Kent and Sussex. Also at the lower end of the village is St Peter's church, largely Norman in structure though heavily restored: the twelfth-century tower is capped with a steep pyramidical oak roof which is well seen from points in Stages 2 and 3. At our turning at Rodmell is the Forge House, home of Frank Dean, the local farrier. We can peep into his smithy and see the forge and the pokers and tweezers and hammers and horseshoes of his trade. It is good that a farrier should operate right on the line

Southease Church

of England's longest official bridle-route, especially one who keeps up the traditions of his craft so well as Mr Dean. Next to the Forge House is the Mill House, where the miller lived when the windmill was close to the village: but Mill Hill is named from a former windmill towards which the lane takes us gently up past hedges increasingly luxurious, with wild plum and cherry.

On Mill Hill we look over the miniature Cricketing Bottom, with Southease Hill just concealing Telscombe (Tytel's valley), an unspoilt village very close to the sea. Somewhere on these hills in 1377 French forces captured the Abbot of Lewes, who opposed them. They then came on across our path and, supported by their ships in the Midwynd, attempted to take Lewes; but withdrew with the approach of Richard II and his army. On Front Hill the route becomes rather dull – not much view and a straight concrete farm-track. The arable fields on either side are thickly covered with flints great and small, and it seems incredible that wheat could grow so well on such stony ground. But in fact the earth below is not so flinty. Quite apart from the effect of ploughing which throws flints and broken chalks to the surface, the reason they lie so thickly is that through millions of years they have in places become deposited on the surface of the downs from higher levels from which the chalk itself has washed away. On Swanborough Hill we come on to downland turf for two miles. Our route now goes right along the edge of the scarp and we can gaze down the steep combes furrowed with sheep tracks which look like rows of seats in a classical amphitheatre. There are badger setts around here, intercommunicating burrows from which the snouty grey-furred creatures emerge at night and move around the combes with ambling trot, pausing frequently to sample the air and sometimes emitting horrendous sounds – 'the rutting brock scream in the night'.

Now come our best views of the Ouse valley. The dominant positions of the fort on Mount Caburn and the castle at Lewes are obvious (see Stage 16). Nearer at hand, along the line of the road, are successively Iford, Swanborough and Kingston-near-Lewes.

Frank Dean and Achnacarry

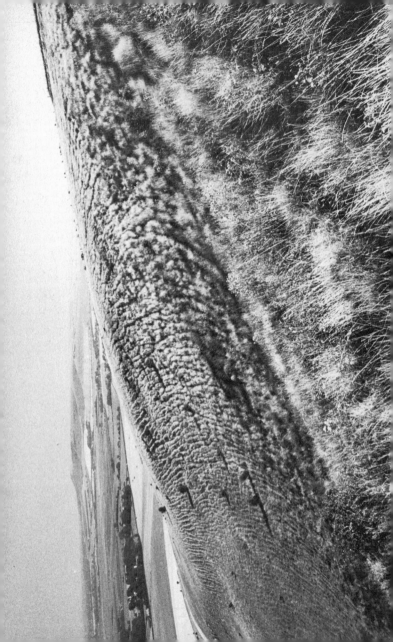

Iford (yew ford) has a beautiful church, St Nicholas's, of which the main impression is that standing in the nave one can see through the double chancel arches of the tower to the east end with its three narrow windows – a vista entirely Norman. Swanborough (peasant's mound) is a manor house built around a twelfth-century hall, a lovely knapped-flint building. Kingston, whose name denotes that it was once a royal manor, has an old core but has recently grown considerably. It was once owned by that Elizabethan hero, Sir Philip Sidney. Each village or parish at the foot of the downs had its own stretch of downland, and the usage of the down was strictly controlled by the landowner. Thus in 1615 the tenants of Lord Abergavenny at Rodmell Manor (some of the houses at Rodmell still have As on them) were each allowed to keep through the winter in their sheds or yards a maximum of three cattle, one horse, and forty sheep. In the summer they could graze their livestock on the down.

After Swanborough Hill comes a neck with views down both sides, where three round barrows are clearly distinguishable. After these we pass a dew-pond and then, at the turning of our route, another. On the hill here once stood Ashcombe Mill, notable in its day for being the only windmill in Sussex with six sweeps instead of the usual four, and, owing to its position, a great landmark. From here we look down on Cold Combe, which we shall now circumambulate. We are now on the line of an old track, Juggs Road, so called because the fisherfolk of Brightelmston (now Brighton), known to the prosperous citizens of Lewes as 'Juggs', brought their fish by this direct route across the downs to the county town. Juggs Road passes through Kingston at a point known as Nan Kemp's corner. A large stone at the parish boundary gave rise to one of those macabre local legends, now proved by patient research to be entirely without foundation. At its most lurid, Nan Kemp was supposed to be a mother who suffered so severely from what we would now call post-natal depression and became so jealous of her husband's affection for their baby, that she roasted it for him to eat; then killed herself at the parish boundary.

Sheep tracks on Swanborough Combe

In August 1899 W.H. Hudson, the naturalist who had already roamed the pampas and rain-forests of South America, lay down here on Kingston Hill and contemplated the softer charms of the South Downs. His eye was caught by the effect of the white tufts of thistledown detaching themselves from their stalks and floating off in the wind on their seed-bearing journeys, which in favourable conditions can extend for miles: 'Looking long and steadily at them – their birth and their flight – one could fancy that they were living things of delicate aerial forms that had existed for a period hidden and unsuspected among the matted roots of the turf, until their time had come to rise like winged ants from the soil and float in the air.' Another scholar earlier wandered over the hills of our Stage 3. This was John Dudeney, a boy who in the 1790s was under-shepherd to a flock of 1,400 sheep whose grazing area was on Newmarket Hill. This boy spent his hours of summer solitude in a remarkable achievement of self-education. He saved up to buy books, which he stored in a cavity of the ground which he called his 'understone library'. By this means he acquired knowledge of algebra, geometry, astronomy, French, and also Hebrew (from a Hebrew text of the Bible). Evidently he also kept a good eye on his flock, for in 1802 he was promoted as head shepherd to a flock on Rottingdean Hill. But soon afterwards he went to Lewes to join a printer's and later founded a school, dying a well-known and honoured member of the local establishment.

Just as intelligent shepherd-boys longed for education, so we who have been educated are curious to know about the shepherds and their flocks. Two hundred years ago it was reckoned that no less than 200,000 ewes were grazing on the South Downs between Eastbourne and Steyning. These were the famous black-faced South Downs sheep, the breed described at the time by Arthur Young:'Their shoulders are wide; they are round and straight in the barrel; broad upon the loin and hips; short well in the twist, which is a projection of flesh in the inner part of the thigh that gives a fullness when viewed from behind, and makes a South Down leg of mutton remarkably round and short, more than most breeds.' The classic flock consisted of about 500 breeding ewes of three ages. With the lambs, the total flock in summer could be as much as 1,500 head, about a quarter of which was culled annually. Great attention was paid to breeding by selected animals; also to winter feed (turnips and hay). Another feature of the husbandry of the sheep was that they were 'folded' each night all year round: i.e. they were enclosed in a space bounded by wooden hurdles which were shifted each day so that the sheep fertilised the fields with their manure; or else in permanent sheep yards. But in the daytime they were up on the downs, munching the turf and moving slowly forward across the open land, unconscious of the ecological miracle created by their grazing, or the magical musical effect of their bleating mingled with their tiny tinkling bells.

Clad in a long cloth cloak, and with a felt hat and crook in hand, the shepherds drove their flocks from the fold at break of day and returned with them at evening, an infinitely long daily routine brilliantly compressed by Milton:

> Together both, ere the high lawns appear'd
> Under the opening eye-lids of the morn,
> We drove afield, and both together heard
> What time the grayfly winds her sultry horn,
> Batt'ning our flock with the fresh dews of night,
> Oft till the star that rose, at evening, bright
> Towards Heaven's descent had sloped his westering wheel.

The shepherd's constant companion was his dog, a highly trained professional. Otherwise he was often alone, an acute observer of nature and steeped in nature-lore. But in May or June he took a subordinate place, when teams of men were hired by the farmers to undertake the shearing. Usually about thirty of them, men and boys, they were led by a 'Captain' and a 'Lieutenant' and sheared several flocks at each centre, kept going from dawn to dusk with liberal quantities of ale and beer and meat and cheese. After which the fleeces went off for sale, the team dispersed, and the shepherd resumed his solitary life.

Newmarket Plantation is the dull name for a fine grove of beeches with surrounding ash and undergrowth of hawthorn. It is second only to Chanctonbury in its isolated splendour, right on our path. As we come down towards it we see the way in which the wood bends away from the prevailing south-westerlies, and if they are blowing hard we can hear it sighing or even roaring. Our route past it is through a pasture bright with clover and ragwort, and rest-harrow, chickweed and toad-flax – a very good place to look at downland flowers. Just before the Plantation we can see the Sussex University buildings, designed by Basil Spence in the 1960s to melt into the park at Stanmer and lie below the level of the large park trees.

Stage 4
Lewes to **Pyecombe** 8½ miles

SPECIFICS

The first 2¾ miles lead up the dip slope and the last 1½ miles cut
down to Pyecombe, but all the rest is along the ridge. Nearly half
the stage is on earth or grass, some unconfined; there are no roads
except a quarter-mile in Pyecombe; and the rest is basically flint
track. Mostly arable. About eleven gates to open, nearly all in the
first part of the stage. Westbound, cumulative ascent 228 m, descent
178 m. Bridle-route throughout. See maps 18 and 17.

Route westbound

From the Newmarket Inn to Pyecombe Plough Inn 8½ miles (13.5
km)

(a) *From the Newmarket Inn to Ditchling Beacon* 5½ miles (8.5 kms)
From the Newmarket Inn cross the A27, then turn right to a path
leading up the embankment to a bridle-gate. Then up a sunken
track along a fence to Ashcombe Plantation. Through the wood
bearing left, then on across grass to a low point where two dry
valleys meet. From here the way is ahead uphill through a metal
bridle-gate to the left of a fence, then maintaining direction for
more than 1½ miles. We pass under electricity wires. Then at a
junction of bridleways, turn right. After a wood to our left, we come
to the turning sharp left on to the main ridge (junction with Stage
16). The confined track continues to the access road to Streathill
Farm. From here it becomes unconfined along a width of grass all
the way to the road at Ditchling Beacon.

(b) *From Ditchling Beacon to Pyecombe Plough Inn* 3 miles (5 km)
Continue along the ridge first on a well-defined track, then on grass,
then back on a track and over a rise. Where the track approaches

the Clayton Windmills, turn sharp left at a metal field-gate. A quarter-mile on, after New Barn Farm, turn right and downhill by a gravel track through Pyecombe golf-course. Cross the A273 to a confined path leading left: then right up a road into Pyecombe. Just before the church, turn left down to the Plough Inn on the A23.

Route eastbound

From Pyecombe Plough Inn to the **Newmarket Inn** $8\frac{1}{2}$ miles (13.5 km)

(a) *From Pyecombe Plough Inn to Ditchling Beacon* 3 miles (5 km) Go up the small road through the village. By the church turn right down to the A273. Left for 200 m by a confined path beside the road; then turn right into Pyecombe Golf Club. A gravel track now leads up through the course. At a bridleway crossing, turn left. A quarter-mile on, after passing New Barn Farm and before the windmills, turn sharp right uphill by a metal field-gate. The track leads up along the ridge of the downs: after a section on grass it resumes as a track to Ditchling Beacon.

(b) *From Ditchling Beacon to the Newmarket Inn* $5\frac{1}{2}$ miles (8.5 km) Across the road the way continues unconfined on a width of grass to the access road to Streathill Farm. Then it becomes a confined track across Plumpton Plain. The way turns sharp right (junction with Stage 16), still confined, with a wood to our right. More than half a mile on, at a bridleway junction, turn left. Then straight downhill, under electricity wires, for $1\frac{1}{2}$ miles. At the bottom, where two dry valleys meet, go through a metal bridle-gate and bear slightly right across grass to enter Ashcombe Plantation, bearing right in the wood. Then down by a sunken track beside a fence to the A27. Cross the road to the Newmarket Inn.

Approach by car

At start: Newmarket Inn is on the A27 between Lewes and
Brighton, 1 mile from Lewes. *At end*: Pyecombe is on the A23,
2 miles short of Brighton. *Also*: at Ditchling Beacon on a small road
over the downs from Ditchling to Brighton.

Approach by other transport

Train: British Rail at Lewes and Falmer (respectively 2½ miles and 2
miles from start of stage), and at Hassocks (2 miles from Jack and
Jill windmills). *Local buses*: Southdown services at Pyecombe to
Haywards Heath, Burgess Hill and Brighton (hourly, about
two-hourly on Sundays), and to Horsham and Brighton (hourly,
infrequent on Sundays); also many buses at Lewes. *Taxis*: Lewes,
S&G Taxis (07916–6116); Brighton, Radio Cabs (0273–24245).

Refreshment

Pubs: Newmarket Inn; Plumpton, Half Moon (real ale, meals);
Pyecombe, Plough (real ale, meals). *Drinking water*: by Newmarket
Inn.

Accommodation

Hotels or guest houses: White Hart Hotel, Lewes BN7 1XE (Cat
5/5/5; 07916–4676); Belvedere Guest House, 2 Albion Street,
Lewes BN7 2ND (Cat 3/2/2; 07916–6057); Lamb House, Chapel
Hill, Lewes BN7 2BB (Cat 1/1/1; 07916–3773); Jack and Jill Inn,
Brighton Road, Clayton, Hassocks BN6 (Cat 3/1/5; 07918–3595).
Other: Patcham Youth Hostel, Patcham Place, Brighton BN1 8YD
(0273–556196); grazing, Beacon House, Beacon Road, Ditchling,
Hassocks BN6 8XB (07918–4294).

Admission

Ditchling Beacon (Sussex Trust for Nature Conservation and
National Trust), open access; Jill (Jack and Jill Windmills Society),
probably open on summer Sundays; Danny (Mutual Householders
Association), May to September, Wednesdays and Thursday
afternoons.

Stage 4
Lewes to **Pyecombe**

O bold majestic downs, smooth, fair, and lonely;
O still solitude, only matched in the skies;
   Perilous in steep places,
   Soft in the level races,
Where sweeping in phantom silence the cloudland flies;
With lovely undulation of fall and rise;
   Entrenched with thickets thorned,
   By delicate miniature dainty flowers adorned!

Robert Bridges (1844–1930)
from 'The Downs'

Once outside the sound-band of the A27 we resume the silences of
the Way. Down to our right is Ashcombe House, largely hidden in
trees, a fine Georgian mansion of grey and red brick with a large
porch, now owned by Sussex University. Ashcombe Wood is
sycamore, with the ground thickly covered with ivy: here too is the
Arum known as 'Lords and Ladies' or 'Cuckoo Pint', easily
recognisable by its long coiled spathe which protects the purple
spadix, or by its brilliant poisonous fruits. After Ashcombe Wood
we descend to a point which by optical illusion appears to be
surrounded by higher ground, though in fact the water flows out by
the lower edge of the wood. From this point we now go gently uphill
for more than two miles on the dip slope. Balmer Down (Balmer
means stronghold pool) rises between two dry valleys – Ashcombe
Bottom and Buckland Hole. Our route up it is beside fences and
between fields, but flowers along the fence include toadflax and
weld. After a concrete pond and before electricity lines, the fields to
the left overlie an extensive lynchet system. Then, after turning

right, we are between hedges of hazel and hawthorn with spearwort and eyebright below. We pass by the posts of a former sheep pound and later, after the wood on our left, comes the sharp turning on to the ridge. The footpaths and bridleways around the slopes of Blackcap (the hill just through the gate at the corner) and Mount Harry beyond it are very good for wild flowers. A point of reference for excursions here is Plumpton, or more specifically the Half Moon, which bears the encouraging notice '*Hikers, walkers, and riders welcome*', and is approachable by bridleway either here or a mile on, just before Streathill Farm (in both cases only three-quarters of a mile off course).

Plumpton is the name of a Saxon village (no prizes for guessing that it means plum farm) now rather strung out. The church (St Michael's) is Norman, with a thirteenth-century chancel, and bears the faint imprints of medieval wall-paintings. The manor (Plumpton Place) is a sixteenth-century house redesigned by Edwin Lutyens, who is particularly associated with Sussex through his work with the pioneer garden-designer Gertrude Jekyll. At Plumpton Place he also built an ornate Mill House and bridge as an approach to the house. Both church and manor can be seen from the Way, though the eye is at first caught by the barrack-like buildings of the Plumpton Agricultural College, which owns some of the land around us.

Confusingly the top of the downs above Plumpton is known as Plumpton Plain and is on our left as we now go along the ridge. After the wood come fields; three-quarters of a mile after the corner, a bridleway leads off to the left. Within a few hundred metres it comes to a most interesting archaeological site. This is a settlement of the late Bronze Age and hence over 2,500 years old. The discovery consists of four embanked enclosures linked by trackways, each with the remains of a circular timber hut of 6 m diameter, which would have had a conical roof supported by a central post. Just south of the settlement is a contemporary field system. This, then, is where, in a drier climate than ours, a group of men and women lived by keeping cattle and pigs, and also sheep and goats; by trapping and hunting; by growing barley and collecting wild fruit. In other larger settlements they tanned leather, wove a primitive form of cloth from nettle fibre, made pottery, and fashioned bronze into spear-heads, sickle-heads, swords, axe-heads, gouges, and knives. And they walked along or beside the South Downs Way, using it as a great highway for movement and for droving flocks or herds.

We cross a surfaced road leading to Streathill Farm (just before it a field to our left contains a medieval stock-enclosure). This is the highest farmstead on the South Downs (200 m) and its name comes from Streat, one and a half miles north, which is on the line of a Roman road along the greensand way below the downs: the Saxon name for a Roman road was a 'streat'. Just after this, invisible from the Way though very prominent from below, is a belt of beeches in the shape of a V, planted in 1887 to commemorate Queen Victoria's golden jubilee. After Streathill Farm we are released from close-confining fences for more than two miles, and the Way ceases to be a narrow track and looks more as it mainly was in the past – a route of general direction across the downland turf. As we approach Ditchling Beacon, where sheep have munched for centuries, the turf is noticeably springy underfoot. This is because it is composed of thick layers of interlaced fibres, their roots entwined in the earth below, and constituting as many as twenty species to a square foot. This is the green carpet which becomes woven with colour in the summer, 'by delicate miniature dainty flowers adorned'. Ditchling Beacon is National Trust property. Around the top is a roughly rectangular earthwork, the outline of a hill-fort of the early Iron Age. At the summit, in place of a beacon – one of a series that were lit at the news of the Spanish Armada – is a trig point (an indication plaque has been stolen). The view is superb, right across the weald to the North Downs, picking out the Hog's Back near Guildford thirty-one miles away. On our route Firle Beacon is eleven miles back and Chanctonbury Ring twelve miles forward in direct line. Unfortunately the Beacon gets very overrun as it is the highest point on the South Downs in East Sussex (248 m), and a scenic road crosses to Brighton.

Robert Bridges' line, 'where sweeping in phantom silence the cloudland flies', reminds us that part of the charm of the natural scene of a ridge walk is in the clouds, those ephemeral shapes of such deceptive size and distance when seen from below, though like the moon much of their mystery has gone now that man flies around them and sees them from all angles. Perhaps the best days for downland views are those when in a fresh clear air the stratocumulus comes rolling across, bringing patches of shade. In *Wild Life in a Southern County* Richard Jefferies ninety years ago exactly described the effect: 'The shadows of the clouds come over the ridge, and glide with seeming sudden increase in speed down-hill, then along the surface of the corn, darkening it as they pass, with a bright band of light following swiftly behind. It is gone, and the beech copse away there is blackened for a moment as the shadow leaps it'.

A mile to the north is the little town of Ditchling, from which the beacon takes its name. Here, where formerly the Romans had a fortified camp, Diccel's people (Diccelingas in Old English) came and established a settlement which grew to be the administrative centre of a large Saxon royal estate. Ditchling remained important in the Middle Ages and possesses a beautiful thirteenth-century church, St Margaret's, cruciform and with a central tower. In later times Ditchling became a centre of religious dissent and many of the inhabitants worshipped not in the church but in the Old Meeting House of the Baptists, which is to be seen along a twitten, or walkway; actually, at one time Baptists walked from Lewes regularly to the Sunday services here. Ditchling has an unspoilt but traffic-soiled centre with several houses of note, including the Elizabethan Wings Place. Nearer below us in Westmeston (the west-most farm): St Martin's church has Norman walls in the chancel, a Norman doorway and font. It is built of flint and topped with a wooden bell-turret.

After Ditchling Beacon our next point of reference is the Keymer post: the arms are liable to get stolen but the post at least remains and has an acorn carved as a finial at the top. At the Keymer post we pass from East to West Sussex, and so from concrete plinths to wooden signposts. Soon afterwards we see the sweeps of the Clayton windmills looming up towards us.

Sheep on Ditchling Beacon

Windmills exercise a special fascination today, partly because they are one of the earliest forms of industrial machinery and partly because their power production is ecologically so satisfactory. How did they originate? They were introduced into England in the twelfth century, probably from observation of Middle Eastern mills during the Crusades. They provided an efficient alternative to water-mills, and in England both water and wind mills were mainly set to grinding corn. Each rural community needed its corn ground locally, so windmills were soon constructed near all villages which lacked fast-running streams, notably those around the South Downs. How did they operate? The original mills were post mills, i.e., they were balanced on a central post so that they could be turned to face the wind. The force of the wind drove the four stocks which were set with sails, and thus the axle or windshaft on which the stocks were supported. To this was fitted the brake wheel to regulate the speed; on its perimeter were gear teeth which drove the stone nut, which drove the stones. The millstones were of such a design that the grain, inserted through the eye of the upper stone which revolved at around 125 revolutions a minute, was ground between them and squeezed out at the rim.

Where I said 'were' I should have said 'are'. For windmills, having become disused almost totally (so that there were only about fifty working in England in 1946) are now staging a comeback. Here at Clayton the Jack and Jill Windmills Society (whose motto is *Remolam* – that I may grind again) is determined that Jill shall be grinding corn again within a few years. So when she comes alive, with the sweeps revolving and the huge driving-wheels turning and the stones grinding, with a clattering, humming, and roaring of all the component parts, those inside will experience the supreme satisfaction of smelling the warm flour as it runs out from the stones – the flour from wheat that has been ground down to a fine wheatmeal, which can be used to make rich brown bread with all the nourishment still in it, and not merely crushed on rollers. Operating a post mill is rather like sailing a ship. Great care must be made to keep her winded, to prevent her getting out of hand with excessive

Jill and Jack, two sweeps up

speed, to regulate the sails, etc. Jill was originally built in 1821 in Brighton and later was towed by oxen up to Clayton and worked here till 1909. Meanwhile her obviously masculine companion Jack, who is a smock mill (i.e. the mill revolves on rollers set in a tower so that externally only the cap moves, the whole appearance of the mill resembling a peasant in his smock) was built here in 1866. He had a nasty accident when he lost two sails and his fantail in a storm, and was converted into a dwelling though restored externally to his former glory. Jack and Jill are possibly the most famous windmills in England because of their position on the horizon by the main railway line to Brighton. They are a special attraction for the South Downs Way, and yet at the same time I must say that I am glad that the smooth lines of the downs are not broken by the harsh silhouettes of windmills, as they would have been 200 years ago.

From the windmills' car-park a bridleway leads down to Clayton, half a mile off: or more precisely to Clayton church, the old village being slightly to our right (Clayton like Plumpton is self-explanatory as a name). The outward aspect of the church of St John Baptist has not changed much for 500 years, with roof, porch, and bell-turret linked to plain walls of flint and lime. But inside, our eyes are held by one of the most remarkable examples of medieval wall-paintings, which gives an inkling of how the interior looked nearly 900 years ago. Technically, the story is that these murals were painted on to fresh plaster as it was laid, soon after 1100, but were later covered over – the area around the Saxon chancel arch by paint in the fifteenth century (to make way for the installation of a rood), and the other walls by whitewash in the seventeenth century (to banish superstition). Artistically, the paintings depict long lean figures in heavy ample garments and with exceedingly small heads, of a style that derives from the artists of Poitou and even Sicily, as well as from the Anglo-Saxon tradition. Theologically, they show the Last Judgement, with Christ in Glory flanked by the apostles, and the procession of humanity moving unequivocally towards heaven or hell. And emotionally, they translate us to a time when illiterate villagers stood and gazed on them and beheld the stern lessons of

Pyecombe pintle-gate and crook

morality, while in the candle-lit chancel the priest chanted in Latin and the deacon swung the censer.

Near the church is Clayton Manor, formerly the rectory, where a fragment of Roman mosaic was found. Of an even earlier date was a bronze brooch found at Clayton. Also near the church is the ornate entrance to the railway tunnel, dating from 1840, of yellow brick and with decorative turrets. It now encloses a little house between the turrets, with bright red paintwork and a cheerful appearance. The first trains roaring through each morning must have an extraordinary effect in the bedroom. In August 1861 a horrible accident occurred in the tunnel, killing 23 people and injuring 175.

Back on the Way, we pass the buildings of New Barn Farm and then go down through the Pyecombe golf-course to a road: this is on the line of a Roman road across the downs. At this point, if we turned up the road for 350 m, then left up a track for one mile, we would come to Wolstonbury Hill (Wulfstan's stronghold). This is a spur projecting from the ridge and hence very prominent. It is the site of an Iron Age hill-fort, and the bank and ditch protecting the spur from the south are still well defined. Within the defensive area are mounds of ancient flint mines. The hill looks down on Danny, an Elizabethan mansion, and beyond to the urbanisation around Keymer, Hurstpierpoint, and Burgess Hill.

Stage 4 ends at Pyecombe. Pyecombe means 'the valley below the peak', the peak being Wolstonbury Hill; though actually it is remarkable for being not in a valley but right up on the ridge of the downs at 100 m high. Appropriately, Pyecombe is mainly known as the place where shepherds' crooks were made, a Pyecombe crook (or hook, as the shepherds called it) being instantly recognisable by its long guide and small neat hook. The blacksmith's forge was just opposite the church, and at one end of the pintle gate into the churchyard a Pyecombe hook has been affixed. Pyecombe church (of the Transfiguration) is Norman, with a thirteenth-century tower with a Sussex cap. The flint walls are covered with pebble-dash. The chief object in this church is the Norman lead font, large and deep in size, and elegant and restrained in style.

Stage 5
Pyecombe to **Upper Beeding** 6½ miles

SPECIFICS

Only 1 mile or so of this stage is along the ridge; the rest takes
shortcuts behind it and ends on the Adur. Over half the route is on
grass or earth, the rest on chalk or flint track: no surfaced road. It is
very largely through arable, with patches of scrub and pasture.
About eight gates to open. Westbound, cumulative ascent 264 m,
descent 350 m. Bridle-route throughout. See maps 17, 16 and 15.

Route westbound

From Pyecombe Plough Inn to **A283** 6½ miles (10.5 km)

(a) *From Pyecombe Plough Inn to Devil's Dyke Hotel access road* 2½
miles (4 km)
Cross the A23 and take a concrete lane opposite, going straight
ahead to a bridle-gate and then uphill on a path between hedges.
After a bridle-gate near the crest of the hill the path maintains
direction for 150 m then veers slightly to the right. Over West Hill,
then down, following the line of a fence. Then ahead into a sunken
lane which leads through a bridle-gate and past the cottages and
barns of Saddlescombe to a road. Cross the road leftwards to a track
leading uphill, passing to the right of a reservoir, then slightly
leftwards and on up through bushes and at first parallel to a road on
our left. The track leads on to cross the Devil's Dyke Hotel access
road at the crest of the hill, at bridle-gates.

(b) *From Devil's Dyke Hotel access road to A283* 4 miles (6.5 km)
Go across the grass pasture directly away from the road, and with
the earth ramparts of the hill-fort to our right. To our left a fence
draws nearer to where we go through a gate. The track then leads
ahead over Fulking Hill and then Perching Hill. Then, where it goes

under electricity wires, it inclines half left to go around Edburton
Hill; and at the saddle beyond, slightly left again up around
Truleigh Hill. Then past the radio masts and buildings on Truleigh
Hill by a broad lane: after a belt of pines continue along the path
parallel to the road, gently downhill to where the road turns. Here
proceed through a bridle-gate ahead, downhill through a pasture
and then by another gate to a path between fences which goes down
to the A283: Stage 6 continues 100 m left.

Route eastbound

From A283 to Pyecombe Plough Inn 6½ miles (10.5 km)

(a) *From A283 to Devil's Dyke Hotel access road* 4 miles (6.5 km)
From the end of Stage 6 cross the A283 and go left for over 100 m;
then right, up Beeding Hill on a track confined between fields and,
after a field-gate, across a pasture to a bridle-gate to join a road.
Continue ahead on a path parallel to the road leading uphill. After a
belt of pines the way goes on past the buildings and radio masts on
Truleigh Hill. The track then descends to a saddle; then half right to
go up around Edburton Hill. After passing under electricity wires, it
is up over Perching Hill and then Fulking Hill. Then, at a gate, go
ahead through the middle of a pasture, with the earth ramparts of a
hill-fort to our left, to a bridle-gate at the Devil's Dyke Hotel access
road.

(b) *From Devil's Dyke Hotel access road to Pyecombe Plough Inn* 2½
miles (4 km)
Cross the road on to a track ahead through bushes, which draws
near to a road on our right, leading gently downhill. Later, where
we come to an open space, the track passes to the left of a reservoir
and comes down to a road. Across the road and past the barns and
cottages of Saddlescombe. Then through a gate and up a sunken
lane; then on uphill, keeping to the line of a fence. On West Hill we
go through two bridle-gates, then downhill, taking the track slightly
leftwards, to a bridle-gate and a track between hedges which leads
down to a concrete lane and the A23.

Approach by car

At start: Pyecombe is on the A23, 2 miles short of Brighton. *At end*: on the A283, 200 m towards Shoreham from the roundabout with the A2037 at Upper Beeding. *Also*: from the secondary road over the downs between Poynings and Brighton, at Saddlescombe and at Devil's Dyke Hotel (car-park); and on the small road from Shoreham up to Tottington Barn.

Approach by other transport

Train: British Rail at Hassocks (2½ miles from start of stage). *Local buses*: Southdown services at Pyecombe to Haywards Heath, Burgess Hill and Brighton (hourly, about two-hourly on Sundays), and to Horsham and Brighton (hourly, infrequent on Sundays); at Devil's Dyke (summer only, Sundays variable); at Beeding cement works to Shoreham and Steyning (hourly). *Taxis*: Brighton, Radio Cabs (0273–24245); Shoreham, rank (07917–2828).

Refreshment

Pubs: Pyecombe, Plough (real ale, meals); Poynings, Royal Oak (real ale, meals); Devil's Dyke Hotel; Fulking, Shepherd and Dog (real ale, meals); Upper Beeding, Bridge (real ale).

Accommodation

Hotels or guest houses: Tottington Manor, Edburton, Henfield BN5 9LJ (Cat 5/4/5; 0903–815757); Follymead, Mill Lane, Poynings BN4 7AE (Cat 1/2/1; 079156–286); Downers Vineyard, Clappers Lane, Fulking, Henfield BN5 9NH (Cat 1/2/1; 079156–484). *Other*: Youth Hostel, Tottington Barn, Truleigh Hill, Shoreham BN4 5FB (0903–813419); grazing, stabling, camping, Brendon Riding School, Pyecombe, Hassocks (07918–2158).

Admission

Newtimber Place (Mrs Clay), May to August, afternoons:
Newtimber Hill (National Trust), open access: Saddlescombe Chalk
Pit (Sussex Trust for Nature Conservation), open access: Devil's
Dyke (Brighton Council), open access.

Stage 5

Pyecombe to **Upper Beeding**

DESCRIPTION

Higher and higher to the north aspire the green smooth-swelling
    unending downs;
East and west on the brave earth's breast glow girdle-jewels of
    gleaming towns;
Southward shining, the lands declining subside in peace that the
    sea's light crowns.

Algernon Charles Swinburne (1837–1909)
from 'On the South Coast'

After crossing the main London to Brighton road (traffic lights
make possible what would otherwise be impossible on summer
weekends) we go past the Brendon Riding School and with luck
may see horses being put over the bright array of jumps – logs,
gates, hedges, banks or dykes, some in double or triple succession
and several over 1.5 m high. Horse shows are often held here, with
immaculate riders in white breeches and red or black jackets adding
colour to the scene.

    We follow the track up past a hawthorn hedge and so on to West
Hill, a hump surrounded by downland on all sides. Just to the north
is Newtimber Hill, owned by the National Trust and with wooded
crest and turfy slopes: there are Stone Age flint workings and early
field systems on it. Beyond it is Newtimber Place, a moated
Elizabethan house and ancestral home of the Buxton family. By
now the roar of the road has yielded to the song of the skylark. The
astonishing performance given us by the lark is eternally fresh, a
loud clear warble uttered from a fluttering flight high above the
ground and sometimes continued for as long as five minutes.
Certainly we all know that this is done basically to distract our

attention from that vulnerable grass-lined nest in the corn; but the song is far more than one of expediency or despair. As heard by the human ear, it is one of the most moving and poignant expressions of defiance, energy and joy. Each of Shelley's twenty-one stanzas on the skylark expresses an aspect of its unpremeditated art, and my excuse for quoting one of them is that he was born and bred in Sussex, at Horsham.

> Higher still and higher
>   From the earth thou springest,
> Like a cloud of fire;
>   The blue deep thou wingest,
> And singing still dost soar, and soaring ever singest.

We now descend to Saddlescombe (the valley by the saddle of land, and pronounced 'Salscum'), going down a sunken lane between ash scrub. As seen from our approach, Saddlescombe is a sleepy hamlet with cottages beside our track and flint farm-buildings. This small place has an ancient history. The manor of Saddlescombe was owned by the abbey of Bosham in Saxon days, then at the Conquest was awarded to the powerful William de Warenne (together with forty-three other Sussex manors): under the Warenne and then Fitzalan overlords it became subfeuded to first the Templars and then the order of St John. At the Dissolution it was purchased by Sir Anthony Browne, an intimate of Henry VIII, as part of the Cowdray estate: from the Brownes it went to the Egremonts, and then in 1921 was sold to the tenant farmer, Mr E. Robinson. From the memoirs of one of the Robinson family we have a charming description of life at Saddlescombe over a hundred years ago. The farm comprised 900 acres and had three flocks of sheep which were driven on to the downland by day. The oxen were formerly of the red Sussex breed, but were later replaced by large black Pembrokes. They worked in pairs, were shod like horses, and responded to their names, such as 'Hawk and Pheasant', 'Quick and Nimble', 'Crisp and Curly', 'Pert and Lively'. Besides the rooks which still dominate

Saddlescombe farm-buildings

the ashes and sycamores at Saddlescombe, there were quail and kestrels and occasional ravens; and besides foxes there were badgers. The Robinsons were Quakers and their home life was extremely spartan, though not so hard as that of their labourers who earned less than £1 a week in the 1860s. But there was hidden treasure all around them: 'A half-groat of Henry VII was pulled up with a mangold-wurzel and a large silver coin of Charles I was found under hill turf.'

From West Hill we have seen ahead the upper slopes of the Devil's Dyke, and the South Downs Way now continues to the left of it. But for those with time to spare and no fear of mud, a worthwhile deviation is to go down to Poynings and then up through the bottom of the Dyke itself. It is half a mile to Poynings by the bridleway which we find by going a few metres up the main road to our right, then down to the left: on the way down through coppices we pass near the old Saddlescombe treadmill which was worked by a donkey. Poynings (Puna's people, and pronounced 'Punnins') is centred on its church, Holy Trinity. This fine cruciform building of knapped flint dates from 1369, and is reminiscent of St Andrew's Alfriston in Stage 2. But whereas the windows of Alfriston are in the Decorated style, those at Poynings have advanced into the Perpendicular, with straight chunky mullions leading upwards to the arches. As at Alfriston, it is the sense of space within that amazes, heightened when entering on a hot day and finding the church cool and quiet. Three hundred metres beyond the church along the underhill lane is the Royal Oak; its sign depicts the mature tree which shielded the royal fugitive, and the acorn from which both tree and Restoration evolved. Just up the road from where our bridleway emerged, the Sussex Trust for Nature Conservation has nurtured a rare colony of junipers – juniper, the cypress with the needle-leaves and fleshy cones and delicate fragrant wood.

From Poynings the route up the bottom of the Dyke starts only a few metres to the left of where we emerged. We go past fields and through ash and then arrive at the foot of the glen. This is the best place to observe the strange little valley which cuts into the

The Devil's Dyke curving upwards

escarpment for three-quarters of a mile, secluding itself when turning. So straight and smooth are its slopes that it seems incredible that they are natural and not man-made. Folk-lore solved this problem by attributing the whole thing to the Devil. Satan was trying to cut a dyke through the downs and bring in the sea to flood the churches in the weald. He had nearly succeeded in his fiendish plan when fortunately he was disturbed by an old woman carrying a candle, which he mistook for the dawn. Since he could only operate in darkness he left his work unfinished, but not before he had made a right mess of the downs; for the earth which he had shovelled out with his great spade had landed all over the place, causing the mounds and tumuli which so intrigue the archaeologists.

The old story has a modern sequel: for who but the Devil would have induced the fearful commercialisation of the Devil's Dyke in recent times? A railway line was built from Brighton up to Devil's Dyke Farm; a double-track funicular was constructed from near Poynings up the north face of Dyke Hill; and a cable-car (whose concrete anchoring-posts we still see) straddled the gorge itself. Massive housing development was then threatened. But these diabolical schemes were thwarted, not by an old woman with a candle but by the Brighton Corporation with a lot of money. The Devil has since been reduced to sending litter-bugs and probing cars and motorbikes into the area. The section of the South Downs Way that leads from Saddlescombe up through the thickets of Summerdown to Dyke Hill is consequently rather grubby, though wooden posts now help restrict car entry. We pass the iron railings of a reservoir, of the sort installed before the last war. With its steep slopes and also its road, car-park and pub at the top, Dyke Hill is a prime site for hang-gliders. Helmeted figures assemble their wings on tripods, then take long strides downhill and are off. Once airborne they hoist themselves into the saddle and stirrups and lie horizontal, controlling the wings purely by balance. Suspended above the scarp, they look like large insects or even prehistoric reptiles such as the pterodactyl. Strangely they don't seem to frighten the birds, but the horses often scare when they come whooshing by. In the pasture above the Dyke we pass the ditch and rampart of the Iron Age fort, still massive after 2,000 years of erosion; (actually the term 'Devil's Dyke' originally referred to this earthwork rather than to the valley below it). This fortification guarded the vulnerable neck of the promontory beyond, and lesser earthworks secured the northern side of the enclosure. Probably Devil's Dyke fort was at one time the main point of control of the whole downland area between Ouse and Adur, though at other times Wolstonbury (only two miles off) or Hollingbury assumedly exercised influence.

We are now back on the crest of the downs which we left back at Clayton in Stage 4, and have views down to the sea over Portslade and Southwick, 'girdle-jewels of gleaming towns'. Below is Fulking (Folca's people) which can be reached either by bridleway from the top pasture or by footpath from the saddle between Fulking and Perching Hills. These bring us steeply down around a combe to the garden of the Shepherd and Dog. This pub is well worth the detour and drop of 100 m. It has a delightful garden set between banks of flowers and it serves good food, featuring old-fashioned herb-flavoured pork sausages and delicious firm chocolate mousses. Just in front of the pub is a red-brick green-roofed structure with water gushing out, and on it the inscription, '*He sendeth springs into the valleys which run among the hills: O that men would therefore praise the Lord for his goodness*' (quotations from psalms 104 and 107). This is a fountain erected as a memorial to John Ruskin, the Victorian arbiter of art and architecture, who when walking here from Brighton had suggested the channelling of nearby springs to the village. The effect of this inspiring monument is rather spoilt by the local council notice that the water isn't safe for drinking. As it must come straight from the chalk it's hard to see how it could be polluted, though in the old days the water here was used by animals and for sheep-dipping.

A pleasant sequence of little rounded hilltops now follows. In only $1\frac{1}{2}$ miles we have Fulking Hill, Perching Hill, Edburton Hill, and Truleigh Hill. Each name relates to a farmstead below the scarp-face. Perching is 'the people of the small enclosure', Truleigh is 'tree clearing', and Edburton 'Eadburga's farmstead': Princess Eadburga, the granddaughter of Alfred the Great, founded a church here. On the summit of Edburton Hill, but out of our sight as

we skirt around it, are the earthworks of a Norman fort which guarded the boundary between the Rapes of Lewes and Bramber. It had a small motte (earth rampart) and in the centre a very small rectangular bailey (tower). Down below at Edburton is St Andrew's church, mainly Early English in style: the interior is whitewashed and contains a Norman lead font (comparable to the font at Pyecombe) and Stuart pulpit and altar-rails. It is said that the downs around Edburton Hill were one of the last areas where – till about 1800 – the great bustard (the largest native British bird in its day, whose habitat was wide-open spaces) was hunted by greyhounds. This was not the only unusual way that birds were killed. All along the downs in spring the shepherds were busy trapping the wheatear. The wheatear, so called from its white rump, was then much more common than now: when intimidated it has the habit of going for cover in the ground. The shepherds therefore made shallow trenches of about a foot long and covered them with turf except for an entrance hole. In these they trapped the wheatear in huge numbers. The birds were sent to the London market packed in fat in barrels, and were usually eaten roasted, wrapped in vine leaves.

Now comes Truleigh Hill with three radio masts extruding, in contrast to the power lines from Portslade which cross the downs discreetly between Perching and Edburton Hills. We pass a large barn, some houses, and Freshcombe and Summerdean Farms. Sheep are kept here and (at the time of writing) horses for escorted rides. At the far end of the complex is Truleigh Hill Youth Hostel, an important staging-post for many South Down walkers. The hostel is on the site of a barn which belonged to Tottington (Totta's farmstead), the next habitation below the scarp. After an avenue of firs comes the path beside the small access road down the side of Beeding Hill: to our right a grassy combe, with old cultivation terraces on it, gives views down to Upper Beeding (Beada's people). At a large Downsmen's signpost the valley of the Adur is spread before us, cutting through the downs to the 'southward shining sea' at Shoreham (where Swinburne wrote 'On the South Coast'). Ignoring the chimney of the cement works, the most

Elegance on Perching Hill

interesting points of reference are the ruins of Bramber Castle
upstream, the Lancing College chapel downstream, and
Chanctonbury Ring ahead, which all belong to Stage 6. We descend
to the main road between fences brightened with poppies,
geranium, camomile, mallow, white campion, and scarlet
pimpernel.

Stage 6
Upper Beeding to **Washington** 7 miles

From the Adur the route goes around the head of Steyning Bowl
and then mostly just behind the ridge and up and over Chanctonbury
Hill. One mile is on small surfaced roads, nearly 1½ miles are on
earth or grass, and the rest on firm chalk or flint track, steep at one
point. Sections of pasture but mostly arable. About six gates to
open. Westbound, cumulative ascent 234 m, descent 146 m.
Bridle-route throughout. See maps 15 and 14.

Route westbound

From A283 to A24 7 miles (11 km)

(a) *From A283 to Steyning Round Hill road* 2 miles (3 km)
From the end of Stage 5 turn left along the A283 for more than 100 m,
then through a bridle-gate on the other side of the road. From
here a confined path leads to the bridle-bridge over the Adur.
Follow the embankment to the right upstream for 150 m, then left
along a track to a gate at a road. Right along the road for half a mile.
Just after Annington House, where the road turns right, go left up a
sunken track between trees. The track turns right and uphill near
farm buildings: then leads steadily up the edge of fields. At a
bridle-gate it briefly turns right, then resumes direction up to the
road on Steyning Round Hill.

(b) *From Steyning Round Hill road to A24* 5 miles (8 km)
Turn right along the road for half a mile; then, where it bears right,
go ahead through a gate along the edge of a field to a bridleway
crossing. Ahead and up on a track between fields. At a fork bear
right, keeping to the crest of the downs and up towards
Chanctonbury Ring. The track then crosses the grass in front of the

ring and leads on past a dew-pond. A quarter-mile beyond the dew-pond turn right at a bridleway junction. The route now goes steeply downhill on chalk and later gravel, and comes to the A24.

Route eastbound

From A24 to A283 7 miles (11 km)

(a) *From A24 to Steyning Round Hill road* 5 miles (8 km)
From the A24 take the track uphill, at a fork bearing right. The track continues steeply up the flank of the down. At the top, shortly after it levels, turn left at a bridleway junction. The track then leads up to pass to the right of Chanctonbury Ring, and continues along the crest of the downs curving gently but maintaining direction, passing a bridleway crossing on the way. Later it comes to another bridleway crossing and goes through the gate ahead, then down to a gate and ahead along the road for half a mile.

(b) *From Steyning Round Hill road to A283* 2 miles (3 km)
Turn left off the road at a wooden gate just before the road turns right. The path leads downwards along the edge of fields, then curves uphill briefly with the line of a fence, then left through a gate to maintain direction. Then downhill at the edge of fields to farm buildings, and so leftward into a tree-lined lane. At a road turn right: half a mile later, where the road turns right shortly before a church, go left through a gate on to a track to the embankment of the Adur. Right downstream for 150 m, then across the bridle-bridge and so by a confined path to the A283.

Approach by car

At start: on the A283, 200 m towards Shoreham from the roundabout with the A2037 at Upper Beeding. *At end*: on the A24, 1 mile south of Washington roundabout, turn off on to a secondary road. *Also*: at Botolphs and above Steyning Bowl (car-park), both on small roads from Steyning.

Approach by other transport

Local buses: Southdown services at Beeding cement works to Shoreham and Steyning (hourly); at Washington to Worthing and Horsham (about hourly to Worthing, two-hourly to Horsham: infrequent on Sundays). *Taxis*: Shoreham, rank (07917–2828); Worthing, Golden Car (0903–38826).

Refreshment

Pubs: Upper Beeding, Bridge (real ale); Steyning, Norfolk Arms (real ale, meals); Washington, Frankland Arms (real ale, meals). *Restaurant*: Steyning, Springwells Hotel.

Accommodation

Hotels or guest houses: Springwells Hotel, High Street, Steyning BN4 3GG (Cat 4/4/5; 0903–812446)

Admission

Bramber, House of Pipes (Anthony Irving), daily: Cissbury (National Trust), open access.

Stage 6
Upper Beeding to Washington

Say what you will, there is not in the world
A nobler sight than from this upper down.
No rugged landscape here, no beauty hurled
From its Creator's hand as with a frown;
But a green plain on which green hills look down
Trim as a garden plot. No other hue
Can hence be seen, save here and there the brown
Of a square fallow, and the horizon's blue.

Wilfrid Scawen Blunt (1840–1922)
from 'Chanclebury Ring'

Through banks of mallow we start this stage by using a modern
bridge to cross a modern river. The bridge was built specially for the
South Downs Way. The river, embanked as we see it, was formerly
an estuary of the sea with wide mud-flats where at high tide large
boats sailed up between the downs. Even the name Adur is fairly
new, coined by Michael Drayton four centuries ago (he assumed
that Shoreham was on the site of the Roman harbour Portus
Adurni, though Portsmouth is more likely): formerly this was called
the Bramber Water. The road, the cement works, the pylons and
the disused railway line we cross just after the river, all these
complete the utilitarian scene; but from our bridge we can see a
mile upstream the clump of trees which cover the mound on which
Bramber (bramble thicket) Castle was built, and the grey flint
section of wall which is all that remains of it. Here was the
strong-point that dominated this locality from Saxon times and

St Botolph's church

which became the chief fortress of the Norman Rape of Bramber under William de Braose. Well within range of the archers and slingers in the towers and turrets, ships unloaded their cargoes at Bramber port, and travellers crossed over to Beeding on a great stone bridge: it was 52 m long and 5 m wide, had four arches resting on huge piers with cutwaters, and over the central pier on the southern side a large chapel capped the construction. In the Civil War the castle was besieged by the Parliamentarians and there was a skirmish at the bridge. Castle and bridge are now no more and Bramber is just an intervening row of buildings adjacent to Steyning. It became one of the more notorious of the rotten boroughs, gradually reducing to only eighteen voters returning two Members of Parliament. When William Wilberforce passed through the village in his coach, someone mentioned to him that it was Bramber. 'Bramber?' he said. 'Why, that's the place I'm Member for.'

From where we join a small road we are in a hamlet called Botolphs after St Botolph's church 200 m to our right (Botolph was an early English missionary). This became a shrunken village in the late Middle Ages, when its economy died from the receding sea which spelt the end of local fishing and salt industry, and mounds and declivities still show where homesteads once were. The church has a Saxon nave, long and tall, and a Saxon chancel arch with roll-moulded rim. The rise and fall of the prosperity of the village is mutely expressed in the three thirteenth-century arches along the north wall, which served to provide a north aisle for the growing population, but later were filled in again when the population fell. The house by the church incorporates some of the fourteenth-century constructions of the original priest's house. Along the hedge-lined lane we next pass Annington Farm and then the manor house, with Georgian brick frontage and an orchard.

By means of a farm lane lined with chestnut and sycamore, we climb gently up Annington Hill between fields with good views. The sea is hardly three miles off: looking towards it we are struck by a large building on the top of a hill. This is Lancing School chapel, built progressively over the past hundred years in the Gothic style. From nearly two miles away we can only see its bulk, and not its stunning proportions, beautiful finish, or impressive set of towers, pinnacles and flying buttresses. The sensation of height and light when entering the chapel is quite unforgettable, induced by the clusters of columns reaching from the floor to the vault and the large windows in aisles and clerestory. Lancing chapel is the Anglican equivalent of the Roman Catholic cathedral at Arundel, since both seek to recreate the medieval in the grand manner: but of the two Lancing is undoubtedly the more dramatic.

As we go up Annington Hill, passing the newly-planted clump of Bramber Beeches, we round the head of Steyning Bowl, at the foot of which is the old town of Steyning (pronounced 'Stenning'). Steyning means the dwellers by a stony place, and may refer to Celtic stones found here. We can reach it either by the lane at Botolphs or by the road we now briefly follow -- either way a diversion of about one mile. Penetrating through the ring of modern homes we come to the old centre only to find that, as is typical in old Sussex towns, there is no real centre but a rambling high street. To savour Steyning one should stand at the corner of the High Street and Church Street. In Church Street is a group of sixteenth- and seventeenth-century houses as good as any in the county. In the High Street are Georgian houses such as the Chequers Inn and Lloyds Bank, and also Chantry House. Standing by itself away from the streets is St Andrew's, Steyning's great Norman church. To sit in the nave and study the arches with their multiple orders, each with separate shafts and capitals and with nothing fumbled or mis-shapen, is to sense the virility and inventiveness of the twelfth-century master-masons. In the porch is a Saxon tomb slab which some have identified with that of Aethelwulf, King Alfred's father. The establishment of a large Norman church on an earlier Saxon foundation is appropriate because Steyning featured as one of the causes of the Conquest, William I having a grievance against Harold for sequestering it from the Abbey of Fécamp in Normandy.

Steyning is also notable in having its own local saint, Cuthman, whose story is curious and charming. Cuthman was a shepherd-boy in the west of England who decided to travel eastwards. But unlike most young men who leave home, Cuthman took his old mum Frippa along with him; and as she was disabled he pulled her along

in a cart with a rope. On the way they passed some men mowing the grass for hay, who were loud in their mockery at this pathetic procession, especially when the rope broke and Cuthman had to replace it with twines of branches and withies: divine retribution instantly visited the mowers with heavy rain. Later, when even the improvised rope broke, Cuthman realised that he must stop: at Steyning he built for himself and his mother a hut and later a church for the local people whom he had converted to the faith.

Back on the Way we pass over Steyning Round Hill: here, when the down was first ploughed in 1949, twenty Bronze Age funeral urns were sliced up by the plough. With two further humps and the crests of hanging woods to the north, our view concentrates southwards, and ever more clearly we can now pick out the earthworks of Cissbury at the end of the long low line of Lychpole Hill. Cissbury can be reached by a bridleway to our left, a diversion of two miles along the line of an old drove road much used by horses (there are racing stables at Findon). On the way there we pass close by Park Brow, where a late Bronze Age settlement of at least eight round huts has been excavated, with extensive field systems around it.

Of all the Iron Age forts on the South Downs, Cissbury is the largest and most impressive: in fact it is the most formidable earth-fort on any English chalk hilltop apart from Maiden Castle in Dorset. An area of 60 acres is enclosed by a massive rampart with an external ditch and smaller counterscarp bank outside the ditch, built around 250 BC. The crest/ditch vertical height is at one point still 12 m; and the wooden palisades would have added further to the height. It is calculated that around 10,000 timber posts were used, each 4.6 m long. As with the other hill-forts, the precise purpose cannot be known, particularly the extent to which it was a refuge in time of danger or a permanently inhabited settlement. Nor can we tell whether it was constructed to defend an area of tribal territory from that of another, or mainly to combat the incursions of new waves of Celtic invaders from the sea. Possibly it fulfilled all these roles at different times, and certainly we know that it was

Church Street, Steyning

refortified in the later Roman period, probably against the Saxons. And we know it by association with the final masters of the fort, the South Saxons, since it came in time to be named after their chief, Cissa. But of that earlier time, just before the dawn of recorded history in Britain, the great ring of earthwork keeps its secrets. All we can say for sure is that whoever ruled here commanded the downland between Adur and Arun. As to his power, authority, personality, or the fortunes of his tribe, we remain ignorant. While the Celtic chieftain sat in his hut of wood, hill-forts had already developed into thriving cities on the shores of the Mediterranean, and on the most brilliant of them all the Athenians had built the eternal temples of their Acropolis.

Another feature of Cissbury is that within the large enclosure are the chalk-waste humps of some 200 flint mines dug here by the people of the late Stone Age, and hence even more remote in time from the Celtic fort-builders than the Celts are from us. Flint was essential to these people, especially for making axes, and the best flint lay in seams within the chalk. At Cissbury the seam was about 12 m below the surface. With nothing better than the antlers of a red deer for a pick (the brow tine served as the pick and the beam as the handle) the primitive miners dug their shafts and tunnels and by the light of tallow candles cut into the seam and extracted the precious flint. Besides the all-important axes, flint was used for arrow-heads, daggers, scythes, scrapers, and chisels. This stone which can produce so sharp a cutting edge remained the basic tool of ordinary people long after their rulers had abandoned it for bronze and later iron.

Now we come up to Chanctonbury Ring, the crown and symbol of the South Downs. In whatever season or weather it is always impressive, whether in clarity from far off, or looming out of the mist; a single mass of grey-black trunks and spindly branches in winter, or in the summer the fragmentation of millions of delicate green leaves. The clump is renowned as a beech grove, planted originally more than two centuries ago expressly to impress and delight the eye. The beeches with their smooth metallic trunks and

Within Chanctonbury Ring

glossy leaves give a clean-cut contrast to the downland turf around and to the grass which unusually grows beneath them. But they have also been supplemented by a few Scots firs, evergreen oaks, and sycamores, as well as more beech saplings: and the tallest of all is a mighty ash, showing what ash can do if favourably treated. The clump bends from the south-west and merges with the hanging woods on the north escarpment.

The Ring itself is a bank and ditch surrounding the central area of about 4 acres: clearly a Celtic fort. In the middle a temple was built during the Roman era; it was 6 m square, was surrounded by a verandah, and would have been used for the submission of votive offerings to some local deity – flowers or food or perhaps the sacrifice of a chicken or goat. The Ring, the great ash tree, the spirits of the gods, the Celtic warriors, all these call to mind Wagnerian themes, not the least those evoking the spring and nature, forest murmurs and birdsong, and the will to wander wide across the land. Chanctonbury (the name means the stronghold near Chancton, the farm near the brushwood thicket) mystically attracts urban man as much as pagan man, and the clump of trees induce an almost religious awe. And from the cool shade of the beeches we get a perfect view of the weald and the downs – 'a green plain on which green hills look down'.

The man responsible for the beeches of Chanctonbury was Charles Goring, the owner of Wiston House which we can just see from the eastern edge of the Ring, a mile away and 180 m below among the large trees of its park. The Goring family still owns a large estate here, though the house itself is used by the government for the laudable purpose of fostering Anglo–German relations. Wiston (Winestane's farmstead, and pronounced 'Wissun') is basically an Elizabethan stone house with large mullion windows. Beside it is St Michael's church, much restored in the last century but now again in rather derelict condition, with an effigy of Sir John de Braose its principal treasure: Sir John is wearing complete plate armour, his head in a basinet (helmet), his waist in a baudric (broad leather belt), and his feet in sollerets (long footguards with pointed

Chalk track on Chanctonbury Hill

toes). At the time the house was built, Wiston belonged to the
Shirley family, and the three sons of Thomas Shirley were colourful
products of a colourful period. Inspired by the exploits of Drake
and Raleigh, Anthony Shirley led a piratical raid into the Caribbean
in 1596, but in spite of looting the towns of St Iago and St Martha, he
returned next year empty-handed. He then travelled to the Levant
and on to Persia, taking his younger brother Robert with him. These
swashbuckling gallants caused a sensation at the court of Shah
Abbas, and Robert so adapted himself to life in this distant land that
he took to wearing Persian dress and married a Caucasian beauty,
Teresia. He returned to England as the Shah's ambassador; and
though this title was largely honorific it enabled him and his wife to
appear on grand occasions at the court of Charles I arrayed, to the
huge amusement of the courtiers, in their exotic silken robes, in
which they have been captured in the canvases of Anthony Van
Dyck at Petworth House. Meanwhile Thomas, the eldest brother,
restive at remaining at home with his old father whilst Anthony and
Robert hit the headlines, as it were, left Wiston and travelled rather
ineffectually himself, to the detriment of his estate.

Five hundred metres beyond Chanctonbury Ring, soon after the
faint remains of a cross-dyke, we come to the best example of a
dew-pond on our route. The word dew-pond is misleading, because
the dew has no special effect on them. 'Mist-pond' would be a better
name, because they are designed to encourage precipitation, though
even this has only a marginal effect. The main attribute of the
dew-pond is that it is extremely efficient in capturing and retaining
rainwater, and in fact this one did not completely dry up even in the
hot summer of 1976. When the pit has been dug, the bottom is lined
with compacted clay tempered with lime to stop worms penetrating.
Then straw is placed over it to prevent the clay from cracking in the
heat of the sun. On top of the straw bed is laid a mixture of chalk
rubble and flints, to prevent cattle and sheep from breaking it up.
The animals by constant use of the dew-pond also keep the verges
cropped so that weeds do not invest it. There is no reference to
dew-ponds before the eighteenth century, but presumably they
existed in some form before. They then fell into disrepair when
water was piped up to the downs. The Chanctonbury dew-pond,

built originally in 1870, has been reconstructed by the Sussex Downsmen, providing a practical aid for riders and an interesting example for everyone, especially in the variety of plants that grow around it.

Soon after, the Way descends steeply down a chalk track through thickets and past the pits of former chalk quarries. On the grassy banks, besides red campion, harebells, centaury, birdsfoot trefoil, and coltsfoot, the common spotted orchid grows profusely. But perhaps the best feature of this descent is the variety of shrubs all in one small area, not cramped in a hedge but growing freely: the hazel with its smooth brown stems and rounded, long-pointed leaves; the hawthorn and the blackthorn with their spiny branches and cascades of white blossom in which the deep colours of their fruits (the bright red haws of the hawthorn or the bluish-black sloes of the blackthorn) are delicately anticipated; the spindle with its green bark and twigs, and scattered star-like flowers; the maple and the guelder-rose, whose best showings are in the autumn when their leaves turn red; and the whitebeam, which in spring presents the white woolly undersides of its leaves to give an almost dreamlike appearance.

Just before the end of this stage, after passing a grass-covered gas-pressure reducing station and a chalk quarry, a footpath leads down to the right for half a mile to Washington (the farmstead of Wassa's people) now secluded from the main road by a bypass: and riders can get there by the old main road, from which they can also cross the A24 by a bridge and thence by bridleway reach Barnsfarm Hill in Stage 7. The old village is built from a variety of materials: some houses are of flint or brick or clunch, and some of sandstone (of which there are two sorts, the green Burgate and the dark brown). St Mary's church was rebuilt in 1865 in the Early English style, very effective and compact, and with plenty of colour from the stained glass and the chancel roof, painted deep blue and studded with stars. Refreshment is to be found at the Frankland Arms. Nowadays they sell Whitbread beers, but when Hilaire Belloc came here and pronounced that 'the swipes they take at the Washington Inn is the very best beer I know', it was Mitchell's ale that was sold. That great imbiber would certainly beckon us down to Washington before going on to tackle Stage 7.

Stage 7
Washington to **Amberley** 6 miles

SPECIFICS

This stage is on or close behind the ridge, descending to the Arun. It
is on firm chalk or gravel except for nearly 1 mile on grass and half a
mile on surfaced road. Nearly all is through arable, but with
scrubland around Amberly Mount. Only about four gates to open.
Westbound, cumulative ascent 156 m, descent 244 m. Bridle-route
throughout. See maps 14, 13, and 12.

Route westbound

From A24 to Amberley Station 6 miles (10 km)

(a) *From A24 to Kithurst Hill road* 3 miles (5 km)
Up Glazeby Lane: where the surfacing ends continue ahead uphill
on a flint track between fields. At the top of Barnsfarm Hill pass
through a gate beside a cattle-grid on to grass, and follow the line of
a fence to a barn. Then through a gate beside another cattle-grid,
ahead on a track up and over Sullington Hill to the car-park by the
Chantry Post. Then ahead along the track which leads over the
flank of Kithurst Hill.

(b) *From Kithurst Hill road to Amberley Station* 3 miles (5 km)
The pronounced track continues westwards along the crest of the
hills. After passing through a clump of trees on Springhead Hill take
the right fork. Then after Rackham Hill the track descends along
Amberley Mount and reduces to a grass path leading steeply
downhill along the line of a fence. After using a farm-track for
about 100 m, the chalk path drops steeply to a surfaced road. Then
down the road and left at a fork and down High Titton Lane to the
B2139. Turn left along the main road: after houses on the right, a
path on the right cuts the final road loop before the railway bridge
at Amberley Station.

Route eastbound

From Amberley Station to A24 6 miles (10 km)

(a) *From Amberley Station to Kithurst Hill road* 3 miles (5 km)
Opposite the station entrance on the B2139 find a path which cuts
the road loop. Then at a house follow the road up for more than
200 m and turn right up High Titton Lane. At a junction bear right
and shortly after find a path leading steeply up to the left. After
using a farm-track for more than 100 m, the path leads steeply up
Amberley Mount to a gate. The way continues as a track between
fences up Rackham Hill and over Springhead Hill, passing through
a clump of trees on the way, to the car-park on Kithurst Hill.

(b) *From Kithurst Hill road to A24* 3 miles (5 km)
The pronounced track leads ahead over the flank of Kithurst Hill
and comes to the car park by the Chantry Post. Then ahead over
Sullington Hill and through a bridle-gate beside a cattle-grid to a
barn. The way is now on grass to the left of the barn, along the line
of a fence at the edge of a field and up on to Barnsfarm Hill.
Through another gate beside a cattle-grid and then ahead on a flint
track, steadily downhill between arable fields. After passing through
trees, the lane becomes surfaced and leads straight down to the A24.

Approach by car

At start: on the A24, 1 mile south of Washington roundabout, turn
off on to a secondary road. *At end*: Amberley Station car-park off
the B2139. *Also*: from Storrington off the A283 on a small road up
to the Chantry Post; and from a point 1 mile west of Storrington off
the B2139 on a small road up to Kithurst Hill.

Approach by other transport

Train: British Rail at Amberley (at end of stage). *Local buses*:
Southdown services at Washington to Worthing and Horsham
(about hourly to Worthing and two-hourly to Horsham, infrequent
on Sundays). *Taxis*: Worthing, Golden Car (0903–38826);
Pulborough, A–Z Taxis (07982–3230).

Refreshment

Pubs: Washington, Frankland Arms (real ale, meals); Amberley,
Black Horse (real ale, meals); Amberley Station, Bridge. *Drinking
water*: in Glazeby Lane.

Accommodation

Hotels or guest houses: Abingworth Hall, Thakenham Road,
Storrington RH20 3EF (Cat 4/4/4; 07983–2257). *Other*: Arundel
Youth Hostel, Warningcamp, Arundel BN18 9QY (0903–882204);
grazing, and stabling, Mrs Hughes, 22 Church Street, Storrington
(09066–2617).

Admission

Parham Gardens (Mr C. Gibson), Easter to September,
Wednesday, Thursday, Saturday and Sunday afternoons. Amberley
Wild Brooks (Sussex Trust for Nature Conservation), restricted
access. Amberley Chalk Pits (Southern Industrial History Trust),
April to October, Wednesdays to Sundays.

DESCRIPTION

And as we came to Pulborough town
   Storm rose from Arundel,
The first hot rain came splashing down,
   Thunder began to knell.
The tempest worked up fever-pace,
   White hissed the bubbles flung;
Wild sudden freshets ran their race,
   The fleetfoot winds were sprung.

Edmund Blunden (1896–1974)
from 'Stane Street'

The main road slices through the downs in a deep chalk cutting still
recent enough to bear grass and flowers unimpeded by shrubs:
marjoram and kidney vetch brighten the banks with tints of purple
and orange scarcely seen by the skimming motorists, and the
delicate spikes of the orchids must be invisible to them. We go up a
lane scruffy with creepers and shacks but with two cheerful features:
a bank of cultivated hypericum and a tap for drinking water. Then
we are out of the trees and climbing gently between the arable. To
the right is the upper fringe of the ashes in Biggen Holt; to the left
the Highden beechwood and below it Highden House (though
Windlesham House, the preparatory school, is shrouded in trees and
seen only from Stage 6). We cross three lines of cross-dykes, now
ploughed over: more obvious is a block of concrete and iron, the
remnant of wartime defences. On Barnsfarm Hill the track
disappears and we edge along the grass pasture instinctively
watching out for cattle, especially if with a dog. As if true to its
name, a black corrugated-iron barn sits on the hill beside the Way –

a tempting place of refuge against wind or rain: but actually the barn recorded is a great seventeenth-century wooden structure, with aisles and braced tie-beam roof, tiled and weatherboarded, which stands below at Sullington (the farmstead by the marshes). Ahead Sullington Hill protrudes rightwards from the ridge: on its nose the pronounced lines of a cross-dyke (225 m long) look like the marks of half-rimmed spectacles, whilst down its side the track of a bostal resembles the line of a tear falling down its cheek. This anthropomorphic tear-drop would surely have come to rest by St Mary's church (with Saxon nave and thirteenth-century tower) in the graveyard under a grove of ancient yews.

On Barnsfarm Hill we see the weald, whose alien geological structure is revealed in the rose-red colours of the Sullington sandpits, contrasting forcibly with the white of the chalk quarries behind us near Washington. Below us is the National Trust property at Sullington Warren. But after Sullington Hill, views are confined to the south and for the next two miles an area of downland progressively unfolds as we move along the ridge: between it and the sea intermediate hills protect our eyes from the urban coastline from Worthing to Littlehampton. On the slopes close by us were extensive field-systems with traces of settlements and Roman buildings; medieval settlement-sites and pottery have also been found. Further off, just over a mile from our route, the cone of Harrow Hill contains a small square earthwork, perhaps a temple, and on its slopes more than a hundred pits of Stone Age flint mines. Just to the west of this is Barpham Hill: Barpham means 'mound settlement' – a settlement by a burial mound. A mile south of Rackham Hill is the Burgh, a large barrow from which a Bronze Age urn was discovered: an ancient track known as the Lepers Way leads past the Burgh and down to the Arun. Of later date is the site of Michelgrove House, a mile beyond Harrow Hill. This was the Tudor mansion of the Shelley family: unfortunately when they sold their estate to the Duke of Norfolk he had their house pulled down (though this obliteration of the Shelleys as landed gentlemen could not dim the renown of their name, thanks to the unworldly son of

Sir Timothy Shelley). Nearly all this sweep of downland is now under plough but previously it was one of the chief sheep-rearing areas. Patching, the village at the southern edge of it, was the main centre for hurdle-making. Wattle hurdles, known locally as flakings, were made from hazel rods and used mainly for folding the sheep at night.

Meanwhile our route goes past the heads of two vantage-points for cars, each marked by a wooden direction post (if not stolen). The Chantry Post points to Amberley, Storrington, Washington, and Lee Farm: the Kithurst Post to Amberley, Parham, Finden, and Burpham. Both have bridleways leading south into the downland, the one from Kithurst three miles down to Burpham being specially attractive – and useful too, since a mile further on is the youth hostel at Warningcamp. Burpham (pronounced 'Burfam' and meaning the settlement by a stronghold) was fortified by Alfred the Great to guard against the Danes, though it is possible that the stronghold itself was first made by the Danes. Between these two posts the Way is a gravelly track along a sunken lane whose banks are covered with scabious and rampion, which vie for first place as the flower that best symbolises the South Downs. For some, the scabious has it – especially the larger Field Scabious – for the mass of tiny individual flowers that compose its pale mauve head; for others the rampion, for its dark-blue head tousled with long slender lobes spreading outwards. Together they contrast rather like the colours of Cambridge and Oxford, and like those two universities neither can really claim pre-eminence. After Kithurst Hill (Kithurst means a wooded hill frequented by kites) comes Springhead Hill, which is crowned with a clump of beech and sycamore: some of the ground here is on clay overlying the chalk. Then after the fork where we keep right (the left-hand fork is another bridleway leading to Burpham) we come on to Rackham Hill and regain our panoramas of the weald.

With a prominent bowl barrow as foreground, the distant scene appears deceptively wooded, as if the great oak forests had never been felled or the land intensively domesticated. This deception is all the greater since nearer below us is quite evidently a fine park of spreading trees and surrounding woods and copses, with the water-meadows of the Arun as a boundary. Deer are grazing in the park and between the trees is the stone frontage of a large Elizabethan house, with gables and mullioned windows. Thus transported back 400 years, we can from the ridge appreciate Parham, the mansion raised by Sir Thomas Palmer in 1557: from our distance it is apparently unchanged, though actually it was much altered in the eighteenth century and since has been judiciously restored. It contains an important collection of pictures by Romney, Lely, and Van Dyck, and has a panelled great hall, a great parlour, saloon, and long gallery; and its estate includes areas of the downs through which we pass. Parham is also known for its former heronry, whose birds originally migrated here from Michelgrove. To the right of Parham (pronounced 'Parrum') are Cootham and Storrington, to the left Rackham, and these four places mean respectively the settlements where the pear trees grow, where the coots and storks nest, and where hay-ricks are set: somehow place-names derived from natural features are ultimately more appealing than those derived from personal names, of which there are so many on our route. A little further on we come to Rackham Banks. Although these earthworks are still strong enough to stop a tank, it appears that they were not constructed for defence so much as to establish a boundary and deter marauders, and they are the best example of cross-dykes on our entire route.

   At this point even the most fanatical walker or furious rider should stop. For here is one of the best views on the South Downs Way, and I shall defer to Hilaire Belloc for its description:

   At this place the flat water-meadows, the same that are flooded and turned to a lake in mid-winter, stretch out a sort of scene or stage, whereupon can be planted the grandeur of the Downs, and one looks athwart the flat from a high place upon the shoulder of Rackham Mount to the broken land, the sand hills, and the pines, the ridge of Egdean side, the uplifted heaths and commons which flank the last of the hills all the way until one comes to the Hampshire border, beyond which there is nothing. This is the foreground of the gap at Arundel, a district of the Downs so made that when one sees it one knows at once that here is a jewel for which the whole county of Sussex was made, and the ornament worthy of so rare a setting.

The water-meadows are known as the Amberley Wildbrooks (i.e. brooks in the weald). These are dyke-drained grazing pastures with a natural peat bog at their northern end, comprising 1,000 acres in all; no roads cross them, and flocks of geese flight in to feed. Mercifully they were saved from being electrically drained and used for intensive farming, by public protest just in the nick of time. The gap is where the Arun flows through the downs, and four miles off, if the light is right, we can see the silhouette of Arundel Castle at the end of the wooded horizon. The 'ridge of Egdean side' means the first of the wealden hills, between Pulborough and Petworth. As for Hampshire, I hope to prove Belloc wrong about that!

Now we ease downwards on to Amberley Mount. Although really only a shoulder of Rackham Hill, Amberley Mount, like Windover Hill in Stage 1, is so rich in interest that it merits its own designation. Archaeologically, the southern slopes of the mount show extensive use by early agriculturalists. A survey in 1957 found a whole system of twenty fields, mostly rectangular and between 1 and 3 acres, of which six had been divided into terraces. These fields were on the upper zone of middle chalk, ground which was relatively free from flints but broken up by seams of marl. To the side of the field-system two huts were excavated some 300 m to our left, and I quote from the findings of the Sussex Archaeological Society Journal for a description of how one of them was built: 'Surface flints were removed from a circular area at the edge of a field, about 36 feet in diameter. A circular platform of about 26 feet was cut into the hillside. Chalk filling was piled around to raise the sides, which were then revetted with the flints. A wooden hut was built on the platform; oval in shape, with a lean-to entrance at the south and a fire pit by the entrance. Footings of the walls were probably strengthened with flints.' The hut, which had a conical roof, eventually burned down. When we consider that it was built about 2,500 years ago, the achievements of the primitive builder as well as the modern archaeologist both seem remarkable. For the naturalist, Amberley Mount is also notable. It is one of the best localities in Sussex for juniper, and on the north scarp is apparently

Parham from Rackham Hill

the only native British station of the Fly Honeysuckle (*Lonicera xylosteum*). Of the orchids, Lady's Tress as well as Early Purple can be found. And besides, lots of thyme, milkwort, scarlet pimpernel, hairy rockcress and yellow-rattle.

Where we come to the fork at the surfaced road, the right-hand turning goes to Amberley, half a mile off our course. On a promontory of greensand amid the alluvial levels of the Arun, Amberley is blessed by having no through road, so no cars press through it: the silence is broken only by the click and swish of the electric railway running past the end of it. Ambling down the village street we pass old houses and cottages admirably maintained and with well-tended gardens, placed irregularly and so offering exciting perspectives and contrasts. They are made from a variety of building materials which reflect the complex geology of this locality: flint, half-timber, brick, and Burgate stone, with roofs of tile and thatch. We pass Old Postings, the village shop till 1974; April Cottage (thatched) and Thatched Cottage (not thatched); Holly Tree House with its tree, and Old Stack Cottage with a large chimney-breast and a flint-walled garden. Stream Cottage dates from the sixteenth century. The street concludes with a certain air of formality by the church. St Michael's has a Norman nave, thirteenth-century chancel, and wall-paintings. Beyond is Amberley Castle. Its massive walls date from the fourteenth century, when the Bishop of Chichester built defences for his manor here, probably against French raids, creating a fortified house rather than a castle in the strict sense of the term. Although they received a battering in the Civil War the walls were not dismantled, and they still look most impressive and include a fine gateway flanked by round bastions. They enclose a jumble of buildings including a great hall, which comprise a much admired castle residence. The meaning of Amberley is obscure: 'ley' is a clearing, but 'amber' is not evident. It might come from a British word meaning river. Certainly Amberley is essentially associated with water, and is commemorated in an old tag that the 'four good things of Sussex' were the Arundel mullet, the Chichester lobster, the Selsey cockle, and the Amberley trout.

The walls of Amberley Castle

High Titten lane has thick hedges on both sides which disguise the fact that behind them are sharp drops into chalk quarries and our lane is on a knife-edge between them. For us the real knife-edge is where we have to go along the main road for 200 m, before reaching the path that leads us to Amberley Station. Just by the station is the Amberley Chalk Pits Museum, on the site of the former Houghton limeworks. Chalk used to be extensively quarried for the production of lime, which was used as a soil fertiliser before the days of chemicals, especially on the sands and clays of the weald. Lime is obtained by burning chalk with coal in kilns. The chalk is rich in minerals due to the action of leaching, the way in which the rainwater drains through the thin acidic topsoil of the downland, taking with it into the chalk the valuable mineral qualities. The whole process of the limeworks is clearly demonstrated here, including all the separate facets such as the brickworks, the narrow-gauge railway, and the shops of the blacksmith, bagmender, and cobbler, as well as the central action of the kilns. But perhaps the most interesting aspect is that in the quarries we can get an excellent visual understanding of the composition of the chalk over which we have been travelling for so many miles. Beneath the soil, known as renzina, lie layers which have been strongly affected by leaching and weathering and where the chalk has become broken. Below is the unaltered bedrock of solid chalk. In the lowest levels of the chalk its purity becomes progressively adulterated with clay to produce a greyish colour. The quarry walls also show the process of slope development, the complex interaction of wind, rain, rock and vegetation which continues imperceptibly, and will soon serve to reduce the exposed rock-faces of these quarries, in contrast to the cliffs on the seashore in Stage 15, which will remain forever sheer and clear.

Stage 8
Amberley to **Upwaltham** 6 miles

SPECIFICS

From the Arun this stage follows the general direction of the scarp
in the first half: but in the second half, where the scarp turns north,
the route eases down into a dry valley. Three-quarters of a mile is
surfaced road (most of it the busy B2139) and virtually all the rest is
firm chalk or flint track. Although mostly between arable, the route
passes sections of wood and scrub. Probably no gates to open
(except some bridle-gates for riders to avoid cattle-grids).
Westbounds cumulative ascent 281 m, descent 163 m. Bridle-route
throughout. See maps 12 and 11.

Route westbound

From Amberley Station to **Littleton Farm** 6 miles (10 km)

(a) *From Amberley Station to Bignor Hill road* 4 miles (6.5 km)
From Amberley Station go along the B2139 under the railway and
over the Arun to Houghton. Soon after the church turn right on the
road to Bury (junction with Stage 17). More than 300 m on, turn
left up a flint track which soon goes right and then left, at first
through fields then up the edge of Coombe Wood. At the A29 go
right for 100 m, then left up a track, near to a fence on the left. At a
fork veer right, drawing away from the wood on the left, and
continue uphill between fields. The track becomes confined and
goes along the side of Westburton Hill, then down to a barn. Here
turn left on to a bridleway and then immediately right: the way is
then a track between hedges uphill. Where it comes by a bridle-gate
to a crossing track, turn right and then up, bearing left with a fence
on the left. Then over Bignor Hill and gently down to the National
Trust land and the Latin signpost (junction with Stages 17 and 18).

(b) *From Bignor Hill road to Littleton Farm* 2 miles (3.5 km)
The way continues ahead along the track leading to the right of the
Latin signpost. Shortly after, where it comes to the bank of Stane
Street, it turns half left to follow beside the bank for 150 m, then
half right. Then along the line of a fence between arable, and out of
National Trust land. The well-defined track then goes gradually
downhill past cattle-grids. Later it descends more steeply as a lane
between hedges to the A285 by Littleton Farm.

Route eastbound

From Littleton Farm to Amberley Station 6 miles (10 km)

(a) *From Littleton Farm to Bignor Hill road* 2 miles (3.5 km)
Opposite Littleton Farm on the A285 the way leads uphill as a
chalk lane between hedges. It continues ahead as a well-defined
flint track, beside and then through arable, passing cattle-grids.
After coming to trees on Burton Down it enters National Trust land
and goes along the line of a fence between arable. At a grass bank
turn half left to follow the line of the bank for 150 m, then half right
to arrive shortly at the Latin signpost and the head of Bignor Hill
road (junction with Stages 17 and 18).

(b) *From Bignor Hill road to Amberley Station* 4 miles (6.5 km)
From the Latin signpost the way leads ahead to leave the bushes as
a flint track between arable gently up Bignor Hill: then downhill as
a grassy track, keeping close to a fence on the right. Shortly after the
fence bears right, find a crossing fence and bridle-gate to the left.
Take the track which leads sharply down to the left between bushes,
to arrive at a barn. The way is then to the right of Westburton Hill,
confined and between arable: then down to the A29. Turn right
along the road for 100 m. Then turn left down beside a wood and
into arable, turning right and then left before reaching a road. Turn
right on the road for more than 300 m into Houghton (junction with
Stage 17). At the B2139 turn left and go along the main road to
cross the Arun, and under the railway to Amberley Station.

Approach by car

At start: Amberley Station car-park off the B2139, 4½ miles from
Storrington. *At end*: on road verge by Littleton Farm on the A285,
2 miles south of Duncton. *Also*: at Houghton; and from Bignor up a
very small road up Bignor Hill.

Approach by other transport

Train: British Rail at Amberley (at start of stage). *Local buses*:
possibility of a special Southdowns Ramblers' bus on summer
Sundays. *Taxis*: Pulborough, A–Z taxis (07982–3230); Arundel,
Arundel Taxi (0903–882418).

Refreshment

Pubs: Amberley Station, Bridge; Houghton, George and Dragon
(real ale, meals). *Drinking water*: at Houghton Bridge.

Accommodation

Hotels or guest houses: Coldharbour Farm, Sutton RH20 1PR (Cat
3/1/2; 07987–200); Duncton House, Duncton, Petworth GU28 0LT
(Cat 1/2/2; 0798–42311). *Other*: Grazing, stabling and camping at
Coldharbour Farm.

Admission

Bignor Roman Villa (Mr H Tupper), March to October, daily
except Mondays; Bignor Hill (National Trust), open access.

Stage 8
Amberley to **Upwaltham**

To this green hill a something dream-like clings,
Where day by day the little blunt sheep graze,
Threading the tussocks and the toad-stool rings,
Nosing the barrows of the olden days.
An air drifts here that's sweet of sea and grass,
And down the combe-side living colour glows;
Spring, Summer, Fall, the chasing seasons pass
To winter, even lovelier than those.
The dream is deep today, when all that's far
Of wandering water and of darkling wood,
Of weald and ghost-like down combined are
In haze below this hill where God has stood.
    Here I, too, stand until the light is gone,
     And feed my wonder, while the sheep graze on!

John Galsworthy (1867–1933)
'Bury Hill'

The Arun is the longest of the little Sussex rivers which drain the
weald through the line of the downs. In geological terms they are all
'subsequent' rivers, in that their erratic courses have been
determined by the wealden sands and clays. But where they flow
through the downs they make use of the gaps created by earlier
'consequent' rivers which originally ran in long furrows from the
chalk dome which overlaid the land. The Arun was linked to the
Wey and the Thames by a canal built for military purposes during
the Napoleonic wars, but now disused. At Houghton bridge it is still

Houghton bridge

strongly tidal. For half a mile we have to go along the main road on the causeway, always an unnerving experience for riders. Houghton (pronounced 'Howtun') means headland farmstead. St Nicholas' church is simple, Early English of Victorian restoration. There are old cottages and, at our right turn, the Old Farmhouse which is of half timber and roofed with thick thatch. Just up the road is the George and Dragon, an excellent pub where one can eat and drink under the shade of a walnut and a pear tree. A plaque says that Charles II stopped here for a drink during his escape after the Battle of Worcester, and the story is one of the most romantic episodes in English history.

Fleeing from the field of battle on 3 September 1651, the twenty-one-year old king spent a couple of desperate days virtually alone, and miraculously avoided capture from the man-hunt by walking nine miles on two successive nights and by hiding in the oak when the soldiers passed by below. Then, disguised as a servant and with his locks shorn, he rode south to Somerset and then east to Wiltshire while his friends searched for a boat to take him to France. For some of the way he carried an attractive girl, Jane Lane, on a pillion behind him: when the horse lost a shoe he had to take it to a farrier, who told him how much he longed to get his hands on that rogue Charles Stuart. On 12 October Lord Wilmot and two servants (one a real servant, Robert Swan, the other the King) rode from near Salisbury to the Meon valley, and on Old Winchester Hill they had a rendezvous with Colonel George Gunter, who took them on to his sister's house at Hambledon: forty miles in all. Next day the four of them rode across the downs via Stansted and towards Arundel. But on the way they nearly bumped into Colonel Morley of Glynde, the military governor of Arundel Castle, who was out hunting: 'I did not much care for his waxed moustaches,' quipped Charles as soon as they were out of earshot. This encounter decided them to cross the Arun instead at Houghton; and at the inn they stopped briefly to take bread and beer, not dismounting, together with some ox-tongue they had with them. From Houghton bridge they rode along the ridge of the downs (our Stages 7 and 6) to

The Latin signpost by Stane Street

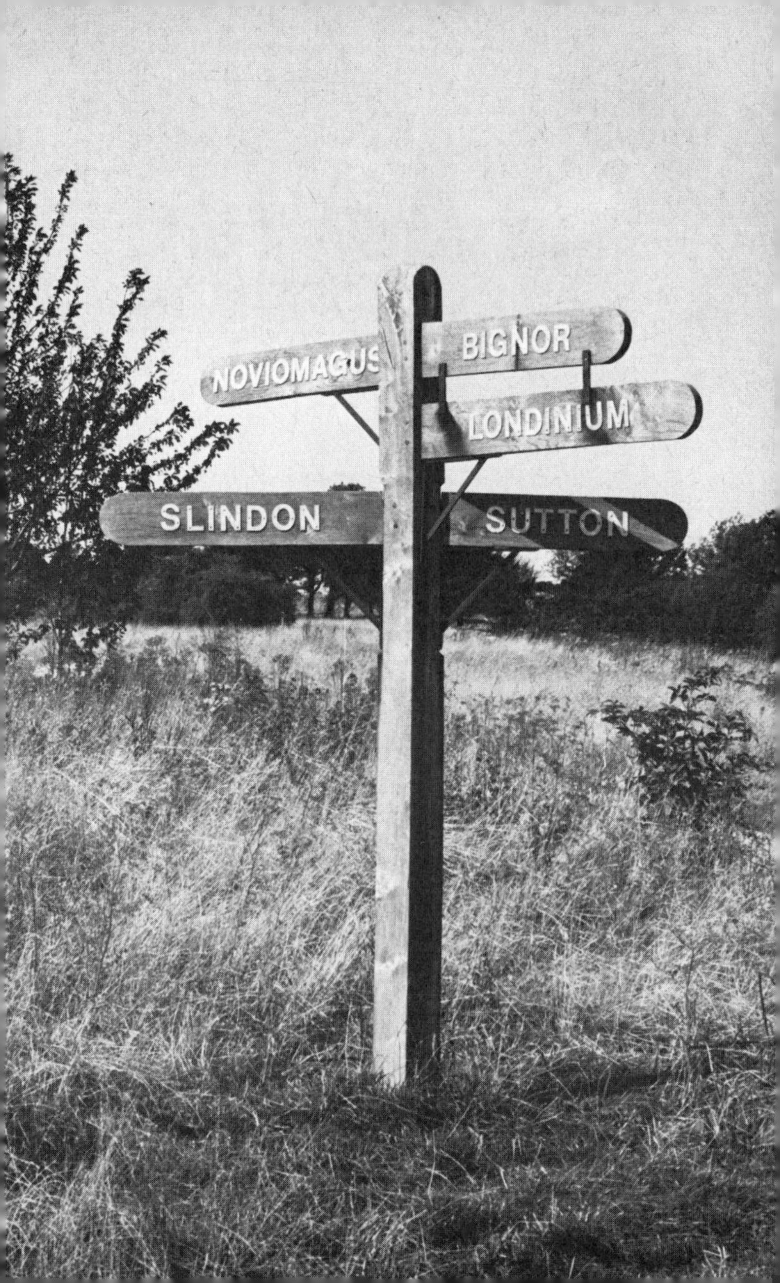
NOVIOMAGUS
BIGNOR
LONDINIUM
SLINDON
SUTTON

Bramber, to cross the Adur. Here they had a shock, for a group of Parliamentarian troopers were standing in the street. There was nothing for it but to trot straight through, which they did with their hearts in their mouths. To their horror a detachment then mounted and cantered up behind them, but only rudely passed by them in the narrow bostal. Then on they went across the downs to Brighthelmston: this day their ride was at least forty-five miles. The next day the royal fugitive embarked from Southwick. This is how King Charles II came to ride the South Downs Way.

Bury (meaning a stronghold and pronounced 'Berry') is three-quarters of a mile north of Houghton. It is the less-visited counterpart to Amberley. Under walnut trees the village street leads down to the banks of the Arun, where stands St John's church, whose thirteenth-century walls support a long low-sloping roof of Horsham stone, whilst the tower is capped with a tall shingle-covered timber spire. John Galsworthy came and lived here in the autumn of his days, and his poem on Bury Hill expresses an old man's feelings when contemplating the natural scene. We ascend Bury Hill at first through fields near where pheasants are bred, then up past Coombe Wood. Beyond the main road we come close to the beeches of Houghton Forest, the remains of the large hunting reserve of Houghton Chase, which was the cause of an almighty row between the Earl of Arundel and the Bishop of Chichester in the thirteenth century. The forest belonged to the church and provided the episcopal venison: so when the Earl's men were caught poaching, it was the final straw in the strained relations between the two magnates, and the Earl was excommunicated. It needed royal intervention and many assurances of good behaviour before the ban was lifted.

The Way passes to the south-west of Bury and Westburton Hills, blocking views to the north. Near Westburton (the farmstead west of a stronghold, i.e. Bury) the bones of elephants were discovered in 1740. It is known that the Emperor Vespasian brought battle-elephants to Britain, and perhaps these were some. After the point where the Way zigzags we go up Bignor Hill to a panorama by 'Toby's Grave'. This is a mounting-block placed here in memory of James ('Toby') Fitzwilliam who was a leading figure with the

Cowdray Hunt and owner of Burton Park, and whose ashes were scattered here on Bignor Hill: the quotation is from R.L. Stevenson.

A large wooden signpost, planted near a round barrow, points the direction to three Saxon settlements – Bignor, Slindon and Sutton – and two Roman cities – Noviomagus and Londinium. It heralds our approach towards two monuments of Romano-British civilisation – the Roman road Stane Street and the Roman villa at Bignor. Here, surely, rather than at Pooks Hill near Burwash, is where the ghost of Parnesius the Centurion of the Thirtieth Legion might appear from behind the yews and hawthorns on a midsummer evening if suitably evoked, and give us flashes of insight into that forgotten world – all those human touches which dry facts alone cannot revive. The bare facts about Stane Street are clear enough. It was constructed some thirty years after the Roman invasion of 43 AD to link Noviomagus (Chichester) with Londinium (London), and driven in as straight a line as possible, taking it in three straight sections of which the first was from Chichester to Pulborough. The road rested on a cambered causeway which on Bignor Hill became a 'dual carriageway'. The composition of the road (or 'agger') varied according to the terrain: on Bignor Hill it was flint set in chalk, in the weald gravel set in clay, and only rarely – near large towns or at bridges or fords – was it paved with stone, despite its Saxon name Stane Street. Coming up the hill from Noviomagus Regnentium and the south-west, the agger was bounded by banks on either side, though not on the north-easterly descent down Bignor Hill. Besides being a military highway, Stane Street was an economic artery and from it smaller roads penetrated into the greensand belts where slaves toiled on the estates, and the wealden forests where grimy charcoal-burners fed the furnaces of the ironworks.

One and a half miles down the road (or from the barn by Westburton Hill) is the Roman villa at Bignor, situated close to the line of Stane Street. It was supported by an agricultural enterprise that comprised around 800 acres of cereals as well as perhaps 200 sheep, 60 cattle, and twelve teams of oxen, in an estate of some 2,000 acres. The owner lived in luxury, and the contrast between his life-style and that of his slaves and peasants was comparable in our times to that of white settlers who until recently owned large farms

in Kenya or Rhodesia – though he was no expatriate. Whereas they might have installed air-conditioning in their main rooms, he had hypocausts which provided an efficient central-heating system. From a furnace outside the room the hot air was conducted through tunnels below the floors and then up flues in the walls to vents below the eaves. He had windows glazed with green glass, and hot baths. For decoration his floors were laid with mosaics, whose design and execution are among the best ever found in Britain. The minute cubes which form the mosaics are made from hard chalk, red brick, sandstone, or limestone, and produce a wide variation in tone, though the dominant colours are red, black and white. Surrounded by elaborate borders, Winter shivers in her cloak; dancing-girls gyrate with flying veils; Venus presides over gladiatorial combats; and an enormous eagle carries Ganymede, the Cretan shepherd-boy, through the skies to meet the gods on Mount Olympus.

Where the Way crosses Stane Street the land is National Trust property. Cowslips, bugle, vipers bugloss, marjoram, and harebells grow here amid the banks and shrubs. Some 300 m south-east of the Latin signpost are the earthworks of a late Stone Age camp, Barkhale. Remoter by far than Roman rule, how hard it is to envisage human scenes here: tribal dances? sacrifices? initiations? anthropophagy? Even Puck would be hard put to revive these to our senses.

Where we leave the property there is a stone drinking-trough for horses, often dry. From here we leave the escarpment, which goes north for two miles beyond the radio masts on Burton Down. The villages below, which are thus enclosed by a rough semi-circle of hills with heavily wooded slopes, are memorably beautiful. There is Bignor itself (Bica's hill-brow) where, around a square of tiny lanes, several cottages lie half hidden by trees: they include the Old Shop, an interesting fifteenth-century house thatched and half-timbered, with brick infilling and sides of flint and stone. The church of the Holy Cross was largely rebuilt in the last century and is characterised by lots of narrow lancet windows set in local

The line of the downs from Bignor Hill

honey-coloured stone: as so often, the oldest part of the church is
the arch dividing nave and chancel, which is Norman. A little
beyond the village is the gate of Bignorpark House, whose large
chestnuts and ilexes add grace to the scene. Half a mile from Bignor
is Sutton, where large windows in the Early English style give light
to the unadorned but fine interior of St John Baptist's church. And
beyond Sutton lies Barlavington:Barlavington (pronounced
'Barlton') means the barley farm of Lafa's people, and Sutton
means the farm just to the south of it.

Our route continues with wide prospects to the south across the
lower hills to the distant sea. Halnacker Mill can be seen three miles
off, and close by but unseen is Gumber Farm, just off Stane Street.
It means Guma's enclosure, and one imagines Guma, having been
allotted this high-level property by his chief, making full use of the
largely disused 'streat' to get his people and his produce up and
down the hill. Then we leave the National Trust land and ease our
way across Sutton Down and Littleton End, looking towards
Littleton Down straight ahead, the highest of the Sussex Downs,
with Bishop's Ring just to the right of it. The upper end of ash
woods are to the right as we wind through arable. Where we go over
a cattle-grid, we cut the line of a cross-dyke. Where we pass through
trees, the hedge is sweet with marjoram: then it is down to the road.
We have an account of a journey along this road 160 years ago. On
2 August 1823 William Cobbett, the radical thinker and scourge of
the Tory squires, passed by here on his horse. As he mounted the
hill from Duncton, the clouds 'came up like judges' wigs': 'Before I
got to the top of the hill at Donton, the white clouds had become
black, had spread themselves all around, and a pretty decent and
sturdy rain began to fall.' Just after passing Littleton Farm he would
have come to the buildings and church of St Mary at Upwaltham –
the upper forest settlement – in whose parish this little valley lies.

This description began with an old man's verses, so let it end with
those of a young man. This is the area of downland best beloved by
Hilaire Belloc, who walked all over these hills and also rode on
them on his horse, Monster. When he fell in love with Elodie, who
became his wife, he wanted somehow to link his love of nature with
his love for her. His joyous expressions of feeling are infectious to

anyone who has walked or ridden across this corner of the downs, so
full of natural beauty and historical romance:

> Lift up your hearts in Gumber, laugh in the weald,
> And you my mother the Valley of Arun sing.
> Here I am homeward from my wandering,
> Here I am homeward and my heart is healed.
> You my companions whom the world has tired,
> Come out and greet me. I have found a face
> More beautiful than gardens; more desired
> Than boys in exile love their native place.
> Lift up your hearts in Gumber, laugh in the weald . . .

Stage 9
Upwaltham to **Cocking** $5\frac{1}{2}$ miles

SPECIFICS

This stage goes along the straight ridge from the dry valley at
Upwaltham to the gap at Cocking. For all except $1\frac{1}{2}$ miles the route
is through or beside woods, the remainder being all arable. The
going is soft through the central wooded section, though there is a
quarter-mile of surfaced road and about $1\frac{1}{2}$ miles of hard flint track.
Only about two gates to open. Westbound, cumulative ascent
143 m. descent 160m. Bridle-route throughout. See maps 11, 9
and 8.

Route westbound

From Littleton Farm to **A286** $5\frac{1}{2}$ miles (8.5 km)

From Littleton Farm go up the confined track to a crossing track at
a hedge. The way then enters the field ahead by a bridle-gate and
goes up through the field, then on by a gate through to the top
corner of another field. Continue ahead on a track through a wood
to the Teglease Post. By a pronounced track, maintain direction for
1 mile to the Lavington Post. Take the right of two paths ahead and
continue along the ridge through woods. Shortly after a junction of
paths the way turns sharp right for a few metres, then left to resume
direction. Later it comes to a strip of arable and goes along the left
side of it, at the edge of beech plantations. At the end of this stretch
we come to a crossing group of trees (junction with Stage 19). Then
ahead and on to a flint track which leads steadily down, and so past
Hill Barn and to the A286.

Route eastbound

From A286 to **Littleton Farm** 5½ miles (8.5 km)

From the road go up Hillbarn Lane, then past Hill Barn by a flint track steadily uphill, with forestry joining on our right. Just after a crossing group of trees (junction with Stage 19) the way continues to the right-hand side of a strip of arable at the edge of beech plantations. Where the arable ends we go left and then immediately right to maintain direction into woods on a rough track. At one point the way is signposted left at a fork, then immediately right to rejoin the main track. After a junction of paths it continues ahead through wood to the Lavington Post: then by a pronounced track to the Teglease Post, and ahead into a wood. From here it goes through the middle of an arable field and down by a gate through another field, to a bridle-gate at the lower end. Cross a track and go ahead down a lane for 200 m to the entrance of Littleton Farm on the A285.

Approach by car

At start: on road verge by Littleton Farm on the A285, 2 miles south of Duncton. *At end*: on verge of A286, ½ mile south of Cocking.

Approach by other transport

Local buses: Southdown services at Cocking to Bognor Regis, Chichester and Midhurst (hourly). *Taxi*: Petworth Taxi (0798–42691).

Refreshment

Pubs: Graffham, Forester's Arms (real ale, meals); Cocking, Richard Cobden (real ale, meals). *Drinking water*: at Hill Barn.

Accommodation

Hotels or guest houses: Woodstock Hotel, Charlton PO18 0HU (Cat 4/4/2; 024363–666); The Hall in the Wood, Graffham, Petworth GU28 0PT (Cat 3/3/4; 07986–436); Eastwood Farm, Graffham, Petworth GU28 0QF (Cat 2/2/1; 07986–317); Nether Hoyle, Heyshott, Midhurst GU29 0DX (Cat 1/1/1; 07986–240). *Other*: grazing and stabling, Upper Norwood Farm, East Lavington, Petworth GU28 0QG (07986–264).

Stage 9
Upwaltham to **Cocking**

DESCRIPTION

O'er Northern Down, all up the wind
   Go on to Burnt Oak Gate
We all of us just there got in
   The hounds ran a great rate.
Away they went for Herring Dean
At Cocking road they turned again
   With a hark forward hark on hark.
Then down the wind o'er Cocking Course
   Each man did push his horse
To Teglease gate, where huntsman-like
   We stopped to see them cross
There first came Veny, Luther next,
Young Trojan, Victor and the rest,
   With a hark forward hark on hark.

from an eighteenth-century doggerel
on the Old Charlton Hunt

Littleton Farm, as its name implies, is quite a small place – and remote too, except for the road. From it we mount 135 m up Littleton Down, which unlike the name is not at all small: in fact it leads up to a point (variously called Littleton Down or Crown Teglease) which, at 255 m, is the highest on the South Downs in Sussex, though as it is in the middle of a forestry plantation it has no views and no interest. For the only occasion on the entire main route we go slap through the middle of an arable field without a track, just a path trodden into the chalk between the corn. Although it may 'go against the grain' to tread through the crop, we have every right to do so; and the action of walking breast-high through

the waving wheat just before the harvest is undeniably satisfying. It is rather like being at sea in a small boat, but instead of the neutral water we are in among the heads of corn with their almost mouth-watering promise of nutrition – rather like sailing on the wine lake or climbing the butter mountain or coming to the house of the sugar-plum fairy. From the field we go through a wood, mainly beech and with dog myrtle below, and once out of it are at the Teglease Post, put up by the Cowdray Hunt and pointing the way to East Dean and Duncton. Teglease means sheep pasture and became the word denoting the right to pasture sheep on the downs in summer. There are no sheep up here now, just trees and corn, and the shepherds and huntsmen wouldn't recognise the place: some of the fields up here were first ploughed as recently as 1980 in unfortunate pasture clearances. For the next mile we get views across the weald to the pine-covered hills which are higher than us: Black Down, now seven miles north, is, at 301 m, the highest point in Sussex. The track is welcoming as ever and on our left, through windbrakes of ash, are wide fields on the dip slope. In this way we come to the Lavington Post, which also points to East Dean southwards, but north to East Lavington and Graffham.

East Lavington and Graffham are two small parishes close below us. East Lavington was formerly called Woolavington, which means the farmstead of Lafa's people by a spring. Graffham means the settlement by a grove. In time East Lavington became the house and park of the land-owning family while Graffham was the village where most of the local people lived. At the time of the Conquest the land was held by six Saxon thanes. They were summarily ousted in favour of four French knights – Robert, Ralph, Roland, and Ernald – who controlled seven villeins, six bordars, scores of serfs, and a probable population of around a hundred. The manor passed through many hands till, in the eighteenth century, its heiress Charlotte Orme married John Sargent. In default of male heirs (amongst other deaths, George Sargent was shot dead by an army deserter up on Graffham Down in 1807), it later went to his grand-daughter Emily who had married Samuel Wilberforce, son of

Orienteering past the Lavington Post

the reformer William Wilberforce. When she died, Samuel became lord of the manor. But this was no ordinary squire, for he was a leading figure in Early Victorian England, an ambitious and successful cleric who became Lord Bishop first of Oxford and then of Winchester. One of the main issues of the day was the changes in worship advocated by the Oxford Movement, and Samuel Wilberforce was deeply preoccupied with it, not only as Bishop of Oxford but for family reasons. Emily's younger sister Caroline had married Henry Manning. He was also a clergyman and held the living of East Lavington and Graffham, where he lived in the rectory. After agonising soul-searching and desperate pleas from Sam, he 'went over to Rome'. Not only Henry Manning but also both Sam's other brothers-in-law 'went over', and Manning (long a widower and hence not precluded from the Roman Catholic priesthood) eventually became Archbishop of Westminster and Cardinal of the Sacred College. How astonished Wilberforce and Manning would be to know that a hundred years later the revised services of the Anglicans and Roman Catholics are barely distinguishable!

For South Downs wanderers who are not concerned with these shadowy battles of the mind, I can record that Samuel Wilberforce has left a practical memorial in the beeches known as the Bishop's Clump and seen from Stages 8 and 18. The track marked for East Lavington leads half a mile down to Graffham church and the lodge into East Lavington Park. The large house, much altered, is now Seaford College, a public school for boys. The church of St Giles was completely rebuilt in the 1870s, and the neat but rather harsh exterior is in the Early English style. Among the 'presentments' of the churchwardens is this entry of 1622: 'We present Joan Harman for being, as it is suspected, an incontinent person, a gadder up and down, a common carry-tale, a maker of lies, one that hath contracted herself to 2 or 3 knaves and is married to none, but still continueth her bad courses.' So much for Joan Harman!

Now follows a mile of wood, followed by another mile along the edge of woodland. Some would like to see the downs bare of all

The Way through scrub on Graffham Down

plantations, others like the variety and the comforting feeling of being in woods; the Masai versus the Kikuyu, as it might be. Dr Johnson supported the latter view when he said that the bare downs around Brighton were so dreary that a man might go and hang himself if only he could find a tree to sling the rope. But all can agree that trees should not be planted in serried ranks along a ridge, nor scrub allowed to get out of hand, as happen in this stretch. We pass first through coppices with plantations to our left and fine hanging woods down to the right. Old yews have been preserved and beech saplings recently planted. The Way tunnels through the branches as a straight path except that just after a prominent bowl-barrow (one of a series of fourteen along the ridge just here, one other also prominent), we are invited to side-step to the right for a few metres – a quirk which few follow since the evident path lies ahead. Along the path we find the common St John's Wort, with its bright yellow petals studded with black dots. Later we go along the edge of the Forestry Commission's plantations, though other trees to the right still prevent views. Charton Forest is mainly beech, and those we see were planted nearly fifty years ago. Dull though the plantations may be, it is good to see so many broad-leaved trees, well outnumbering conifers. The large forest shelters herds of fallow deer, and also the smaller roe deer and the muntjac, a new arrival now well established in thickets along the north scarp west of the Arun. Jays and magpies flap through the branches harshly crying, but in summer the visiting turtle-dove lulls us with its pleasant dreamy purring. On the ground, often hidden in the carpet of leaves, are toadstools and mushrooms, including the extremely poisonous Death Cap (*Amanita phalloides*), which can lead to a slow and painful death: fortunately its appearance is so ugly that few are tempted to experiment – a white or yellowish-green cap, white gills, and a loose membranous cup at the base.

But the new Charlton Forest only covers part of the area of downland once so called, for the word 'forest' didn't mean just a lot of trees but land protected by law for the benefit of hunting. Originally this meant hunting the deer, but 300 years ago a group of noblemen discovered that to hunt the fox was far more exciting and challenging. The deer had mostly become confined within walled parks, where with elaborate ritual the hart could easily be hunted down, and outside the parks the felling of trees had largely destroyed their ancient habitat. But the fox was fast and cunning, and could only be successfully hunted with effort and attention to the control and breeding of hounds. The Duke of Monmouth, illegitimate son of Charles II, kept a pack of hounds at Charlton: he said that when he became King of England (which he did his best to become by invading the West Country in 1685) he would come and keep his court at Charlton. But the greatest days of the hunt were in the mid-eighteenth century, with the pack of the second Duke of Richmond (illegitimate grandson). A flavour of the thrills and spills of the chase comes from an account of the remarkable run of Friday 26 January 1738, on which the pack hunted a succession of scents over a total of at least thirty-five miles, ending with a kill by South Stoke on the Arun. The first part of the run was all over our Stage 9, and some of Stage 19 as well:

At a quarter before eight in the morning the fox was found in Eastdean Wood, and ran an hour in that cover; then into the Forest, up to Puntice Coppice through Herringdean to the Marlows, up to Coney Coppice, back to the Marlows, to the Forest West Gate, over the fields to Nightingale Bottom, to Cobden's at Draught, up his Pine Pit Hanger, where His Grace of St Alban's got a fall; through My Lady Lewknor's Puttocks, and missed the earth; through Westdean Forest to the corner of Collar Down (where Lord Harcourt blew his first horse), crossed the Hackney-place down the length of Coney Coppice, through the Marlows to Herringdean, into the Forest and Puntice Coppice, Eastdean Wood, through the Lower Teglease across by Cocking Course down between Graffham and Woolavington, through Mr Orme's Park and Paddock over the Heath to Fielder's Furzes, to the Harlands, Selham, Ambersham, through Todham Furzes, over Todham Heath, almost to Cowdray Park, there turned to the limekiln at the end of Cocking Causeway, through Cocking Park and Furzes; there crossed the road and up the hills between Bepton and Cocking.

By now we are on Heyshott Down. Heyshott means a
heather-covered corner of land but this refers to the northern part
of the parish rather than to the down. There is a Nature Reserve on
the scarp here, in which there are known to be eleven species of
orchids as well as a great variety of mosses and liverworts. Plough
has furrowed the bald head of Manorfarm Down, to our right as we
start our descent. But to our left the woodland stretches away over
Herringdean and the Marlows. As we come down, the grassy bank
beside the track has campion, kidney vetch, and later scabious,
harebells, marjoram, and the ubiquitous lady's bedstraw. We come
to Hill Barn, where there is an English Woodlands sawmill: this
receives hardwoods from an area of about fifty miles around and
saws them into planks and lengths which will mostly be used for
joinery and furniture-making. Just by the buildings is a tap for
drinking water, set in a cairn of stones. It bears the inscription: *This
tap for walkers is placed here in memory of Peter Wren aged 14
years. He loved the English countryside and walked the South Downs
Way in the summer of 1978.*

A bridleway to the right at Peter Wren's memorial would take us
half a mile down to Cocking. Cocking means Cocca's people,
though 'people' is an inadequate term for the gang or extended
family that actually came here under Cocca's leadership some 1300
years ago, carving their way into the soggy forest to places where
the British had not ventured. There is something very basic about
this assertion of ownership – probably a crude carve-up of
uninhabited areas by the tribal chief in the earliest centuries of
Saxon settlement, and relating usually to land away from the
navigable rivers that they had come up in their flat-bottomed boats.
The territory of each of these settlements just north of the downs
extended indefinitely northward into the forest. The most
remarkable achievement of early pioneering seems to have been
that of Beada's people whose settlement at Lower Beeding is fully
ten miles north of Upper Beeding (Stage 5).

At Cocking we come to where a little stream of clear water glides
past the churchyard. The water has only just emerged from the

Chalk spring by Cocking church

springs at the foot of the chalk, which were one reason why Cocca's people settled here in the first place. To us surface dwellers who see the chalk so dry and the clay soils so wet, it is paradoxical that it is the chalk which receives the rainwater and allows the moisture to percolate through it, whilst it is the clays which reject it and so force it out sideways as springs. Cocking church is finely situated on higher ground beyond the water and at the edge of the village. It was originally built for the Benedictines, and when they left the patron saint evidently left also. The tower and south aisle were added to a Norman nave in the early fourteenth century, at which time an unneeded window was blocked. When the blocking masonry was recently removed it uncovered a fragment of wall-painting showing the angel saying to the shepherds (and their dog), 'I bring you good tidings of great joy.' In the church tower hang three medieval bells, so when they ring out, the sounds are the same as would have been heard 600 years ago. And so into Cocking, which is remarkably unspoilt despite being on a main road, the yellow paint on the woodwork of several houses denoting that they are part of the large Cowdray estate. The pub is named after Richard Cobden, the advocate of free trade, who was born at Heyshott. His policies involved the end of the protectionism enjoyed by the farmers for their wheat, and a century of agricultural decline. But now the cycle is completed, since the farms of Cocking and Heyshott are prosperous again, whilst it is the cotton-mills of Lancashire that are ruinous.

Stage 10
Cocking to **South Harting** $7\frac{1}{2}$ miles

SPECIFICS

The route goes straight along the ridge except that it makes U-turns around Treyford Hill and Beacon Hill. It is through arable except for $1\frac{1}{2}$ miles of woodland and $2\frac{1}{2}$ miles of scrubland and pasture, on some of which it is unconfined. The track is firm chalk or flint for some $2\frac{1}{2}$ miles and for the rest it is firm earth path or track. Only about two gates to open. Westbound, cumulative ascent 253 m, descent 221 m. Bridle-route throughout. See maps 8 and 7.

Route westbound

From A286 to B2146 $7\frac{1}{2}$ miles (12.5 km)

Go along Middlefield Lane between farm buildings and up between hedges. The chalk track continues ahead up Linch Down (to the left of the summit) becoming flinty and then grassy. It then goes over the small hump of Didling Hill and then ahead to enter woods. After passing wire enclosures, the path descends gently. In an area of large beech trees it turns sharp right at a bridleway junction. Later it emerges from the wood and descends to the access road to Buriton Farm. A few metres to the left is a bridle-gate to a confined path, which then goes through a copse and along the lower edge of arable. The route then turns leftwards and upwards over the ridge of Pen Hill, and steeply down again. It then leads around to the left, curving away from Beacon Hill. By a gateway it turns sharp right (junction with Stage 19) and returns around the side of Beacon Hill to the ridge. Then left and up Harting Down, and by a bridle-gate to the B2141 and car-park. Across the road find the path through hanging woods to the B2146.

Route eastbound

From B2146 to A286 7½ miles (12.5 km)

The path leads through hanging woods, to cross the B2141. Then as a grass track it goes from beside a car-park through a bridle-gate and along the crest of Harting Down. Where the ridge comes down to a saddle, turn right along a track which gradually ascends the hill. The way then takes a sharp left turn (junction with Stage 19) to contour round Beacon Hill and regain the ridge. Then steeply over Pen Hill: on the descent the path curves round to the right at the lower edge of arable, then left through a copse to a confined path between fields, and to a bridle-gate. Turn left for a few metres on the access road to Buriton Farm, then right on to a track which bears right: maintain direction up into a wood, ignoring paths to right and left. In an area of large beech trees at a bridleway junction, turn left. The path now goes gently uphill in wood past wire enclosures, then emerges between arable. For the rest of the stage the route is straight ahead, up over Didling Hill, then Linch Down (to the right of the summit), changing from grass to flint and chalk, and descending into a sunken lane and to the A286.

Approach by car

At start: on road verge of the A286, ½ mile south of Cocking. *At end*: on verge of the B2146, ½ mile south of South Harting at the top of the hill. *Also*: on the B2141 1 mile south of South Harting at the car-park on Harting Down.

Approach by other transport

Local buses: Southdown services at Cocking to Bognor Regis, Chichester and Midhurst (hourly); at South Harting to Midhurst and Petersfield (infrequent, not on Sundays). *Taxis*: Cocking, Midhurst Taxi (073081–3988); Petersfield, Clarkes Taxi (0730–62364).

Refreshment

Pubs: Cocking, Richard Cobden (real ale, meals); Bepton, Shamrock (real ale); Hooksway, Royal Oak (real ale, meals); South Harting, White Hart (real ale, meals).

Accommodation

Hotels or guest houses: Southdowns Country House Hotel, Trotton, Rogate, Petersfield GU31 5JN (Cat 5/5/5; 073080–521); Chalk Way Cottage, Cocking, Midhurst GU29 0HN (Cat 1/1/1; 073081–4204). *Other*: grazing and individual camping at Manor Farm, Cocking (073081–2784).

Admission

Uppark (National Trust), April to September, Wednesdays, Thursdays and Sunday afternoons.

Stage 10
Cocking to **South Harting**

DESCRIPTION

The great hills of the south country
    They stand along the sea:
And it's walking there in the high woods
    That I would wish to be,
And the men that were boys when I was a boy
    Walking along with me.

Hilaire Belloc (1870–1953)
from 'The South Country'

The Midhurst–Chichester road makes use of the lowest pass across the downs between the Arun and Meon rivers, only 100 m high. So it's not surprising that a Roman road (Chichester to Silchester) came by here long ago, and a short while ago a railway also. Just under the old flint steading and new metal barn at the start of this stage lies the tunnel of the London, Brighton, and South Coast line between Midhurst and Chichester, with stations at Cocking and Singleton. The board of directors of this company clearly got their market research wrong, and were also unduly swayed by the glamour of the Goodwood races which in July brought the rich and famous to Singleton station: passenger services ran only from 1881–1935.

Middlefield Lane is well and truly sunk into the chalk by the action of centuries of cart-wheels, hoofs, and feet; it takes us gently up the face of Cocking Down and is bordered by a mature hedge which, to judge by the number of shrubs in it, must have been here for a long time. Besides hawthorn and blackthorn it contains field maple, dogwood, briony, dog-rose, spindle, and elder. In autumn the yellows and reds of leaves and berries make a fine display, a tapestry of strong colours placed for our close inspection, and lasting late into November. The dull wire fences which succeed the hedge go between fields now mostly arable, including the entire brow of Linch Down (Linch meaning rising ground). These are farmed by the Cowdray estate, which owns a lot of land to the north. Beyond it are good views across the Rother to the hills of sand and clay now directly on our right. To the south are the conifer plantations of the West Dean estate, bordered by hedges smothered in clematis. Since they lie a little to our left we can see over them to the Solent and the Isle of Wight, with the Chichester cathedral spire and the masts on the Trundle as prominent points of reference in a view which covers most of Stage 19. Bridleways lead down to our right to two tiny settlements, Bepton and Didling, both less than a mile off our course. Bepton (Baebba's farmstead) is an unspoilt corner where St Mary's church, with a squat tower under a Sussex cap, sits among trees beside a pond. Didling means 'Dyddel's people', though it calls to mind a diddle or a doodle or a dawdle. A dawdle to Didling is to be recommended, for halfway between the houses and the steep chalk scarp stands the little church of St Andrew, known from its position as 'The Shepherds' Church'. The simple whitewashed interior, the medieval benches and the seventeenth-century pulpit and altar rails are offset by views of the lines of the downs through the plain glass windows, and you don't have to be religious to feel a spiritual calm as you sit and look at them. Outside the church is a fine old yew tree which once was nearly cut down by mistake, as can be seen.

We now enter a wood and find a tall wire-mesh fence on our left. From it come strange bird-sounds, and through the foliage are bright flashes of blue and green and red. Peacocks display their long trains of exotic feathers and Himalayan pheasants strut about. In winter we can just see the chimney of a house as if camouflaged. This is Monkton House, the secluded retreat of Edward James, once owner of the West Dean estate. Back in the 1930s the young Edward James conceived the fancy of converting a traditional shooting lodge (designed by Lutyens) into a surrealist dream – or, some would say, nightmare. The brick walls are painted blotchy purple, the colour of copper beeches. Below the first-floor windows are pink plaster-mouldings in the shape of towels hung out to dry.

The drainpipes are mock bamboos. Inside, the walls are of silk or worsted; the stair carpet has the pattern of paw marks as if an enormous hound had just mounted them; the dining-room has a dome and windows of alabaster; the four-poster bed has palm-tree posts; the bathroom, a crystal which reflects changing colours; and the sitting-room, a sofa shaped like Mae West's lips. Perhaps it is not surprising that Edward James has never lived in Monkton House, whose curtains are permanently drawn and which is as closed to the world as Tutankhamun's tomb. Instead this eccentric, a patron of Salvador Dali, has elected to live in the Mexican jungle where, amid the luxuriant vegetation of a steep valley, he directs the construction of a concrete pleasure-dome.

The Way now turns southwards to loop around Treyford Hill. Just where woodland resumes on our right, a stile gives access to the Devil's Jumps. This is the name given to a group of burial mounds which are roughly in line with each other. They are amazingly large and pronounced, one being the highest in Sussex. They date from the early Bronze Age, around 1600 BC, and are all of the bell-barrow type. They would originally have contained 'a single primary cremation' – i.e., they were built to house the ashes of just one tribal chief, placed in a jar of pottery and accompanied by various artefacts for his journey to the other world: a hoard of bronze implements has been recovered from them. The Devil's Jumps have recently been cleared of undergrowth and generally tidied by the voluntary efforts of the Sussex Downsmen, and it is satisfactory that this imposing site can only be seen by those who walk (or ride) at least a mile to it. Most of those who do, come up from Hooksway and the Royal Oak (see Stage 19), which is where we will find ourselves also if we miss the important right turn in Phillis Wood.

This upper end of Phillis Wood has fine old beech trees with sturdy roots and branches, as well as oaks and birch. In it we don't feel entirely confined because we get occasional vistas through or over them. There are wild raspberries, free for the picking. These are the sort of high woods where Hilaire Belloc 'would wish to be',

The high woods on Treyford Hill

singing and striding along. We have heard his echoes on other stages, but this is the stage to record his walk across the county of Sussex which started at Robertsbridge on the Kent border on 29 October 1902 and ended close by here at Harting five days later. He imagined three companions, referred to as Grizzlebeard, the Sailor, and the Poet, and his account of their journey is in *The Four Men*, in which he exudes his Rabelaisian attitudes and appetites, but also his deep emotional patriotism, here manifested in lyrical descriptions of the Sussex scenery. His walk took place just before the Age of the Car, probably the last occasion when road-walking could still be a pleasure: if he walked today, Hilaire Belloc would be up here on the South Downs Way.

At the access road to Buriton Farm (so called, though it is fully five miles from Buriton), a right turn would lead us to Treyford and Elsted, half a mile and 1½ miles off. These are two more small settlements along the underhill lane which follows the upper greensand belt parallel to us throughout this stage. Treyford (pronounced 'Trefford') means tree ford; assumedly there was originally a tree which lay across a stream. It has no church but two churchyards. Elsted means Aella's place, and probably refers to Aella, first king of the South Saxons. Appropriately the church (of St Paul) is basically Saxon, and one of the finest examples of their 'herringbone' masonry. St Paul's is also unusual in having been restored from a ruinous condition not – as is normal – more than a hundred years ago, but in the 1950s, and done in such a way that all the old masonry is preserved without being copied or altered. From the clear north windows one gazes out across the weald, for the greensand belt has its own little bench-level before it gives way to the lower clays. Between Elsted and the chalk downs is the site of a Romano–British farmstead, including a rectangular building and a courtyard, and occupied from the first to the fourth centuries. On Pen Hill we go along a cross-dyke, which served here probably as the boundary of a sheep-run or cattle pasture. The hump of Pen Hill gives fine views of the higher summits of Beacon Hill ahead and Treyford Hill behind and the line of the downs beyond it. Below us

Milkpond Bottom

to the north are hanging woods of ash, and to the south the unspoilt combe of Milkpond Bottom where, beside the Way at any rate, large numbers of rabbits have replaced the sheep as the main agency against woodland regeneration. Beacon Hill has more distant views, and on it are more earthworks enclosing 40 acres. A bridleway leads up and over it and could shorten our route by three-quarters of a mile, but it involves a steep ascent and descent and the top is rather flat and lacking foreground. So it is better to stick to the attractive section that zigzags south.

The sharp turning comes in a gorsey corner. This is the junction with Stage 19, and just beyond the gate is Telegraph House. The house is on the site of one of the stations of the London–Portsmouth telegraph system which was set up to keep the Admiralty in quick touch with the fleet at Portsmouth. The original system, invented by George Murray, was installed in 1800 and so carried the news of the Battle of Trafalgar. It involved a tall structure with shutters that opened and shut to a code. The shutters were worked by former seamen, and each station had a retired naval officer in command. In 1823 the shutters were replaced by the more efficient semaphores, with movable arms. Although the semaphores could transmit a message between London and Portsmouth in three minutes in ideal conditions, both systems were dependent on visibility. They were superseded by the electric telegraph, installed in 1849 along the railway line. The derelict telegraph house was bought by Earl Russell in 1900, and on the site he built the present house, including the tower which is its principal feature. When Lord Russell came into financial difficulties (he was later imprisoned for bigamy in a judgement which was the last occasion when the House of Lords acted as jury for 'one of their peers'), his brother Bertrand Russell took it over in order to found a school here on the principles advocated by him and his wife, Dora. These involved abandoning discipline and letting the children do as they pleased. They were encouraged also to abandon their clothes on warm summer days; and the story goes of a conventional couple who drove up to the school with a view to placing their delinquent child in it. The father got out of his car and rang the bell, which was opened by a sixteen-year-old girl, stark naked. 'Good God!' exclaimed the parent. 'There is no God,' the girl replied, and firmly shut the door. The great philosopher soon began to doubt the wisdom of his educational theories, and the school departed with Dora in 1934. Russell returned alone to Telegraph House. 'For about two months, purely to afford myself distraction, I worked on the problem of the twenty-seven straight lines on a cubic surface.'

Ranks of rosebay willowherb now line our route. This tall bright pink flower is very common along the Way. In August the tiny silk-parachuted seeds are continually letting go their frail anchorage and drifting away on the summer breeze. In twilight the colour lights up the dark green of the undergrowth, looking like a forest fire. The path takes us along the side of Bramsholt Bottom, another natural valley, unploughed and unfenced, in this upland paradise profuse with flowers. The theme continues over Harting Down to the road, but it is probable that more fencing will soon be erected in this area. Gone are the days when a farmer could instruct a shepherd to take a flock of sheep for the day on to unenclosed land, so the open ground is now sheepless. Although rabbits may do their bit, the ground inevitably deteriorates. The landowner here has been discussing with the local authorities and the Downsmen how best to re-introduce sheep on to Harting Down without detracting too much from the natural scene.

Harting now comes into view. There are three Hartings, West, East, and South. Of these, South is the original. Harting (Heort's people) is reached by a bridleway just at the very end of this stage, by the second road: it leads for half a mile through beechwoods down to the village. The main street is mostly of old houses of brick and limestone clunch, not so much of flint as we would find in villages further east. The White Hart Inn has my recommendation: on a cold winter day it had no less than three open wood fires, excellent hot shepherd's pie, and no music. Overlooking the village street is the church of St Mary and St Gabriel, a fine cruciform building of the fourteenth century. In a cruciform church the nave and chancel are of equal length and the tower is in the centre. At Harting the chancel, separated by a lofty arch, seems remote from the rest of the church, like a church of its own, as at the Roman Catholic chapel at St Nicholas, Arundel. Actually the Roman

Catholic connection with Harting is strong: the Carylls (see Stage 20) had a Catholic chapel built for themselves in the south-east corner of the church, and Reginald Pole, Cardinal and last Roman Catholic Archbishop of Canterbury, held the vicarage of Harting, amongst other appointments. This church is also memorable for its roof, rebuilt after a fire in 1576, and is a splendid example of the art of Elizabethan carpentry, especially in the chancel with elaborate pendants to the wall-posts and beams. Outside are two strong modern verticals: the 43 m copper-sheathed broach spire and the tall churchyard cross, an unusual and sensitive war memorial. Anthony Trollope lived at Harting for some months before he died, and Gilbert White's family owned land on the south slopes of Harting Down, around Kildevil Copse. But as a salutary reminder of what life meant to the ordinary villagers – not men of education like Anthony Trollope or men of wealth like Harry Fetherstonhaugh – here is the description by an old Harting man of his daily round at harvest time some 200 years ago: 'Out in morning at four o'clock. Mouthful of bread and cheese and pint of ale. Then off to the harvest field. Reaping and mowing till eight. Then morning breakfast and small beer. Breakfast – a piece of fat pork as thick as your hat is wide. Then work till ten o'clock: then mouthful of bread and cheese and a pint of strong beer. Work till twelve. Then at dinner in the farm house; sometimes a leg of mutton, sometimes a piece of ham and plum pudding. Then work till five: then a nunch (cheese) and a quart of ale. Then work till sunset: then home and have supper and a pint of ale.'

Back on the South Downs Way we come to the first of two roads which climb the hill from Harting. This one leads to Chichester. Up this hill in around 1694 came that intrepid lady, Celia Fiennes, riding side-saddle and with perhaps a couple of mounted servants and a spare horse. Although herself unmarried, she had a network of relations and friends throughout England, coming as she did from an aristocratic Roundhead family that had married into the new merchant classes. On this occasion she had stayed at Nursted near Petersfield with 'Mr Holt that married my mother's sister': 'from

South Harting church from West Harting Down

thence I went to Chichester through a very fine Park of the Lord Tankerville's, stately woods and shady tall trees at least 2 mile.' Lord Tankerville was the then owner of Uppark, approached up our second road; but from where we cross the first road it is possible to walk up through a field to Uppark Tower, now a ruin. It must have looked splendid when built, an octagonal Gothic structure of two stories on top of the hill, designed by the architect Henry Keene. It was built to the orders of Sir Matthew Fetherstonhaugh to commemorate his stake in a syndicate which sought to establish a new colony in America, to be called Vandalia (now part of Virginia). Hence the folly was called the Vandalian Tower. It was burnt by arsonists (vandals?) in the troubled times of 1842.

The last half-mile of this stage is through more 'high woods', this time on the steep scarp slope; beech and ash and also chestnut, their height accentuated by the hill. Nowhere on the Way do we get a better impression of the hanging woods than here, in a grove called The Bosom. They are not silent, though, for just below us are the roads which fork out from Harting and all the cars are changing gear. At the second road we can think of the Duke of Wellington being drawn up by toiling horses in a carriage, and calculating, in his usual practical way, how the hill would wear them out if they had to do it often. This was one reason why he refused the offer of Uppark as a gift from the nation and chose instead Stratfield Saye in Hampshire.

The drive entrance to Uppark itself is only a quarter of a mile left along the road, and of all the great houses along the Way this is the most expressive for those who walk or ride. Whereas Firle is folded into the foot of the down, its park and garden retaining hidden charms and with the sun late to reach its windows, Uppark stands boldly on the top, capturing all available sun in its rooms and gazing at the Channel. This situation, in any case unusual for an eighteenth-century house, was also impracticable on the chalk because of lack of water, except if hauled up from a deep well. The building of a great house at Uppark was assisted by the installation of a pump at St Richard's spring at Harting (the engine-house still

View from the Vandalian Tower

stands) and pipes of lead and iron to bring the water to the house – a device developed from the invention of the owner's grandfather in pumping water into London. From the Fords the estate passed to the newly-rich Fetherstonhaughs. Sir Matthew redecorated the house splendidly and filled it with magnificent carpets, furniture and works of art. Sir Harry, his son, was a rake who hunted, raced, gambled, and entertained lavishly. For a year he had a sixteen-year-old girl at Uppark as his mistress, but then dropped her. She wrote to his friend Charles Greville, 'O God, what shall I dow? what shall I dow? O God that I was in your possession or in Sir H. Either. What a happy girl I should be . . .' Emma Hart passed into other possessions, including Sir William Hamilton's and Nelson's, and so into history. Sir Harry postponed his marriage till he was seventy, and then wedded Mary Ann Bullock, his head dairy-maid. Thus it was that Uppark was preserved from Victorian 'improvements', for Mary Ann and then her sister Frances, who only died in 1895, kept the place 'as Sir 'Arry 'ad it', he that had been born in 1754! With 'the two elderly ladies in the parlour following their shrunken routines,' the young H.G. Wells, whose mother was their housekeeper, was flirting with the maids downstairs.

The sun-catching windows of Uppark

Stage 11
South Harting to HMS Mercury 8½ miles

SPECIFICS

The first part of this stage is along the ridge by tracks confined by
hedges or woods: the official South Downs Way ends at Sunwood
Farm. The second part is through forest and off the ridge. The third
part is mostly bare of wood and unconfined where it ascends Butser
Hill to regain the ridge. There are 2 miles of small surfaced road, 1½
miles of hard gravel track, and the rest is well-defined earth track or
grass. There are about five gates to open. Westbound, cumulative
ascent 245 m, descent 185 m. Bridle-route throughout (with
alternative bridle-track in the Queen Elizabeth Forest). See maps 7,
5 and 4.

Route westbound

From B2146 to HMS Mercury 8½ miles (13.5 km)

(a) *From B2146 to the Buriton-Chalton road* 3½ miles (5.5 km)
The track leads along the ridge with a hedge on the left: after
three-quarters of a mile it continues between hedges, then through a
copse to Sunwood Farm. Then left and immediately right along the
surfaced road. At a fork keep right into a wood, then follow the
road round to its end at Coulter's Dean (junction with Stage 20).
From here the route is under the electricity wires by a confined
track which converts to a lane, and so to the Buriton–Chalton road.

(b) *From the Buriton-Chalton road to the Queen Elizabeth Park
Centre* 2 miles (3 km)
Continue ahead through a car-park and bridle-gate into the Queen
Elizabeth Forest on a track uphill. Where the track starts to descend
take the right fork down Gravelhill Bottom: this eventually leads to
a gate and then on to a forest road downhill to the edge of the

forest. (Riders and walkers can alternatively use the more attractive trail through the woods, skirting just to the left of this route and waymarked with red posts with white horseshoes.) At the forest edge, follow the marked riding trail rightwards past the Park Centre.

(c) *From the Queen Elizabeth Park Centre to HMS Mercury* 3 miles (5 km)

Go through the tunnel under the A3, then veer left off the access road to find a track through two bridle-gates down to the grass. From here go through the middle of the grass area steadily uphill, gaining the higher ground between two wooded areas, and through a gate. Then near the top of Butser Hill (with telecommunications mast) follow the riding trail waymarks leftwards to a gate by a car-park entrance. The route is then along the access road away from Butser Hill and ignoring a road sharp right to East Meon. At the next junction take the road to the right marked '*Unsuitable for Motor Vehicles*' and go past Homelands Farm. The road then deteriorates to a confined track along the ridge over Tegdown, then along the edge of Hyden Wood to the East Meon–Horndean road by HMS *Mercury*.

Route eastbound

From HMS Mercury to **B2146** 8½ miles (13.5 km)

(a) *From HMS Mercury to the Queen Elizabeth Park Centre* 3 miles (5 km)

From HMS *Mercury* cross an initial road junction to come to the East Meon–Horndean road. Cross this onto a confined track marked '*Unsuitable for Motor Vehicles*'. This leads by the edge of Hyden Wood, then along the ridge over Tegdown. The track later converts to a road, passing Homelands Farm, and comes to a junction. Here take the road leftward towards Butser Hill (and its telecommunications mast) and to the access road to a car-park. Here leave the road by a bridle-gate ahead on to grass and follow the riding trail, waymarked with red posts with white horseshoes, rightward and away from the summit down between two wooded areas, through a gate and then down to the lowest point by the A3. Then through two bridle-gates, up on to an access road, and through the tunnel under the A3 to the Park Centre.

(b) *From the Queen Elizabeth Park Centre to the Buriton–Chalton road* 2 miles (3 km)

Follow the riding trail behind the Park Centre, so that the centre is on your right. Turn left at a park road up into the forest: our route, at this point, is surfaced. Then, where the road turns sharp left, continue ahead up Gravelhill Bottom through a gate and along a flint track. At the upper end veer left at a crossing path, then take a right fork on to a track at the edge of the forest, down to a gate and car-park at the Buriton–Chalton road. (Riders and walkers may alternatively use the more attractive waymarked trail through the woods, skirting to the right of Gravelhill Bottom).

(c) *From the Buriton–Chalton road to B2146* 3½ miles (5.5 km)

The small road indicating the South Downs Way soon converts to a confined track: after passing under electricity wires it comes to Coulter's Dean and converts back to surfacing (junction with Stage 20) as far as Sunwood Farm. From here the way maintains direction as a track through wood and between hedges, and later, with a hedge to the right, to the B2146.

Approach by car

At start: on verge of the B2146, ½ mile south of South Harting at the top of the hill. *At end*: on the secondary road between East Meon and Horndean, by HMS *Mercury*. *Also*: off the B2146 between South Harting and Nursted, on a very small road to Sunwood Farm and Coulter's Dean; a quarter-mile from Buriton on the small road to Chalton; at the Queen Elizabeth Country Park car-park off the A3; and on Butser Hill car-park.

Approach by other transport

Train: British Rail at Petersfield ($2\frac{1}{2}$ miles from the route at the Buriton–Chalton road). *Local buses*: Southdown service on the A3 by the Queen Elizabeth Park Centre to Portsmouth and Petersfield (hourly); at South Harting to Midhurst and Petersfield (infrequent, not on Sundays); many local buses at Petersfield. *Taxi*: Petersfield, Clarkes Taxi (0730–62364).

Refreshment

Pubs: South Harting, White Hart (real ale, meals); Buriton, Five Bells (real ale, meals). *Snacks*: Queen Elizabeth Country Park Centre, Coach House Café.

Accommodation

Hotels or guest houses: Drovers, Barham Road, Petersfield GG32 3EX (Cat 1/1/1; 0730–67573). *Other*: grazing at Glebe Farm House, Buriton (0730–63805).

Admission

Queen Elizabeth Country Park (Hampshire County Council and Forestry Commission), open access; Park Centre open March to November, daily; Ancient Farm Demonstration Area open May to September, afternoon.

Stage 11
South Harting to **HMS Mercury**

DESCRIPTION

After night's thunder far away had rolled
The fiery day had a kernel sweet of cold,
And in the perfect blue the clouds uncurled,
Like the first gods before they made the world
And misery, swimming the stormless sea
In beauty and in divine gaiety.

Edward Thomas (1878–1917)
from 'Haymaking'

This stage begins as a track with unimpeded views to the north:
below is the green copper spire of South Harting church and beyond
the village is the hump of Torberry Hill: Torberry means a
stronghold by a high rock, and was the site of an Iron Age fort,
though no traces now remain. Just beyond this hill is Bohemia
Hollow where, according to a notice in the church, 'the Queen of
the Gypsies used to hold court up to the middle of the last century'.
To the south, through a hedge, is the wooded line of West Harting
Down drawing towards us. But after a crossing-lane our track is
bordered by impenetrable hedges covered by clematis. In the
process of reversion caused by the abandonment of hedge-trimming
in many places on the downs, this parasitic climber is so successful
that it threatens to dominate whole areas of scrub, and by its
monotony is the very reverse of its common name, Travellers' Joy.
When one thinks of the thorn trees and hazels being slowly
suffocated underneath, even the bright features of the clematis – the
greeny-cream flowers with their sweet scent, and the masses of
feathery fruits known as Old Man's Beard – appear unattractive.
    Just before Sunwood Farm (Sunna was the first farmer here), we

cross into Hampshire and here the official South Downs Way comes to an abrupt and pointless end. Undeterred by this bureaucratic barrier we continue past the workmanlike dairy-farm with its barns, milking shed and well-tended gardens, along a surfaced lane lined with copper beeches, the chlorophyll of their leaves masked with anthocyanin pigment. Then after the lane descends through a wood, a track leads three-quarters of a mile down to Buriton: this starts as a bridleway charmingly called Milky Way, but then the direct route to the village is a footpath across several fields, so for riders the best way to Buriton is by the bridleway at the Buriton–Chalton road. The old village centre is by the duck-pond in front of the church (St Mary's, with a fine interior including four-bay Norman arcades), and is well preserved by private occupancy and strict planning controls. Externally the complex doesn't look much changed from 150 years ago; but of course, as with all the other villages along our way, it is utterly changed in sociological terms. Whereas the old village then comprised a self-centred community of agricultural labourers and domestic servants run by tenant farmers and landowners, it is now occupied by mainly professional or retired people disconnected from any purely local economic structure. Whereas the cottages were crammed with many people (whole families sometimes sharing one room), each house now usually contains at the most a nuclear family group. And whereas in those days each man's status was proclaimed by his clothes, it is now impossible to tell – especially at weekends – which is the distinguished general or which the old farm-hand. For us who pass by, the architectural deception is beguiling and one can easily imagine figures from the past, in smocks or long dresses, sitting by the pond: village people whose forthright names are recorded in old documents – names such as William Lovechild, Thomas Hogesflesh, Richard Nayno, Francis Blackear, or Elizabeth Pretty. The manor house just behind the church was the seat of the father of Edward Gibbon, but that smooth classical historian was no real admirer of nature, as his grudging and pompous description reveals: 'The spot was not happily chosen, at the end of the village and at the bottom of the hill; but the aspect of the adjacent grounds was various and cheerful: the downs commanded a noble prospect, and the long

hanging woods in sight of the house could not perhaps have been improved by art or experience.' (I like that 'perhaps'.) He was clearly not an outdoor type: 'For the sports of the country I had no relish: I seldom mounted a horse, I never handled a gun; and when my father galloped away on a fleet hunter to join the Duke of Richmond's foxhounds, *my* walk was soon terminated by some shady bench, where I forgot the hours in the conversation of Horace or Xenophon.'

The greatest visual change at Buriton is up on the downs along our route: for after a section of track between hedges (passing one of the prettiest of cottage gardens) and going over the railway tunnel, we come to the Queen Elizabeth Country Park. Just before this we cross the Buriton–Chalton road and the last of the South Downs Way signs which points towards the Sussex border. The eastern end of this park is a forest covering War Down and Holt Down, two substantial hills now invisible under the trees. The plantations date from the 1930s. On War Down (to our right) they are virtually all deciduous, since the topsoil is only around 15 cm deep and the native beech is one of the few trees that will tolerate the very dry chalky soil. So to our right it is mainly beech, though the initial plantation is ash as well; there is then some Scots pine, and ash is also planted along the route down Gravelhill Bottom. On Holt Down (to our left) the thicker topsoil has permitted the planting of Western red cedar, Corsican pine, and Western hemlock, as well as beech, and the riding trail passes by these importations from the Mediterranean and North America. They will only be allowed to live for about sixty years before they go to the sawmill, since they reach maturity quickly. The slow-growing beeches, however, may be kept growing for as much as 150 years, so a century from now many of them will still be here. The beech also has the better fate of being used for furniture, while the softwoods may suffer the degradation of being broken into fibre and then reshaped into dull though useful products such as chip- or insulation-board. In these woods we may see golden pheasants.

The Park Centre is the 'honey-pot' for the swarms of car-borne

The green at Buriton

people, young and old, who visit the park. As such it is very
necessary and is excellently arranged in every way, being
educational, informative, well designed, well run. But for us it is
merely a point of reference as we go through the park, moving from
the wooded east to the open west by a tunnel under the roaring
London–Portsmouth road. Times have changed since 300 years ago
when the first coaches offered a regular service between London
and Portsmouth: it was announced that '*Ye Portsmouth Machine
sets out from Ye Elephant and Castell and arrives presently by the
Grace of God*': 'presently' meant at least two days. We now come to
the demonstration area of the Ancient Farm (the experimental farm
itself is not open to the public, and is on the other side of Butser
Hill).

This is the best place to understand the lives of the Celtic tribes of
the Iron Age, for instead of trying rather ineffectually to visualise
from an archaeological site which shows merely postholes or bones,
here before our eyes are the house, the livestock, the crops, the
herbs, the fence and the pits – almost everything except the people
themselves. The round hut reconstructed is a sort of Celtic manor
house in which the local head-man lived with his family and
retainers, squatting around the central fire or sleeping near the wall
behind flimsy partitions. It is made of an outer wall of stakes and
an inner ring of oak posts which support a continuous lintel, and the
rafters are of elm. So many trunks and hazel rods were needed that
200 trees were used, as well as four tonnes of wheat straw for the
thatch. Already, after the few years of its existence, it is clear that
such a building is more durable than the round houses of the
African tribes, which look so similar. The Soay sheep, so wild that
they are impervious to dog-control and so rough that their wool is
plucked not sheared, and the small Dexter cattle complete the
scene: and among the herbs growing is the woad which the Celts
used to dye their clothes and sometimes their bodies. Of other
experiments conducted, einkorn, the first wheat grown in
prehistory, has been successfully cultivated without artificial
pesticides or fertilisers. This meant regularly hoeing or weeding it.

Celtic manor house

The crop yielded 1.4 tonnes per hectare, but since einkorn is more nutritious than modern corn that figure understates the value of the crop. In fact the Celts developed the einkorn into the even more nutritious emmer and spelt. Emmer has a protein value of 20.0% per gram dry weight, compared to modern wheat's 8.9%. The only amino-acid missing from the chain was lycine, found abundantly in fish, which supplemented the diet. The grain pits that so intrigued the Roman conquerors have been found by experiment to preserve the grain through the winter, sealed within the chalk rock and beneath a tight covering of clay. Oxen have been used to plough under a yoke. All these experiments are undertaken by an enthusiastic and intelligent team who themselves lead perfectly normal modern lives, so don't imagine them painted in woad and chewing the Soay around the hut fire in an Iron Age commune on the other side of Butser!

Now we mount the turfy slope of Butser Hill, 150 m up. In some ways this ascent gives us the best impression of downland in the whole length of our route, for it is throughout on grass close-cropped by sheep. As a result the flowers are profuse, the cowslips, kidney-vetches, and rockroses supplying the yellow, the rampions, scabious, and harebells the blue, and the thyme, salad burnet and bee orchids the reds, which dot the greens of the leaves in a natural pointillism: and, as if to obscure the brilliance, the tall plantains cover the ground like a mist. We go over the traces of lynchets, of which there are many more to our right, as well as behind us on Chalton Down where several square miles of them were recorded by air photographs just before they were all ploughed during or after the war. Incidentally, the photographs also showed settlements of the Romano–British era, which were often laid out in a regular pattern and the houses were rectangular – a palpable advance over the circular hut. The sound band of the A3 spoils the effect, but in compensation we can see the extensive yew woods on Hillhampton Down, whose dark-green lines provide the perfect contrast for the bright turf and flowers. Also on Butser are substantial prehistoric earthworks, ditches and banks that divide the central plateau from the spurs: these were not for fortification, but for stock control.

Although Butser (Beorht's hill) is 'old as time and tide' its summit is geologically not as old as the other downs along our route because it is capped with a layer of tertiary debris known as 'clay with flints'. This helps Butser to be the highest point of the South Downs at 270 m: it is also the culmination of the main ridge, which becomes much less pronounced westwards. So from the trig point on its flat top we get a fine panorama and a last backward look at the straight scarp that we have come along, with Chanctonbury still visible. Sadly, Butser, like Devil's Dyke, has been desecrated by modern man. An immense telecommunications mast is planted on its head. A well-publicised road brings thousands daily in their cars, and for them amenities are now planned: surely this is the wrong place for a 'honey-pot'. But one pleasant feature of Butser is the wooden post and metal bracket that constituted the beacon that was once placed on this and other prominent hills. In times of emergency the fire would be ready for lighting at immediate notice, guarded by an armed horseman known as a 'hobiler'. The mast is a link in the national telecommunications system, part of which is the use of microwaves for telephone trunk calls. Most microwave radio systems operate on frequencies in the 4 to 6 GHz range, i.e. wavelengths of only 7.5 to 5.0 cm. The beams behave essentially like rays of light, in that they follow straight-line paths, and it is therefore necessary to place their aerials high enough to see one another. These aerials are either horns or dishes, and they concentrate the transmitted signals into narrow beams less than one degree across. Each microwave system has eight channels, six of which are normally used for traffic purposes and two kept as standby. Each channel can carry 1,800 simultaneous telephone calls.

From the edge of the plateau we can see Petersfield, the chief town of this locality. Those wanting to walk to Petersfield will best do so from Buriton, either by the road or more adventurously along a footpath by the banks of the stream: two miles. Petersfield is a market town, and was a coaching town which declined in relative importance when the railways were built. The main square is called the Spain, after Spanish merchants, and a statue of William III stands in the centre of it: here and in the High Street are many eighteenth-century houses. At the far end of Petersfield is the village of Steep, where Edward Thomas lived. In his prose he wrote perceptively about the South Downs, though in his poetry they for some reason escaped his vision. Still, the opening lines from 'Haymaking' give a marvellous sense of freshness, helped by that casual extra syllable in the second line, though as in all his poems the joy of nature is tempered with the recollection of misery: and the clouds he saw at Steep surely uncurled also over Butser.

Tegdown concludes this stage. After a section of road, preceded by a fine display of vipers bugloss, we come to an earth track with good views north and south, running between grass fields and then along the edge of Hyden Wood. For over half a mile a line of oaks has recently been planted, their growth helped by the clayey soil just here: in fifty years' time they will look magnificent from near and far.

Stage 12
HMS Mercury to **Exton** 7$\frac{1}{2}$ miles

This stage weaves through a valley and then around Old Winchester
Hill so as to provide a walking-route from Wether Down to the
Meon. It is not a bridle-route, though riders (or walkers wanting an
easy short cut) can get to Exton along 5 miles of small roads. There
is a rough patch on Henwood Down, and the final section down
Garden Hill Lane can be waterlogged. The enclosed fields are
mostly pasture, though there is some arable. There are 1$\frac{1}{4}$ miles of
small surfaced roads, another 1$\frac{1}{2}$ miles on well-defined track, and
the rest is paths, mostly hedge-lined apart from the unconfined grass
on Old Winchester Hill. There are about six gates to open and one
stile to cross. Westbound, cumulative ascent 144 m, descent 280 m.
See maps 4 and 3.

Route westbound

From HMS Mercury to **Exton Church** 7$\frac{1}{2}$ miles (12 km)

(a) *From HMS Mercury to Old Winchester Hill* 4$\frac{1}{2}$ miles (7 km)
Cross the East Meon–Horndean road and follow the road marked
for Droxford which leads through HMS *Mercury*. Just after the
building Anson and before a sportsfield, turn right into a small road
which leads up towards the radio masts, converting to a track which
then goes down between thick hedges as a sunken lane to Coombe
Cross. Cross a road and continue on the track, which soon veers
right and then left amid brushwood. Well under half a mile from
Coombe Cross, watch carefully for a crossing footpath, now
overgrown. We turn left on this through a metal field-gate, then
through undergrowth along the line of a fence to a gate, and on
down by a concrete farm-track. At a road turn right: then left into
the drive of Whitewool Farm and on around the farm buildings.

Then right along a concrete track, becoming flint after a gate. The track reaches the hill and mounts it obliquely rightwards to a gate at the far top corner of a grass field. Here, at a road junction, turn sharp left along the road for 200 m to the northern entry to the Old Winchester Hill Nature Reserve.

(b) *From Old Winchester Hill to Exton Church* 3 miles (5 km)
From the road turn right into the reserve, then left and parallel with the road along the ridge. At the southern end of the reserve take a flint track rightwards above the line of the yew wood: this leads to the hill-fort. Go through the middle of the hill-fort, keeping to the right of the trig-point, and ahead downhill to a stile. The path now leads down the edge of a wood and then along a hedge beside a field. Turn right on to a winding grass track, then by a footpath between brushwood. Just after reaching a concrete farm-track after a gate, turn left on to a flint track (Garden Hill Lane). This soon converts to a sunken lane which becomes a stream in wet weather; but the hedge has been cleared to allow for walking along the banks. On the way we pass across a disused railway line. At a crossing path, turn right and go by a footbridge over the Meon to the A32: cross this to enter Exton and so to the church.

Route eastbound

From Exton Church to HMS Mercury 7½ miles (12 km)

(a) *From Exton Church to Old Winchester Hill* 3 miles (5 km)
From the church take the road leftwards out of the village to the A32. Across the road a track leads by a footbridge across the Meon: 100 m on, turn left up a rough path (Garden Hill Lane): this becomes a stream in wet weather, but the hedge has been cleared to allow for walking on the banks. On the way we pass across a disused railway line. The lane later improves to a flint track. At its end turn right through a gate, and then up a footpath between brushwood to a winding grassy track. At the corner of a field the path turns left up along a hedge, then through a bridle-gate up the edge of a wood to a

stile, and so up to the summit of the hill in the Nature Reserve.
Continue ahead through the hill-fort, to find a flint track leading
above the line of a yew wood. Turn left from this along the ridge
parallel to a road, then gain the road at the end of the reserve.

(b) *From Old Winchester Hill to HMS Mercury* 4½ miles (7 km)
Continue northwards now on the road for 200 m to a fork. Here
turn sharp right through a gate and then incline down across a grass
field on a track. The track then leads away from the hill through a
gate towards Whitewool Farm. Skirt to the left of the farm
buildings, along a drive to a road. Turn right along the road for over
400 m, then left up a concrete farm-track. After a gate this
deteriorates to a path in undergrowth along the line of a fence, to a
metal gate on a crossing hedge. Turn right on to the path between
the brushwood, which within half a mile comes to a road at Coombe
Cross. Cross the road up a sunken lane between hedges to the top of
Wether Down, and past radio masts to a road at buildings. Left
along the road through HMS *Mercury* to the East Meon–Horndean
road.

Approach by car

At start: on the secondary road between East Meon and Horndean,
by HMS *Mercury*. *At end*: in Exton just off the A32, 1 mile south of
Warnford. *Also*: at Coombe Cross on a small road a mile from East
Meon; and at Old Winchester Hill, approachable from the A32 at
Warnford or West Meon.

Approach by other transport

Local buses: Hampshire Bus services at East Meon to Winchester
and Petersfield (about every two hours, not on Sundays); and at
Exton to Southampton and Petersfield (infrequent, not on
Sundays). *Taxi*: Petersfield, Clarkes Taxi (0730–62364).

Refreshment

Pubs: East Meon, George (real ale, meals); Exton, Shoe (real ale).

Accommodation

Hotels or guest houses: Langrish House Hotel, Langrish, Petersfield (0730–66941); Barrow Hill Farm, Ramsdean, Petersfield GU32 1RW (Cat 1/1/1; 073087–340); Giants Farm, Harvesting Lane, East Meon GU32 1QR (Cat 1/3/2; 073087–205).

Admission

Old Winchester Hill (National Nature Reserve), partially open daily.

Stage 12

HMS Mercury to **Exton**

DESCRIPTION

There on the pastoral Downs without a track
To guide me, or along the bare white roads
Lengthening in solitude their dreary line,
While through those vestiges of ancient times
I ranged, and by the solitude overcome,
I had a reverie and saw the past,
Saw multitudes of men, and here and there,
A single Briton in his wolf-skin vest
With shield and stone-axe, stride across the Wold.

William Wordsworth (1770–1850)
from 'The Prelude'

Her Majesty's Ship *Mercury* will never sail the seas. She is a shore
establishment, or 'stone frigate', stranded like Noah's Ark on the
top of a hill, and in fact a naval school of instruction in
communications, operations and navigation. The white ensign flies
from the yard-arm, the bugles call, and the buildings are named
after naval heroes – Anson, Hawke, Kamperfelt. Before the arrival
of HMS *Mercury* in the last war, this spot was the site of a large
country house called Leydene, owned by the Peel family. Infinitely
older than these modern structures is the fragment of an Iron Age
multiple-boundary earthwork which survived the building of both
Leydene House and HMS *Mercury*, and is preserved just by our
route as an example of primitive methods of fortification. A mile
and a half to the south is Broadhalfpenny Down, famous to
cricketers as the place where the men of Hambledon played the
game from the mid-eighteenth century. The Hambledon Cricket
Club established its rules in 1774, and in 1777 came the great
moment when Hambledon beat All England by an innings and 168

runs in a match at Sevenoaks. Hambledon is renowned also for another pioneering achievement: in 1951 Sir Guy Salisbury–Jones planted the first of the modern vineyards in England, despite the general belief that the climate would be too cold and grey for viniculture.

Our route now turns northwards across Wether Down and over Salt Hill, passing the radio masts and the site of a long barrow. We can now see ahead into a valley seemingly surrounded by downs, a bowl through which we will now be walking, though in fact the water flows out to the north. From our rim we go down a sunken lane which takes us from the soft white flinty upper chalk, through the hard white middle chalk, down to the grey marly lower chalk – though these underlying formations are mostly hidden under the surface soil. This lane – or bostal – comes to a road at Coombe Cross, a remote place with a post-box set in the wall. (This reminds me that Wordsworth often walked six miles just to post a letter. I have chosen his quote for this non-bridleway stage because he was the pre-eminent walkers' poet, and scorned to ride a horse). A mile to the right along the road is East Meon.

East Meon can certainly vie with any of the Sussex villages along the way. The Meon rises only a mile to the south and is still merely a small stream, but it is awarded a place of honour in an embankment through the centre of the village, with several bridges to span it, a genial feature all too uncommon in England. The brick houses, some red and some whitewashed, are offset by trees; and several are of the eighteenth century. The Court House is in origin fifteenth-century, and has a stone fireplace and corbelled stone head. But the main sight in East Meon is All Saints church. This church stands in an unusual position to the side of the village and up against the steep slope of Park Hill, so that however you look at it, it seems framed in green. The colouring is even more remarkable in that besides the light-grey of the walls of stone and flint, the roof and spire are of white lead, the broach spire having diagonal joints that give an extra twist. But these features are merely adjuncts to a fine display of Norman architecture in the tower, seen from the

East Meon church

exterior in the triple arches on each side, and from the interior in
the four great arches which support it. A font, made of black marble
from Tournai, is one of the best examples of Norman sculpture, rich
in Christian symbols of vines, doves and crosses. And the church is
completed with later work in the Gothic style.

   After Coombe Cross and the track known as Halnacker Lane
comes a rough patch as we turn across the side of Henwood Down
through thistles towering over hawkbit and ox-eye daisies. Now we
are on Whitewool Farm, which comprises the greater part of the
valley. It provides a good example of farming methods: we see the
pig-sheds, silos, granary, and milking-parlours, and barns with
cleanly thatched roofs. A large herd of Friesians grazes the fields
around the farm, and in mid-afternoon we will see them on their
way to milking, strutting contentedly towards their twice-daily
routine: (a healthy cow will produce as much as 7,000 litres a year,
45 litres a day at the peak). The farmhouse and cottages are neat,
with gardens shaded by some fine oaks and ashes. Now we mount
Whitewool Hanger up a sunken lane. At the top, where the road
forks, the right-hand lane goes down to West Meon and the
left-hand to Warnford. Our route gets rather closer to Warnford
(stallion ford) later in the stage, but not accessibly, so this is the
place to mention the church of Our Lady which stands in peaceful
isolation in the grounds of Warnford Park. It is isolated because the
nearby manor house of the St John family fell into ruins, and also
because the entire village was moved half a mile to its present
position when the trunk road was originally built, by French
prisoners during the Napoleonic wars. The church has a massive
Norman tower and a pure Early English nave, with Jacobean
screen and monuments. As for West Meon, the realities of life there
200 years ago are glimpsed in this extract from the entry for 11 July
1783 in the journal of Gilbert White over at Sherborne: 'The
tempest on friday night did much damage at West-meon, & burnt
down three houses and a barn. The tempests round on thursday and
friday nights were very aweful! There was a vast hail on friday night
at several places.'

Friesians after milking at Whitewool Farm

Old Winchester Hill is the name of a westward spur of the chalk down, crowned by an Iron Age fort. Since Winchester is eleven miles away, this name is confusing. The fort is of medium size (14 acres), univallate with counterscarp bank, with east and west gate entrances, and with a present crest/ditch maximum height of 6.4 m: wooden palisades surmounted the inner rampart. It was built around 250 BC. Celtic residence is indicated in a few depressions within the fort suggestive of hut circles; but more noticeable are the humps of Bronze Age barrows, which antedated the hill-fort by about 1,000 years and so were relics of the silent past as much to the Celts as to us. The panorama is extensive, with our best view of the Isle of Wight. It was here that on 12 October 1644 two gentlemen – Colonel Gunter and Lord Wilmot – with horses, servants, and dogs, met as if by chance out coursing: an unremarkable occurrence, except that one of the 'servants' was Charles II (as described in Stage 8).

For the past thirty years, Old Winchester Hill and the adjoining combe has been a National Nature Reserve of 150 acres. Into this small area an amazing variety of wildlife and plants is concentrated by careful management. Grassland, shrub, and woodland are all to be seen at their very best – the grassland kept clean by sheep and carpeted with flowers; the shrub displaying all the main species, including juniper; and the woodland including a large grove of yews. Lepidopterists will see the butterflies that are no longer common on the downs: in May the Common Blues and Small Heaths, and the Duke of Burgundy fritillary that feeds on the cowslips; in early summer the Chalkhill Blues, whose food is the horseshoe vetch; and in July the brown butterflies and the Cinnabar moths. Meanwhile large mammals such as deer, foxes, and badgers, as well as weasels and stoats, lurk in the undergrowth and prowl nocturnally.

The last section of this stage is down from Old Winchester Hill to the Meon, past the coppices, pastures and hedges of Peake Farm, and then down Garden Hill Lane. From this name one may imagine a pleasant gravelled lane leading gently past gardens: but beware! It

Yews on Old Winchester Hill

is one of the roughest parts of the entire route. It starts off all right
as a lane, but soon deteriorates into a stream bed. If it hadn't been
for the action of the local ramblers in hacking out a path along the
hedge, it would be nearly impassible when the stream is running.
The stream flows under the brick arch of a former railway, the
disused track of which provides a green path south towards
Meonstoke and Droxford. Though not a public right of way, this
railway route is much used by riders. The former station at
Droxford is where, in railway sidings, the coaches of the Allied
commanders were located on 'D-day' 6 June 1944, the
Anglo–American invasion of Normandy. Droxford also is the site of
a large pagan cemetery of the Jutes: this tribe arrived as part of the
generally Saxon invasions of the sixth century, and was prominent
in the settlement of the Meon valley. Finally, we cross the Meon
itself by a white-railed footbridge, a crystal-clear little river flowing
between the reeds. No one knows the meaning of its name, but it is
of British origin. So when the Celtic warriors in the hill-fort looked
down to the valley, it was 'the Meon' they spoke of as well as saw,
and we thus have another link with those 'multitudes of men' who
hunted and fought over the land (though by that time anyone armed
with a flint axe would have been using it only for peaceful
purposes).

Stage 13
Exton to **Cheesefoot Head** 8½ miles

The first half leads from the Meon up and along the now indistinct ridge: the second half goes over lower ground before turning to Cheesefoot Head. There are 3¼ miles on surfaced roads, mostly very minor ones, and the rest is virtually all well-defined earth or flint track, with a short section on grass. The route is lined with hedges nearly all the way and leads through fields, part pasture and part arable. About five gates to open. Westbound, cumulative ascent 226 m, descent 128 m. Bridle-route, though riders must take separate route for 1½ miles. See maps 3 and 2.

Route westbound

From Exton Church to **Cheesefoot Head** 8½ miles (14 km)

(a) *From Exton Church to Beauworth crossroads* 3 miles (5 km)
From Exton church take the lane up to the right which leads around the village. At a fork turn right, then keep right again up a narrow lane, then right once more at a junction. The lane now takes us up for nearly 1½ miles on to Beacon Hill. After a joining lane, keep right at a junction. Then, after passing a car-park area and then a wood on our right, where the road bears right at the end of the wood, go ahead on to a confined track which leads to Lomer Farm (but riders must keep to the road, turning left at the next junction and thence on by road for 1 mile to Wind Farm). At Lomer Farm, go to the left of cottages to maintain direction beyond. The confined track leads on to a wood and to the road at Wind Farm. Turn left along the line of the road, but using where possible the separate verge. Ignoring the turning to Kilmeston, we soon arrive at the Beauworth crossroads.

(b) *From Beauworth crossroads to Cheesefoot Head* 5½ miles (9 km)
At the crossroads turn right on the road marked for Beauworth past
the Millbarrow Inn: 100 m beyond the inn, turn left at a fork. Later,
where this small lane turns right, keep ahead on a farm-track which
leads through a copse, and so to Holding Farm and the A272. Cross
the road on to a track to a metal gate. Turn right into the field, to
the corner by a gate: then turn left, still in the field and near to the
fence on the right, to pick up the faint line of a former track. At the
end of the field, with the barn of Ganderdown Farm to our left, we
go through two field-gates and maintain direction under electricity
wires down to a bridle-gate leading to a wide confined track. This
track continues straight ahead for 1½ miles, crossing a small road on
the way. At a T-junction turn left up the track signed for Morestead,
past cottages and through a wood, then at the side of a field to a
bridle-gate into a confined path up the edge of Great Clump, and to
the A272 near Cheesefoot Head car-park.

Route eastbound

From Cheesefoot Head to **Exton Church** 8½ miles (14 km)

(a) *From Cheesefoot Head to Beauworth crossroads* 5½ miles (9 km)
Cross the A272 (80 m downhill from the car-park) to a bridle-gate
and confined path which leads down and along the edge of Great
Clump. The track then goes beside a field and into a wood. Just past
cottages at a junction of tracks, turn right on to a confined wide
track signed for Ganderdown. This goes straight for 1½ miles,
crossing a small road on the way. Where the close hedges cease,
continue up ahead under electricity wires to a crossing hedge at
field-gates. The route is now ahead in the grass field. At the end of
the field, before a gate, turn right still in the field for some 200 m to
a metal gate: go through this by a track down, to cross the A272.
Then along the road through Holding Farm and ahead by the track.
Where a small lane comes in from the left, continue ahead on it. At
a junction turn right past the Millbarrow Inn to the Beauworth
crossroads.

(b) *From Beauworth crossroads to Exton church* 3 miles (5 km)
Turn left on the road signed for Warnford. Ignore a road leading
left for Kilmeston: then continue where possible along the separate
path beside the road. Turn right into the entrance of Wind Farm,
then bear left on to a track through a copse, then confined between
fields to Lomer Farm: then to the right of cottages to maintain
direction on a confined track beyond. (Riders must stay on the road
before Wind Farm for a further mile, then right at a junction to pick
up the route). The confined track comes to a road with a wood on
the left: after a car-park area it bears right. Turn left at the junction,
then left at a fork: the small lane leads down from Beacon Hill to
Exton. Keep turning left to enter the village and gain the church.

Approach by car

At start: in Exton just off the A32 a mile south of Warnford. *At end*:
the car-park at Cheesefoot Head on the A272, 2½ miles from
Winchester. *Also*: at the Beauworth crossroads by small roads off
the A272; and on the A272 verge by Holding Farm.

Approach by other transport

Local buses: Hampshire bus service at Cheriton to Winchester and
Petersfield (about two-hourly, not on Sundays); and at Exton to
Southampton and Petersfield (infrequent, not on Sundays). *Taxi*:
Winchester, Colliss Cars (0962–53000).

Refreshment

Pubs: Exton, Shoe (real ale); Beauworth, Milbury's (real ale,
meals); Cheriton, Hampshire Hunt (real ale).

Accommodation

Hotels or guest houses: Little Uplands, Droxford SO3 1QL (Cat
3/3/3; 04897–8507). *Other*: grazing and stabling at Little Uplands.

Stage 13
Exton to **Cheesefoot Head**

DESCRIPTION

There are some heights in Wessex, shaped as if by a kindly hand
For thinking, dreaming, dying on, and at crises when I stand,
Say, on Ingpen Beacon eastward, or at Wylls-Neck westwardly,
I seem where I was before my birth, and after death may be.

Thomas Hardy (1840–1928)
from 'Wessex Heights'

Exton has abbreviated from Essessentune and before that East
Seaxnatune, which makes clear its meaning – the farmstead of the
East Saxons. Since this name would only have been given if such
occupation was unusual, it implies that the other settlements around
here were of the West Saxons. So we are well and truly in Wessex,
and indeed technically we entered it at the Hampshire border. The
old village straggles around ample gardens – groups of cottages,
some terraced, most detached. The Meon flows along one side of it,
and happily the A32 traffic flows even further off. The church of St
Peter and St Paul is basically thirteenth-century, but largely rebuilt.
It is flint-knapped, has a wooden belfry and a timber barrel-type
roof over the nave, which is set at an angle to the chancel. A more
remarkable church is to be found at Corhampton (corn homestead),
only half a mile away down the A32. This church (dedication
unknown) was built shortly after the year 1000, and the Saxon walls
and chancel arch are untouched by restoration. The walls are of
plastered whole flints, and their corners are of long and short
stones. The church contains fragments of elaborate
thirteenth-century wall-paintings, one of which depicts the story of
St Swithun of Winchester miraculously preserving unbroken the
eggs which fell from the old woman's basket. Outside is a Saxon

sundial (it is interesting to note that they divided the day not into twelve hours, but eight tides) and a gigantic yew which may be even as old as the church itself.

The two miles of lane from Exton up to Beacon Hill are so narrow that if there is any traffic it has to move extremely slowly. The lane is called the White Way, and must have looked delightful when it was still chalky and unsurfaced. For nearly all the way it is confined between hedges, and in fact the whole stage is characterised by the hedges which border our path. The best of these are the mature hedges which are kept trimmed, the worst those now out of control and smothered in clematis. In among the thorns and hazels flutter the birds of the hedgerow: the blackbird, highly territorialised, busily defending its patch with noisy rattle and fluty song from the first light of dawn; the robins in their red and olive-brown unisex plumage, uttering their diffident refrain; the stocky little wren, with its loud clear warble; the flocks of tits, with the bright yellows of the blue-tits and great-tits specially noticeable; and the song-thrush, who 'sings his song twice over, lest you should think he never could recapture his first fine careless rapture'. All these birds are either wholly or partly resident, so we can see them in all the stages of the year – pairing, nesting, mating, hatching, and always searching for food. The hedge provides them with rich pickings in seeds and berries, and in the worms, spiders, ants, slugs, centipedes, bees, moths and various larvae that are to be found in it.

Beacon Hill is a counterpart to Old Winchester Hill back across the valley – a jutting promontory that would have served equally well for a Celtic fort. The Celts at least made use of Beacon Hill agriculturally, and traces of their fields appear on its north-eastern face: in fact the low-lying land in the valley was at that time marshy and thickly wooded. Although now only one of many Beacon Hills, it was formerly called Lomer Beacon after the village of Lomer which lay just behind it, and which we now pass about a quarter of a mile after leaving the road – or rather, where Lomer was. For this is one of those abandoned villages that lie hidden in the countryside (there are ninety in Hampshire alone), and absolutely no bricks, stones, or flints of it are to be seen: just grassy mounds in a field to our left that has never since been ploughed, of which the largest is

the site of the church. It is poignant to think of the thriving, albeit small, settlement in this lonely spot. Lomer (meaning loam pool) duly had its entry in Domesday Book: 'Ruald holds Lomer of the Abbey of St Peter Winchester, and Alwald held it of the Abbot. He bought it in the time of King Edward for his life and paid the Abbot six sextaries of wine yearly. It was then, as now, assessed at three hides. Here are five ploughlands, one in desmesne, and six villeins and three bordarers with three ploughlands. Also a church, three acres of meadow and two servants. Of this land, one homager of the Abbot holds one yardland. The value of the whole at the time of King Edward and afterwards was six pounds.' This implies a population of around fifty. The property continued in the possession of the Abbey at Winchester until the Reformation, when it passed to the local landowners, Paulets then Wriothesleys. But contrary to later legend, Lomer did not die out at the Black Death nor become a beggars' community ('some in rags and some in tags and some in velvet gown'); it was rather the victim of slow changes in agriculture induced by enclosures and the clearances of the valley. It isn't surprising that so little remains, since the ordinary houses were built of only timber or of wattle-and-daub on a flint foundation or on posts driven into the ground, and so had to be replaced every twenty years or so, even if they had not burned down before.

A quarter-mile beyond the site is the present Lomer Farm, the farmhouse dating from the early seventeenth century, with Victorian alterations. It is part of the big Preshaw estate, as are also Wind Farm and Stony Hard Farm, both with commendably explicit names. Preshaw, like Lomer, was a small downland settlement: unusually, its name is thought to be of partly Celtic origin (*prys* meaning brushwood). In Preshaw Wood there is a large earthwork, probably of the Romano–British period. A mile to the south is a declivity called Betty Mundy's Bottom, flanked by Sergeant's Copse and Sailor's Wood, and thereby hangs a jolly tale. It seems that unsuspecting servicemen – flushed with arrears of pay and months of sexual starvation – were enticed up to this remote place to savour the fabulous delights of Betty Mundy; but when they were well and truly in Betty's arms they were usually robbed and some never returned, their bodies later being found buried in the woods. Buried also near Wind Farm are the bones or ashes of Bronze Age chieftains in their barrows, who presumably died in more heroic circumstances.

Where we rejoin the road at Wind Farm, a pause to look through the hedge northwards will give an excellent view. Immediately in front is a stile across which leads the Wessex Way, whose black double W has been with us since Lomer Farm. This is one of the new unofficial long-distance trails recently devised, and goes seventy miles from Emsworth behind us northwards to Ingpen Beacon in Berkshire, so giving us a further link with Thomas Hardy's lines about Wessex Heights. A mile or so ahead is Kilmeston (Cynehelm's farmstead). When William Cobbett rode through it in November 1822 he found it 'mouldered into two farms, and a few miserable tumble-down houses for the labourers'. The brick Manor House is sixteenth-century, with large eighteenth-century wings added to convert it into a hunting-lodge for the Hampshire Hunt. Among the important people who slept here was George IV, when Prince of Wales. He had a reason besides merely hunting the fox, for his paramour, Maria Fitzherbert, was staying at the time with her family (the Smythes) at Cheriton. Directly beyond Kilmeston can be seen the façade of a large house set in the trees: this is Hinton Ampner (the high farm of the almoner, i.e. the almoner of the monastery of St Swithun at Winchester), and it has one of the finest Hampshire chalk gardens, with vistas flowing into each other, framed by laurel and yew. Just beside the house is the source of the Itchen. Then $2\frac{1}{2}$ miles from us, and slightly left of Kilmeston, is Cheriton (farmstead belonging to a church). This is yet another lovely old village, the tiny Itchen flowing through it, with several old brick or timber houses flanking St Michael's church, which is mainly thirteenth-century. Among the activities at Cheriton in the last century – besides farming – were a timberyard and watercress beds, and it was also one of the last

The mounds of Lomer

places where several families supported themselves by training dogs (a cross between a terrier and a poodle) to hunt for truffles in the beechwoods. Cheriton was originally part of the large manor of Tichbourne, famous for the legal actions 100 years ago when a man claimed unsuccessfully to be the rightful heir to the estate.

On the misty morning of 29 March 1644 the Battle of Cheriton took place just to the east of the village – a small battle, but a crucial one. Sir William Waller and his Parliamentarian army had advanced from Surrey and were confronted by Lord Hopeton's Royalist army from Winchester, with about 10,000 men each. Essentially the Royalists lost the day because of the undisciplined, unco-ordinated attacks made by their cavalry commanders, which failed to break Waller's lines. His cuirassiers and musketeers exacted a terrible revenge, and by the afternoon Hopeton was in full retreat to Basing and Winchester:

> Ho! comrades, scour the plain; and ere ye strip the slain,
> First give another stab to make your search secure,
> Then shake from sleeves and pockets their broad-pieces and
> lockets,
> The tokens of the wanton, the plunder of the poor.

Beauworth (bee farm) is another small village just below us. In the last century children playing near the ancient chapel found thousands of small bright objects which they thought were buttons, but which were really a major hoard of medieval silver coins: though the landowner claimed the hoard, the village people managed to keep quite a few coins for themselves. We come to the Beauworth crossroads where the pub is called Milbury's, a corruption of Millbarrow, a name which records by both the windmill that once stood here and the Bronze Age barrow nearby. Holding Farm is also in the parish of Beauworth, and our transit through it leads under an avenue of mature beeches and close by the site of a Roman Building. The final section of the stage goes

The track towards Holding Farm

across Gander Down, along a fine straight unsurfaced lane for over one and a half miles: but to reach this there is the slightly confusing point where we have to skirt around a field. The gate at the apex of the field, which we pass by, leads to the bridleway to Cheriton, now only one and a half miles off. After Gander Down it is up Temple Valley to Cheesefoot Head, where besides the large wood called Great Clump there are two smaller clumps of beeches, one by the car-park, which make the place a landmark for miles around. Just below is the combe which forms a natural amphitheatre, and where General Eisenhower addressed the Allied troops before the invasion of Normandy.

Stage 14
Cheesefoot Head to **Winchester** 6½ miles

SPECIFICS

This final stage of the main route leads into the old centre of
Winchester by two dog-legs across the low-lying downs and around
St Catherine's Hill to the Itchen. The downland is mostly arable,
and gives way to an unspoilt combe and then the water-meadows.
There is 1¼ miles on surfaced road or pavement, the rest all
well-defined track or path. About seven gates to open. Westbound,
cumulative ascent 81 m, descent 208 m. Bridle-route, though riders
must use a separate route for the final mile into Winchester. The
Cathedral Close is closed at night. See Maps 2 and 1.

Route westbound

From Cheesefoot Head to **Winchester Cathedral** 6½ miles (10 km)

(a) *From Cheesefoot Head to St Catherine's Hill* 4 miles (6.5 km)
Cross the A272 (80 m down hill from the car-park) through a gate
to a track and continue straight ahead across the line of a hedge and
between arable on Fawley Down. The track becomes enclosed, and
after Hydes Cottages it is surfaced. At a road junction at Morestead
go ahead along the road signed for Twyford. Less than half a mile
later, just by a small road junction, turn right up a confined path.
This leads straight towards St Catherine's Hill, passing through
parkland, then arable, then the edge of the Hockley golf-course.
The path finally goes down, in scrub, to a road. (It is expected that
within two years work will start on the M3 here: bridleway transit
will be maintained throughout, and a bridle-bridge will be
constructed.)

(b) *From St Catherine's Hill to Winchester Cathedral* 2½ miles (3.5 km)
From the road below St Catherine's Hill, reverse steps to find a sunken lane leading around to the left of the wire fence of municipal works (see note above on M3 construction). This leads downhill into Plague Pits Valley with St Catherine's Hill on our right, and emerges under the A3 at the Itchen Navigation. Turn right upstream by the towpath to Tun Bridge: (riders must go left here on the road across the Itchen, then right into the city). Continue up the towpath to Wharf Bridge. Then left across the bridge into College Walk and around along College Street. Turn right through St Swithun's Gate into the Close, and through to the Cathedral Green.

Route eastbound

From Winchester Cathedral to **Cheesefoot Head** 6½ miles (10 km)

(a) *From Winchester Cathedral to St Catherine's Hill* 2½ miles (3.5 km)
From the Cathedral Green go through the Close and out by St Swithun's Gate into College Street. This leads around to College Walk and over Wharf Bridge. Across the bridge, turn right on the path down the left bank of the Itchen Navigation. Continue past Tun Bridge (from here the route is bridle): half a mile on, turn left under the A33 arch, then take the path up the base of Plague Pits Valley, with St Catherine's Hill to our left. At the top end pick up the wire fence of the municipal works and keep by them till arriving at a road. (It is expected that within two years work will start on the M3 here: bridleway transit will be maintained throughout and a bridle-bridge will be constructed.)

(b) *From St Catherine's Hill to Cheesefoot Head* 4 miles (6.5 km)
Reverse steps to find a path climbing the slope (see note above on M3 construction) leading up through bushes to emerge on Twyford Down. The route now goes straight for more than 1½ miles, passing the edge of the Hockley golf-course, then between arable, and then as a confined path through parkland. At a road turn left: then, less

than half a mile on, at a road junction go ahead up a small surfaced
lane. This reduces to a confined track after Hydes Cottages (forking
left) and later emerges to go through the arable on Fawley Down.
After crossing the line of a hedge, it comes to the A272 by
Cheesefoot Head.

Approach by car

At start: car-park at Cheesefoot Head on the A272, 2½ miles from
Winchester. *At end*: at Winchester (multi-storey car-parks). *Also*: at
Morestead, 2½ miles from Winchester on a secondary road.

Approach by other transport

Train: British Rail at Winchester (½ mile from end of stage). *Local
buses*: Hampshire Bus and Alder Valley at Winchester to many
places; at Morestead to Winchester and Southampton (infrequent,
not on Sundays). *Taxi*: Winchester, Colliss Cars (0962–53000).

Refreshment

Pubs: Winchester, Old Vine Inn (real ale, meals); Owlesbury,
Shearers Arms (real ale). *Restaurants and snacks*: many in
Winchester.

Accommodation

Hotels or guest houses: Wessex Hotel, Paternoster Row, Winchester
SO23 9LQ (Cat 6/5/5; 0962–61611); Southgate Hotel, Southgate
Street, Winchester SO23 9EF (Cat 3/5/6; 0962–51243); Glasspools
Farmhouse, Longwood Estate, Owlesbury SO21 1JS (Cat 1/2/2;
096274–218).

Admission

Winchester College, daily, Sunday afternoons; St Cross, weekdays;
Winchester Great Hall, daily, Sunday afternoons.

Stage 14
Cheesefoot Head to **Winchester**

DESCRIPTION

Where are the songs of Spring? Ay, where are they?
    Think not of them, thou hast thy music too –
While barred clouds bloom the soft-dying day,
    And touch the stubble-plains with rosy hue;
Then in a wailful choir the small gnats mourn
    Among the river sallows, borne aloft
    Or sinking as the light wind lives or dies;
And full grown lambs loud bleat from hilly bourn;
    Hedge-crickets sing; and now with treble soft
The redbreast whistles from a garden-croft;
    And gathering swallows twitter in the skies.

John Keats (1795–1821)
from 'To Autumn'

In August 1819 John Keats came to Winchester and stayed a couple
of months. His purpose was to make use of the library and also to
concentrate on writing 'Otho the Great'. Every day he took a walk,
and it was the same walk every day. He went through the Cathedral
Close, past the College, across the meadows to St Cross: 'Then I
pass across St Cross meadows till you come to the most beautifully
clear river,' and thence on for two miles more, before he retraced
his steps. From this there is little doubt that his regular walk took
him on to Twyford Down and Hazeley Down, and so to most of our
Stage 14. On 22 September he wrote: 'How beautiful the season is
now. How fine the air. A temperate sharpness about it. Really,
without joking, chaste weather – Dian skies – I never liked
stubble-fields so much as now – Aye, better than the chilly green of
Spring. Somehow a stubble-field looks warm – the same way that

some pictures look warm. This struck me so much that I composed upon it.' The result was his serene, sensuous and imaginative 'Ode to Autumn', which provides a fitting quotation for the last of the stages on our hundred-mile route.

At any time of the year the bridleway across Fawley Down is impressive, unconfined and with uncluttered views ahead across the Itchen valley towards the New Forest. Although lower in altitude than the main ridge behind us, these broad slopes are still emphatically downland, and still on upper chalk. In Keats's day they were mostly grassland grazed by sheep, but now of course they are mostly large fields of arable. The alarming warning signs to the north relate to the extremely remote possibility of spent bullets coming over from the Chilcomb firing-range beyond Deacon Hill. After Hyde Cottages our lane is bordered by shrubs and trees including natural yew. We come to the houses at Morestead (marshy place) and cross the main road which is on the course of a Roman road: then under a beech grove and past the pond at Morestead Grange, and so on to Hazeley Down. Hazeley Down has an unusual appearance, for all the trees in the park and around the house appear to be about thirty years old – a massive planting which includes sycamore, beech, poplar and Midland thorn: though not actually hazels (Hazeley means hazel wood). The reason is that this was formerly a large military camp in which all previous trees had been cut down, and in fact the solitary stone wayside cross to our left is a memorial to the dead of the London Regiment who were stationed here in the First World War. In the Middle Ages all this land was owned by the powerful priory of St Swithun at Winchester, named after St Swithun who was bishop from 852 to 862. St Swithun's day is 15 July and the old superstition is that if it rains on St Swithun's day it will rain each day for forty days thereafter. After Hazeley Down it is Twyford Down – Twyford means double-ford (i.e., over the Itchen) – with the Hockley golf-course on it. Incidentally, the place-names in Stages 13 and 14 are noticeably free from the personal prefixes that predominate in Stages 1–12: perhaps this is because in these stages the land was controlled more directly by the overlord at Winchester, and later by the church at Winchester too, and indeed was less of a pioneering country for the

Saxons, having had intensive Romano–British settlement on it previously. Then we come over the rise and see the squat mass of the spireless cathedral, now hardly more than a mile away in direct line.

Our line, however, is not direct, and we still have two miles to go. Getting into St Catherine's combe is rather complicated and may be more so when construction of this section of the M3 starts. The lovely combe below St Catherine's Hill is technically called Plague Pits Valley, but I think it an unworthy name for this final unspoilt downland corner, with thorn bushes scattered about the banks, sheep grazing, and flowers profuse. To our right is St Catherine's Hill, and the extra effort of going up it is well worthwhile for those with time to spare. The slopes are thickly covered with cowslips in spring and harebells in summer and the top is capped with a clump of beech and surrounding sycamore planted by the Gloucester Militia in 1762 on the site of the former St Catherine's Chapel: near it a small maze of paths is cut in the earth. (Winchester has for long been a military town, and is the home of the Greenjackets, whose parade march is at 160 paces to the minute.) From it we look down on Winchester, that is, unless, as happened to Anthony Trollope when he came up here, we gaze down 'at the white mist that entirely concealed city and valley'. The modern city spreads around, but the nearest part to us is the old centre with the Cathedral Close and College buildings merging into the poplars and water-meadows of the Itchen, which then flows on past St Cross. Traditionally St Catherine's Hill was the limit to which Winchester College boys could wander, and each term a special ceremony called Hills took place in which the entire school came up here, led by the headmaster. When they reached the top he would lead them in prayers and recite Psalm 121 which begins: '*I will lift up mine eyes unto the hills from whence cometh my help: my help cometh even from the Lord who hath made heaven and earth*.' St Catherine's Hill is also the site of the last of our series of Iron Age forts. The ramparts are still massive and we can also clearly see the in-turned entrances and the setting for twin guard-chambers. Unusually, these

Winchester Cathedral from St Catherine's Hill.

circular fortifications are not all at the same level but tip slightly upward on the eastern side where the approach-ground is less steep and so is more vulnerable. Inside the domed summit area within the fort are numerous depressions of about 15 m across, which may be the traces of hut circles. Although the name is misleadingly given to the fort overlooking the Meon in Stage 12, St Catherine's is in truth 'Old Winchester Hill', the prehistoric strong-point which antedated the Roman City.

A tunnel under a road brings us to the Itchen; or rather, the Itchen Navigation, formerly used for barge traffic but now just as attractive as the main river which flows a few hundred metres away. Between the two are the famous water-meadows, and when we see them we realise how passionately the people of Winchester – town and gown – feel about their preservation from development. Tall poplars line the banks, cattle graze in the succulent grass, and the translucent water, free from silt by its passage over the chalk, clearly reveals a fascinating world of fishes, newts, and green weed. At present the A33 roars past between the meadows and St Catherine's Hill, but when the M3 is completed this roar will be silenced. When this happens, our route up the Itchen will be as peaceful as it appeared to Isaac Walton, the father of trout-fishing, who came here and caught up to forty 'samlet or skagger trout' (trout are attracted to the chalk rivers) at a standing, and who wrote of the Itchen in *The Compleat Angler*:

> I in these flowery meads would be:
> These crystal streams should solace me;
> To whose harmonious bubbling noise,
> I with my angle would rejoice,
> Sit here and see the turtle-dove
> Court his chaste mate to acts of love.

Where we cross a small road, a half-mile deviation left over Tun Bridge and along the road, then left again through the meadows, will lead us to St Cross. The Hospital of the Holy Cross was founded

by Henry de Blois, Bishop of Winchester, in 1137 for 'thirteen poor impotent men so reduced in strength as rarely or never able to raise themselves without the assistance of one another'. (Come to think of it, this sounds like people who have just completed the Downsman Hundred.) The remarkable thing is that their foundation still continues for much its original purpose – though nowadays the pensioners are more likely to be retired clergymen than the disabled. Robed in black gowns, with the silver cross of Jerusalem, they inhabit a medieval range with gatehouse, hall, and collegiate staircases, and worship in one of the finest churches in England. Standing at the angle of aisle and transept, one seems enveloped in a forest of mighty trunks as the lines of arches plane away in perspective, from Norman to Early English. At St Cross was also one of the many water-mills that checked the flow of the Itchen.

   Now we come closer to the city, past playing-fields and a line of sycamores, and then after riverside houses we cross Wharf Bridge and approach Winchester College. At this point we can see back towards the meadows and St Catherine's Hill, a view described by Thomas Hardy: 'Behind the city swept the rotund upland of St Catherine's Hill; further off, landscape upon landscape, till the horizon was lost in the radiance of the sun hanging above it.' The College playing-fields are around to the left, with names such as Gater, Logy, Doggers, and Meads. The large stone mansion through gates to our right is Wolvesey Palace, the residence of the bishop: it has its private chapel and is surrounded by the thick walls of the former Wolvesey Castle. We pass the entrance to the College, founded by William of Wykeham in 1382, making it the senior of all the public schools. Its high standards set it at the top of the academic league for many decades, and it produced a breed who progressed through Wykeham's other foundation, New College, Oxford, to dominate particularly the civil service: though curiously in politics Winchester has not shone so brightly, having contributed only one Prime Minister (Addington) as compared to Eton's twenty. Behind the frontage, which includes the Headmaster's House (Victorian, of knapped square flint), are many school buildings, including the fourteenth-century chapel and a fine building of red brick and much stone dressing which might be called 'School of Christopher Wren'. In College Street is also a house with a plaque recording that Jane Austen died here in 1817, working to the end on the last of her novels, *Persuasion*: she wrote, 'We have a neat little drawing-room with a bow window overlooking Dr Gabell's garden.'

The concluding steps of our walk are through St Swithun's Gate – a formidable stone archway with original fifteenth-century traceried and studded doors – into the Cathedral Close. We pass the Georgian frontage of the Pilgrim School, the medieval deanery with its triple arch of open bays, and Cheyney Court, a fine Tudor building. From here we come to the west front of the Cathedral, and see across the green the ancient town centre around the High Street. Winchester admirably encapsulates the many strands of history that we have absorbed in our hundred-mile journey. Its very name is derived from the Roman city here – Venta Belgarum – which means the market town of the Belgii, or Celtic tribes. So it has witnessed Celtic, Roman, Saxon, Norman and English rule, and indeed played an important part in each of them. Particularly it was the chief town or capital of Wessex, which became the predominant kingdom in England and, under Alfred the Great, turned back the invasions of the Danes – Alfred, who is shown defiantly holding his sword in the shape of the cross in the splendid statue (Hamo Thorneycroft, 1901) which challenges the High Street. The city was for a time joint capital of England with London, under the Normans. Kings were crowned here and kept their treasuries here, and Arthur's round table conveniently appeared, helping them to claim a link with the ancient world and the dawn of Christianity. As with other cities, Winchester was inwardly torn by the traumatic issues of the Reformation and later the Civil War, but on the whole it emerged from both relatively unscathed and with a commendable spirit of moderation among the citizens which usually prevented the fanatics on either side from pressing to extremes.

Winchester Cathedral is the culmination of our journey along the South Downs. Of all the churches and cathedrals in the south of England, Winchester is the majestic king, just as Salisbury is the brilliant queen. Entering by the west door, we gaze up the nave and

through the presbytery to the choir and high altar – a vista which, with the Lady Chapel beyond, gives a total length of 169 m, making this the longest cathedral in Europe. Begun in 1079 and with the nave only completed 350 years later, it displays the changing styles of the Middle Ages, though all had the same basic aim in producing a great impression of space and a sense of awe and wonder. Although stripped of most of its medieval furnishings and decoration, that sense is still overwhelming, especially as we are surrounded by stone – floor, walls, arches, mullions and vault. Along the walls of the aisles are elegant eighteenth-century monuments, with many an urn, obelisk, garland, wreath and weeping figure, a rather pale substitute for the uncompromising tombs that formerly littered the sanctuary. Of these the most splendid was the shrine of St Swithun, whose cult attracted pilgrims as did that of St Thomas Becket at Canterbury. Although only few of them came by way of the ridge of the South Downs, and their motives and minds were utterly different to those of modern people, anyone – whether or not with any religious convictions – who has walked the full length of the South Downs Way and arrived at Winchester Cathedral surely cannot fail to feel a touch of timelessness and a perception, shared with the pilgrims, that the physical effort and endurance of the long-distance walk heighten an awareness of the immaterial, and provide liberating release from the trivialities of ordinary daily life, an experience to be recalled nostalgically in later years.

West Front of Winchester Cathedral

Stage 15
Seven Sisters Loop 10 miles

SPECIFICS

This is the official South Downs Way footpath, and is not a
bridle-route. The first 6 miles are along the cliffs of the coast. The
remaining 4 miles are up the Cuckmere valley, fairly evenly split
between river bank, woodland, arable and village street.
Three-quarters of a mile is on surfaced roads, another three-quarter
mile is on flint track, and the rest is on grass or earth. About nine
gates to open and five stiles to cross, many in the final part of the
stage. Westbound, cumulative ascent 417 m, descent 458 m.
Together with the main route of $7\frac{1}{2}$ miles, it produces a circle of $17\frac{1}{2}$
miles. See maps 22 and 21.

Route westbound

From Holywell to **Plonk Barn Alfriston** 10 miles (16.5 km)

(a) *From Holywell to Birling Gap* $3\frac{1}{2}$ miles (6 km)
Where Dukes Drive in Eastbourne turns from the sea-front at
Holywell, find the South Downs Way notice and mount the hill,
initially by concrete steps. Then where the path divides, take the
left-hand path through scrub, always climbing gently. Rounding the
top of Whitbread Hole, find the path which contours through the
bushes, then rounds the seaward face of Heathy Brow, now
climbing gradually, to emerge at the top of Beachy Head. From
Beachy Head the route is along the top of the cliffs as far as the
walls of the former lighthouse at Belle Tout. Then landward past
the walls, and through an area of scrub between road and sea,
nearing a coastguard hut. Then right, to descend to the houses at
Birling Gap.

(b) *From Birling Gap to Exceat Farm* 4 miles (6.5 km)
The way continues up a flinty track landward of the houses, then
dodges inland for a few metres before going left across grass to
regain the cliffs. The route is now along the clifftops all the way
along the Seven Sisters. Then down and slightly rightward, to
descend a steep chalk track to a stile. Here pick up the grass
embankment which later becomes the left bank (right as you look
upstream) of the Cuckmere. Follow the river up to Exceat Bridge;
then right by a path beside the A259 to Exceat Farm.

(c) *From Exceat Farm to Plonk Barn Alfriston* 2½ miles (4 km)
Just beyond the farm buildings find the sign and stile for the way
steeply up a field: then over a stone stile and down through forestry
to West Dean. Go up the small road ahead to the right of Forge
Cottage, then maintain direction on concrete, then earth, into the
forest. Take the first track left along a forest ride, later forking right.
Where the ride turns sharp right, go ahead across a stile by a path
down into a wood, soon veering left. Find a sign and stile leading
right and uphill between arable: then straight ahead between fields,
and then down through pasture to Litlington and along the village.
Later a confined path goes beside the road. The way then goes
through two fields, skirts around a pond, then continues close by the
road along the edge of another field to join Stage 1 at Plonk Barn by
Alfriston Bridge (see Stage 1).

Route eastbound

From Plonk Barn Alfriston to **Holywell** 10 miles (16.5 km)

(a) *From Plonk Barn Alfriston to Exceat Farm* 2½ miles (4 km)
From Alfriston footbridge go towards Plonk Barn (see Stage 1).
Then leave Stage 1 just before the road and turn right and along the
edge of a field. Then, by the road, skirt around a pond and go across
two further fields. Pick up the confined path which leads beside the
road, and then on through Litlington. Towards the end of the village
at a small junction turn left, then right through a kissing-gate. The

route is now up through pasture and then ahead over the brow of
the hill between arable fields. At a wood, turn left on to a path
which soon veers right and climbs up to a stile. Continue ahead
along a forest ride, keeping to the wider track. Where the ride ends
at a junction, turn right and down into West Dean. Maintain
direction and climb steps through the forestry, then down across a
field to Exceat Farm.

(b) *From Exceat Farm to Birling Gap* 4 miles (6.5 km)
Go by a path beside the A259 across the marshes to Exceat Bridge.
Here turn left before the bridge and follow the left bank of the
Cuckmere. At the end, before the beach, continue leftwards on the
grass embankment towards the hump of Haven Brow. Climb the
steep chalk track, then go along the top of the cliffs all the way to
Birling Gap, approaching Birling Gap on the landward side by a
flinty track.

(c) *From Birling Gap to Holywell* 3½ miles (6 km)
The way continues to the landward of the buildings, up on to
scrubland towards a coastguard hut: then leftwards along a path
through gorse towards the former lighthouse at Belle Tout. Passing
to the landward of its walls, continue along the top of the cliffs all
the way up to Beachy Head. From the octagonal walled seat at the
summit go on to find a path of asphalt, then flint, which leads gently
down across the seaward face of Heathy Brow, later contouring
round the side of Whitbread Hole. From here the route is by a grass
track descending gently through scrub, then more steeply to the
edge of Eastbourne at Holywell.

Approach by car

At start: Eastbourne is at the end of the A22, and the start is along
the seafront at the turning of Duke's Drive near Holywell (parking
usually possible). *At end*: Alfriston is a mile off the A27 between
Eastbourne and Lewes (car-park at approach to village). *Also*: at
Birling Gap, a mile off the A259; and at Exceat car-park on the
A259.

Approach by other transport

Train: British Rail at Eastbourne (1½ miles from start of stage), and Berwick (2 miles from end of stage). *Local buses*: Southdown services at Eastbourne to many places; at Beachy Head and Birling Gap (summer only, Sundays variable) and at Exceat Farm (half-hourly, Sundays hourly), to Eastbourne, Newhaven and Brighton. *Taxis*: Eastbourne, Town and Country (0323–27766); Alfriston, Berwick Taxi (0323–870239).

Refreshment

Pubs: Eastbourne, Bertie's Bar on Grand Parade (real ale); at Beachy Head; at Birling Gap; Exceat Bridge, Golden Galleon (real ale, meals); Litlington, Plough and Harrow (real ale, meals); Alfriston, Star Inn (real ale, meals). *Restaurants*: many in Eastbourne; Alfriston, Star Inn. *Snacks*: Eastbourne, Holywell Chalet; at Beachy Head; at Birling Gap; Litlington, Tea Garden.

Accommodation

As for Stage 1 (except Wilmington).

Admission

Seven Sisters Country Park, open access; Park Centre, Easter to October, daily; Exhibition of invertebrates and marine biology, daily. Charleston Manor, garden open occasionally.

DESCRIPTION

Beachy Head rises out of Eastbourne, and from where we leave the
streets and houses we climb steadily up its flank, immediately on
turf and among hawthorn, ilex, gorse and raspberry canes; and from
the start are aware of the sea – sight, sound, and salt air. The path
mounts around the rim of Whitebread Hole, where the level green of
a playing-field is set between hill and sea, and then around Heathy
Brow by a chalk path between thistles and bushes, mainly gorse,
blackthorn and elder, now looking straight down to the shore and
with the blue horizon stretching with every step: strangely remote,
this 'Shepherd's Path' (really a coastguard path) up the hillside, with
nothing man-made visible. At the top, Beachy Head is rather
different. We are back in the realm of the car, and thousands ride up
daily to see the view; for them there are car-parks and refreshments.
At the hightest point an octagonal enclosure with seats inside is
what remains of a Lloyds signal station. This would always have
been a place for sighting ships or for raising the alarm in times of
danger, and (according to Macaulay's description) it was so at the
arrival of the Spanish Armada:

> For swift to east and swift to west the ghastly war-flame spread,
> High on St Michael's Mount it shone: it shone on Beachy Head.
> Far in the deep the Spaniard saw, along each southern shire,
> Cape beyond cape, in endless range, those twinkling points of
> fire.

Nowadays it is the lighthouses which twinkle out to sea, and far
below the headland (where it is less prone to sea-mist than up on the
cliff) is the red-and-white tower built in 1902, looking like a

Beachy Head lighthouse

salt-cellar which has fallen off the table. It is fully automated, and its 240V/400W electricity is converted into 880 thousand candelas, in a lantern which gives two white flashes every twenty seconds: seven miles offshore is the Royal Sovereign Tower which gives one flash every twenty seconds. Anticipating modern lighthouses, Parson Darby of East Dean 200 years ago had a cave made in one of the chalk pinnacles, where a primitive light could be lit in bad weather.

Beachy means 'beau chef', or beautiful headland; beautiful, that is, from the sea where its 163 m white chalk face with head of green turf, rising sheer from the shore, is seen to best effect. But the view from the top is also very fine: the Channel on three sides with its ever-changing colour and ever-moving surface, and ships and boats ranging from supertankers out at sea to rubber dinghies close inshore. At 163 m the horizon is thirty miles, and beyond it the French coast a further thirty-five. Flocks of jackdaws dominate the grassy headland. On the cliffs are ledges and crannies where the gulls perch and nest, loud in their screeches, barks, and mews. Over the water the huge gannets display their spectacular dives, plunging head-first into the sea from a great height. The stub-nosed fulmars, whose structure and behaviour has served them so well that they have spread to every suitable sea-cliff in Britain from having been confined to the remote island of St Kilda off the Hebrides 100 years ago, cruise around with stiffly flapping motion. In May, swallows make their landfall here after their astonishing migration from the Transvaal – those that have survived the searing sands and scorching sun of the Sahara – on their way back to the mud cups which they abandoned the previous year. On these cliffs Edward Whymper first tested his climbing skills as a boy, and the crumbling chalk of the Devil's Chimney was far more hazardous than the granite of the Matterhorn.

So on, gently downhill on grass along the top of the cliffs. Common sense will prevent us treading on the brink, especially since from time to time there are great fissures in the ground near it. By the inexorable action of the sea the chalk face is continually breaking bit by bit: before a section falls it often shifts and cracks first. Looking at these small individual faults in the ground and then ahead along the line of the coast, we realise the tremendous effect of marine erosion over the millennia. Where we walk was once the rounded dome of downland, sloping gradually southwards: the sea has bitten the chalk like cake, and is continually advancing, at the rate of around 35 cm annually. Britain only finally became an island around 8,000 years ago, and its shape is still changing imperceptibly, but in few places is this more dramatically apparent than at Beachy Head and the Seven Sisters. Down where the rollers break is the rocky shore platform formed by the advancing sea, planed nearly level, though with rock pools, steps, and runnels set in it, through which the tide ebbs and flows, and crabs and mussels settle in nooks of seaweed and sea-anemonies. On a falling tide it is possible to walk along the base of the cliffs, but it is exhausting and dangerous. We come to Belle Tout, a tower of Aberdeen granite: it is the base of the former lighthouse, built in 1831. Beyond it we pass within the enclosure of earthworks, probably Bronze Age (only one bank remains, the other has fallen to the sea) and go through gorse, its harsh shape and crude colouring offset in summer by wildflowers within the clearings. Notable among these is the vipers bugloss, whose pink stamens protruding from the blue corollas produce a truly electric effect.

Birling (Baerel's people) Gap is the only access to the shore between Eastbourne and Cuckmere. A group of cottages and a small hotel, wooden steps down to the sea: a lonely place, preserved by the National Trust which now controls the entire coastline of this stage from Beachy Head. This little, hidden, almost secret, access to the sea would have been a point where many dramas were played out. Besides the smugglers, there were the wreckers, bands of men who mercilessly descended from the villages to loot wrecked ships, and in earlier times to kill the shipwrecked sailors too. Congreve wrote:

> As Sussex men that dwell upon the shore
> Look out when storms arise and billows roar;
> Devoutly praying with uplifted hands
> That some well-laden ship may strike the sands;
> To whose rich cargo they may make pretence
> And fatten on the spoil of Providence,
> So critics throng to see a new play split
> And thrive and prosper on the wrecks of wit.

Wreckers' prayers were answered when on 29 November 1747 the *Nympha Americana*, a Spanish ship that had been captured by the English navy and was on its way to London with a prize crew of 130 on board, crashed on the rocks below Flagstaff Point. Despite the prize crew, the Sussex wreckers made off with most of her cargo of velvets, cloths, silver laces, and also gold and quicksilver, before the magistrates could gather the forces of the law to the scene. Doubtless the wreckers also profited after the battle of Beachy Head, a full-scale naval engagement on 30 June 1690 when an Anglo–Dutch fleet of forty-six ships was defeated by the French with eighty-two sail, a defeat rendered ignominious by the fact that the English Admiral Torrington set the Dutch in the van while his ships lay behind. But even apart from dramatic moments such as these, the sea has always yielded up all sorts of usable goods in flotsam or jetsam – that is, until recently when it has more usually deposited the ugly refuse of modern shipping.

The next two miles of shore line is the domain of the famous Seven Sisters. Their names are respectively Went Hill Brow, Baily's Brow, Flagstaff Point, Brass Point, Rough Brow, Short Brow, and finally Haven Brow – the tallest at 78 m. They have a half-sister (Flat Hill, between Baily's and Flagstaff) but she isn't recognised, as she would spoil the magic number of seven. Went Hill is so named because an ancient path, the Went Way (Went means to wend or wander), came down it to Birling Gap; beyond it is Michel Dean, a valley now deserted but where earlier this century the philanthropic Mrs Mary Gilbert founded her 'agricultural school'. Brass Point means where a brazier was set. On Baily's Brow is an obelisk commemorating the gift of this land in memory of two young men who were killed in the First World War (and the sinister thunder of the guns in the Flanders offensives could be heard here quite distinctly); and on Flagstaff Point a sarsen stone records another gift of land. Indeed, the whole length of our walk along the coast is marvellously preserved, much of the turf cropped by sheep and bearing flowers such as scabious, thyme and centaury. The walk over the Seven Sisters is made even more delightful by the curious

sensation of being actually in the swell of a static sea, as we crest each brow and then plunge down each valley, perhaps running. And all the time we have the real sea at our side, the elemental force in which the chalk downs were formed in the first place, but which has now returned as the engine of their destruction.

Haven Brow is where we look down on Cuckmere Haven, another amazingly natural feature in this stretch of unspoilt coastline, with no roads or cars at it and looking much the same as when the Saxon invaders beached their boats there. The river flows into the sea through a shingle beach composed of flints from the eroded chalk cliffs, pounded and rounded by the action of the waves. In them grow shingle plants such as the yellow horned poppy and the large-leaved seakale. Along the embankment behind the beach is a small lake specially made for birds to nest and feed. Here are the wading birds such as the shelduck, boldly marked in white and black and chestnut, nibbling away in the mud; the large black cormorant swimming low in the water; and the grey heron standing motionless and waiting for fish to swim within reach of its dagger-bill. The Cuckmere is now confined in a straight channel: at low tide a salt marsh can be seen within the channel, with bands of grey-leaved sea purslane and the nobbly stems of glasswort growing from it. This new cut of the river was excavated manually by local gangs in the 1840s, but to our right the original meandering course still snakes through the flat alluvial silts and clays. After Exceat Bridge and the Golden Galleon we go across the water-meadows and reed-beds to the old flint farm buildings at Exceat (meaning oak grove and pronounced 'Eckset'), all that remains of a medieval village which became deserted in the fifteenth century. Here are the offices and exhibition hall of the Seven Sisters Country Park, under whose watchful eye nature is conserved for our delight; and also an excellent exhibition of marine life.

Now the scene changes as we go over a hump of ground and enter the edge of Friston Forest, a recent afforestation of over 1,500 acres planted mainly with beeches – over three million of them. Just here there is sycamore and ash among the beeches. Descending 227

The meanders of the Cuckmere

steps, we come upon the flint houses of West Dean (west valley),
now secluded between the trees, the telephone box discreetly
painted grey. After the wild scenery of the coast, how
heart-warming to see this group of ancient cottages so neatly set
around the duck-pond in their own little valley, safe from the
ravages of the sea and the southwesterly gales, the picture of
tranquillity which storm-tossed mariners would have sighed to think
of. The dwelling of greatest antiquity is the rectory: set in the flint
walls of this 600-year-old building are the narrow lancet windows
which light a hall and solar. Across the churchyard, with a great yew
tree in it, stands All Saints' church. Its oblong flint tower is Norman
in its lower part and porch, as is also the nave. The church contains a
fine alabaster monument of the seventeenth century, besides two
excellent examples of modern sculpture in heads of Oswald Birley
the artist, by Clare Sheridan, and John Anderson the politician, by
Epstein.

Back in the forest, we pass between plantations of beech now
thirty years old, some of them nursed with Corsican pines, though
our path is lined by hazel, larch and cypress. Soon we are out of the
woods and go down across Charleston Bottom by a path around the
edge of the trees surrounding Charleston Manor. This is an
exquisite Georgian house of Norman origin, which has a great barn
alongside it (54 m long) with a tiled roof, and a circular dovecote,
the two standard evidences of manorial authority: the barn to store
the produce and the dovecote to keep the pigeons which fed on the
land and then were grabbed for eating. Our route continues up
through arable, then down through pasture to Litlington. On the
way there are good views of the Cuckmere in its valley, and on the
opposite side the steep bank called Hindover (high and over) and a
white horse cut in the chalk. A mile to our right, but out of sight, is a
late Stone Age long barrow. Litlington (Lytela's farmstead, and
pronounced 'Lillington') is another village mainly of flint, with
well-tended houses and gardens, an excellent pub, and a plant
nursery where a wide variety of plants and shrubs are for sale;
adjoining it is a tea-garden set between topiary. Just by the pub a

West Dean rectory

path leads to a footbridge across the river, and over to Frog Firle, by the youth hostel. We pass St Michael's church, which has a Norman nave and chancel and a weatherboarded bell-turret. The rectory has stone facings, as does also Church Farm house.

By means of a path beside the road we go over the Ham (here meaning the dry ground by the bend of the river) and then cut a corner behind Lullington. By now we are in sight of Alfriston, walking along the meadow's edge and closing in on the river we first saw back at Haven Brow. Cuckmere means living pool (cwic mere), which describes the effect of its fast-flowing water as it appeared towards its mouth before it was embanked. It is still fast, fresh, and lively, even if now more constrained. The sea intrudes twice daily, with the salt-water flowing in the opposite direction to the fresh water below. Houses, woods, hedges, fields come and go; but the river flows on, the vital element in this landscape which was formed by it, and the most satisfying.

Stage 16
Lewes loop 8½ miles

This stage provides an alternative walking-route across the Ouse. It does not provide a riding-route, although it is a bridle-route except between Glynde and Lewes. It involves two descents and two ascents, going over Mount Caburn in the middle. There are 2½ miles on surfaced roads on pavements, 1½ miles on hard track, the rest on earth or grass. Mostly grassland, some arable, and an urban section of 1¼ miles through the old centre of Lewes. About three gates to open and seven stiles to cross. Westbound, cumulative ascent 370 m, descent 350 m. Together with the main route of 11 miles, it produces a circle of 19½ miles. See maps 20, 19, and 18.

Route westbound

From Beddingham Hill to **Plumpton Plain** 8½ miles (13.5 km)

(a) *From Beddingham Hill to Lewes War Memorial* 5 miles (8 km)
Leaving Stage 2 on Beddingham Hill 200 m west of the radio masts (grid reference 455060) take the farm-road northwards downhill, continuing on past houses to the A27: then straight ahead and across the railway into Glynde. Left into Ranscombe Lane; a few metres on cross a stile on the right on to a footpath leading up through fields to a ridge. Then ahead down through further fields into Oxteddle Bottom, and to a pond at the base. The path then goes diagonally across a field on to the flank of Cliffe Hill, then on gradually up on to level ground and to the Lewes Golf Club. Then down the lane (Chapel Hill) and across South Street into Cliffe High Street, and so up the High Street to the War Memorial.

(b) *From Lewes War Memorial to Plumpton Plain* 3½ miles (5.5 km)
Continue up Lewes High Street and Western Road, forking to

Spital Road. Cross Nevill Road and go along a lane with the prison walls to our left. Where the lane ends, continue up the central of three tracks, leading gently upwards and to the right. The grass path then passes to the right of the former racecourse buildings and stables. Maintain direction uphill on a pronounced track, passing under electricity wires and keeping to the left of the summits of Mount Harry and Blackcap. The track then joins Stage 4 at the edge of Plumpton Plain, just where Stage 4 turns direction sharply (grid reference 370126).

Route eastbound

From Plumpton Plain to **Beddingham Hill** 8½ miles (13.5 km)

(a) *From Plumpton Plain to Lewes War Memorial* 3½ miles (5.5 km)
Just where Stage 4 turns direction sharply (grid reference 370126), go through a gate and take the grass track leading ahead but gradually downhill, keeping to the right of the summits of Blackcap and Mount Harry. The track becomes more pronounced and passes under electricity wires, and then leads along just to the left of the buildings and stables of the former racecourse. Maintain direction on a grass path which descends gradually, then bears left to enter Lewes past the walls of the prison. Cross Nevill Road into Spital Road, then along Western Road and the High Street to the War Memorial.

(b) *From Lewes War Memorial to Beddingham Hill* 5 miles (8 km)
Go down the High Street and then along Cliffe High Street. Cross South Street and go up Chapel Hill. At the Lewes Golf Club cross a stile on to a footpath: this starts on the level, then inclines gently down the side of Cliffe Hill and later, at a stile, crosses a field diagonally towards a pond in Oxteddle Bottom. From here the path goes to the right of the pond and around to where it steeply mounts the hill. Go over the ridge, and maintain direction downhill to Glynde. At the road turn left, then immediately right, on the road through Glynde and over the railway; then at a fork keep right.

Cross the A27 and continue up the small road to its extremity at the top of Beddingham Hill, joining Stage 2 (grid reference 455060).

Approach by car

At start: nearest car approach to Beddingham Hill is at Firle access road, off A27. *At end*: nearest car approach is at Plumpton on B2116, 3 miles from Lewes. *Also*: at Lewes (car-parks).

Approach by other transport

Train: British Rail at Lewes and Glynde (both on the route). *Local buses*: Southdown services at Lewes to many places; also at Firle Lane to Eastbourne, Lewes and Brighton (two-hourly, not on Sundays). *Taxi*: Lewes, S&G Taxis (07916–6116).

Refreshment

Pubs: Glynde, Trevor Arms (real ale, meals); Lewes, Brewers Arms (real ale). *Restaurants and snacks*: many in Lewes.

Accommodation
As for Stage 4 in Lewes.

Admission

Glynde Place (Viscount Hampden), mid-May to mid-October, Wednesday and Thursday afternoons. Lewes Castle (museum of Sussex Archaeology), weekdays and summer Sundays. Lewes, Anne of Cleves House (museum of local history), March to November, weekdays and summer Sundays.

Stage 16
Lewes loop

DESCRIPTION

Looking northward from the start of this stage on Beddingham Hill, a group of small hills separated from the main range can be clearly seen. A grass slope ascends to a rounded summit. This is Mount Caburn, and the group is often loosely called the Caburn, though it comprises Saxon Down and Cliffe Hill beyond. Our walk will lead us through these miniature hills and into Lewes, whose castle, dominating the gap of the Ouse, is also conspicuous.

We freewheel down the easy incline of the once-surfaced bostal which leads around the head of a lovely rounded combe in whose green bottom the Friesians browse, then straight down, past pussy-willow thorn and elder, to the base of the scarp. After a belt of Scots pines and ash to the left, and to the right a line of trees in a field from which a spring gushes from the base of the chalk, we pass the houses and cottages of Little Dene, their verges bright in spring with daffodil and narcissus, and then the entrance to Preston Court farmhouse. Beyond the A27, a pavement separates us from traffic, and so we enter the village of Glynde. The uniformity of the stout flint-faced cottages with their blue woodwork indicates that this is an estate-owned village; and affirmation of historical ownership comes from the eight quarterings on the sign of the Trevor Arms, an excellent pub with a saloon bar that has the characteristics of a restaurant. Once over the railway line and the Glynde Reach (now no longer tidal), and past the playing-field, we come to the original village centre. Rambler, Rosemary, Orchard, and Rookery Cottages constitute the core, and the present Post Office and village shop was once the inn.

Glynde (meaning a fenced enclosure, and pronounced 'Gline') is the village pertaining to a great house, Glynde Place, whose

Glynde – cupola and bell-turret

entrance is only 300 m up the hill. If the house is open we can walk
through the stable block and under the clock-tower with its shining
cupola of blue and gold, and thence – between pillars surmounted
by lead dragons – to the front of the house, which faces a beautiful
park. The sixteenth-century house is built around a courtyard,
though with eighteenth-century renovations. Like Firle, it is of
stone shipped from Caen in Normandy, together with Sussex flint.
Its great mullioned windows give light to several important rooms,
including a large front hall with two screens of Tuscan columns, and
an even larger gallery on the first floor with panelling and a
sumptuous chimneypiece. The estate has passed by descent for 500
years successively through three families – Morleys, Trevors, and
Brands. Their portraits gaze sternly at us, with a faint impression
that the versatile face of Alec Guinness might be behind all those
kind hearts and coronets. Three achieved national importance.
These were Harbert Morley, a Parliamentarian commander (whom
we have met in Stage 8) related to John Hampden the Patriot who
defied Charles I; Richard Trevor, Bishop of Durham, who
renovated the house; and Henry Brand, a Liberal politician, for
many years Speaker of the House of Commons. Next to Glynde
Place is St Mary's church, an eighteenth-century edifice in the
Palladian style, unusually grand for the Sussex countryside (thanks
to Bishop Trevor). It is more like a private aristocratic chapel than a
parish church, and contains box pews, pulpit, screen, and
communion rail all of the period. In the churchyard is the fine tomb
of John Ellman. He was tenant farmer here for nearly fifty years till
his death in 1829, and during this time by intelligent husbandry he
perfected the famous South Downs breed of sheep. His
experimental flock grazed on Beddingham Hill – there is still
Ellman's Combe – and progressive agriculturalists such as Arthur
Young and the Duke of Richmond came here to Glynde to see,
learn, and pay tribute. John Ellman lived in the Old Farm House,
next to the church.

   Although out of sight from our route (except distantly from
Beddingham Hill) we could not pass through Glynde without
recalling Glyndebourne, only a mile up the road. Sussex, in history,
was a particularly unmusical place: for whatever the reason (was it

the harsh vocal processes and matter-of-fact attitudes of the
Saxons? Or the rich development of the English language, which
made for prose and poetry rather than music?) neither the peasants
or the gentry had any notable tradition of song or tune, unlike the
Welsh or the Gaels. Now that music is everywhere around us, it is
hard to imagine the general astonishment sixty years ago when John
Christie of Glyndebourne began to mount ambitious musical events
in the house: the neighbours felt that the only worthy occupations
for a rich gentleman were hunting, shooting and fishing, and some
of them had hardly heard of Mozart! Anyway, thanks to this
admirable and obstinate man, aided by his marriage to the soprano
Audrey Mildmay ('If you're going to spend all that money, John, for
God's sake do the thing properly!') a full-blown opera season was
launched in 1934: and the highest standards of German musicians
were transposed to Sussex by three talented refugees from Nazi
Germany – Carl Ebert, Fritz Busch and Rudolph Bing. Opera is a
highly sophisticated art-form, and at Glyndebourne its charms are
enhanced by the simplicity and beauty of the natural scene – the
gardens and the downs, and the opera house (designed by John
Christie and Edmund Warre) which stylistically is derived from a
Sussex barn.

From Glynde our path leads straight up to the shoulder of
Caburn, an ascent of 145 m. Women toiling up this slope should feel
profoundly thankful they were not born 2,000 years ago, when all
the water and provisions for the fort at the top had to be carried up:
observation of primitive ethnic groups leaves little doubt that it was
the women who would have done the carrying. We pass belts of pine
and ash; then at the ridge the route dips ahead. But we should here
divert to the left to walk on to Mount Caburn. Caburn means
fortified hill. Originally it was an unfortified open village occupied
by the Celts of the early Iron Age. Then, around 100 BC, an area of
$3\frac{1}{2}$ acres was enclosed by a ditch and rampart, with an entrance on
the north-east: the traces of this rampart, now hardly 30 cm high,
can be seen within the central area. Some 150 years later Caburn
was refortified with a massive outer bank and ditch. Both the inner
and the outer faces of the ditch were revetted with upright posts,
secured to horizontal beams within the bank. It requires an effort to

imagine the original strength and height of these walls, now that
they are reduced to hefty ripples forever flowing outwards from a
grassy pool. But they were strong enough to establish Caburn as the
chief fortress of an area twenty miles or so in radius, commanding
the eastern downs and the Ouse valley. Within them was a crowded
settlement of huts made of chalk rubble with timber framework: it is
estimated that at one time about 300 people lived within the fort.
By this time it was no longer a village so much as a seat of power,
supported by specialist artisans such as potters, tanners, and smiths.
It survived as such into the era of Roman rule, but eventually was
abandoned when Lewes was founded.

Our route now descends into the dry valley hidden in the Caburn
group of hills: on our way down we should look out for the bank and
ditch on Ranscombe Hill (part of the Caburn fortified complex) to
our left, and the traces of lynchets on Saxon Down to our right. We
come to Oxteddle Bottom, where horses graze on the steep turf and
drink at the dew-pond. Then it is up the flank of Cliffe Hill to the
Lewes Golf Course (there is a long barrow near the tenth tee, but
out of our sight). Now comes a surprise, for at the edge of the chalk
cliff – cut away by the quarrying for the former cement works – we
suddenly see Lewes spread before us, with the Ouse flowing right
below. There is the Norman Castle at the highest point; the railway
station with trains gliding through like lizards; the bright white
building of the East Sussex County Council; and, at the far end, the
prison. But to the south of the town (between the houses and the
bypass) lawns and trees are all that denote the site of the great
priory of St Pancras, in size comparable to a cathedral. In its day it
was the most important Clunaic monastery in England, of immense
power and prestige: but after the dissolution of the monasteries it
was demolished.

For the next mile we enjoy one of the most pleasant and
interesting urban walks in England. Perhaps the most fascinating
aspect is the variety of texture of the frontages of the buildings.
Besides the predictable brick, stone, flint, and stucco, there are the
less usual wooden-boardings and shingle-coverings and hangings of

The path down to Oxteddle Bottom

tiles or slates; and the definitely unpredictable imitation bricks and stones. These were means by which the respectable burghers of Lewes built or renovated their houses on the cheap. The apparent bricks are really 'Mathematical Tiles' – thin facings over less dressy walls. Indeed the whole length of the High Street is basically an architectural deception, for the seemingly eighteenth- and nineteenth-century edifices often disguise older structures, and the line of the street is medieval, a long backbone from which narrow lanes or twittens descend on either side like ribs.

The first section is along Cliffe High Street, originally a causeway across the river marshes. We pass the church of St Thomas Becket (fifteenth-century tower, and earlier construction within the nave) and should also note on our right Elphicks, an eighteenth-century building whose ground floor is colonnaded and upper floors hung with 'beaver-tail' tiles. After crossing the Ouse (with Harvey's Brewery visible upstream, the independent brewers who have been producing real ale since 1790), we have Dial House on the right, a fine symmetrical design of the late eighteenth century, with a sundial. So up School Hill, past bow-windowed shops: Lewes (pronounced 'Lewis') derives its name from the Old English *hlaew*, a hill. This brings us to the centre of the town at the flamboyant War Memorial, which is also the place where several Protestants were burnt at the stake in the reign of Mary I. In fact Sussex was strongly anti-Catholic at the time of the Reformation, and ever since those days Guy Fawkes night (commemorating the discovery of the Catholic plot to blow up Parliament in 1605) has been celebrated in Lewes with unusual fervour, now transformed into a popular festival. From here we pass the Crown Courts, a fine formal composition of 1812; and opposite, the White Hart Hotel, formerly the town house of the powerful Pelham family. Other notable residential buildings include number 77–79 (the home of Dr Richard Russell, whose advocacy of sea-bathing and the drinking of salt water as cures for glandular and muscular complaints helped the conversion of the fishing village of Brighthelmston into the resort of Brighton), and Castle Place (home of Dr Gideon Mantell, who first stimulated archaeology in the area by his discovery of the fossil bones of the Iguanodon: the capitals of the two pillars at either end of the house depict fossils).

Lewes Castle is approached from the High Street and under the barbican, from which we can climb up to the top of the keep. The view from this vantage-point betters any written description of the significance of the castle as controlling the Ouse, the approaches to the sea, and the inland weald. The Normans divided Sussex into six 'rapes', or administrative divisions, each with its line of coast and territory stretching inland. That of Lewes was awarded to the Conqueror's friend and trusted councellor, William de Warenne, who had married Gundrada, possibly the Conqueror's daughter. The tombs of this aristocratic couple, rediscovered in the grounds of the priory during excavations for the railway station, are now in St John's church in the residential area of Southover. William de Warenne caused the original castle to be built: this comprised an outer ditch; wooden defensive walls which enclosed a bailey, or courtyard; and, very unusually, two mounds instead of the usual one. Under his successors (there were seven Warenne earls, lasting till 1347) the castle was progressively strengthened with stone keep, towers, and walls. An insight into life in Lewes under Norman rule comes from these two excerpts from Domesday Book. 'Whoever sells a horse in the borough gives to the reeve a penny and the buyer gives another; for an ox a halfpenny; for a man, in whatever place he may buy him within the rape, 4 pence.' 'He who sheds blood pays a fine of 7 shillings and 4 pence. A man who commits adultery or rape pays a fine of 8 shillings and 4 pence, and a woman the same. The king has the penalty from the adulterous man, the archbishop from the woman.' From these we may conclude that VAT was at quite a low rate, slavery rife, and that the penalties for misbehaviour, though onerous, were mild as compared to those in some Middle Eastern countries even today.

Continuing up the High Street, we pass St Michael's church, where Anglo-Catholicism now thrives again after centuries of neglect, and then to the Westgate and Bull House, where Tom Paine, the radical who so strongly supported the French Revolution that he became a member of the National Convention and voted for the execution of Louis XVI, ran a tobacconist's shop. Then on, passing the pedestrian Keere Street and a fifteenth-century half-timbered building, and up St Anne's Hill, with more attractive houses and St Anne's church with Norman tower and nave. Our

urban walk through Lewes culminates beneath the walls of the prison which, because they too are built of flint, seem less forbidding and grim than they ought.

At the point where we pass the prison walls and emerge on to the downland, we walk on history. For this is the spot where the main fighting of the Battle of Lewes took place in the morning of Wednesday 14 May 1264. This battle shook further the monarchical authority already shaken by Magna Carta forty-nine years before: and although the barons had no thoughts of democracy, it is significant that in the following year a 'third estate' of representatives of boroughs and shires was for the first time summoned, together with the prelates and barons, to a parliament. From the higher ground ahead came the baronial army, particularly the two central 'battles' (close formations of cavalry, with foot-soldiers supporting) under Gilbert de Clare and Henry de Montfort. Out from Lewes to defend the town came the Royalist army under Henry III himself and his brother Richard, Earl of Cornwall, who had accepted the honorific title of King of the Romans (popularly known as King of Alemaine). The Royalists had been taken by surprise, and although on their right flank the cavalry under Prince Edward routed the left-most baronial 'battle' composed mainly of untrained Londoners, in the centre they lost ground. At which moment the *coup de grâce* was administered by Simon de Montfort and his cavalry reserve, coming round from the area of the racecourse. The knights were mounted on horses bred for strength: they were clad in mail (small interlocking metal rings) – cap, coat, gloves and hose: their heads were encased in round-topped helmets with slits for vision: and they carried sixteen-foot lances, short swords, and shields. Here, then, was hand-to-hand fighting with lances, swords, spiked maces and savage battle-axes. Heads and limbs were severed, the wounded trampled and mutilated. King and Prince fled back to the town and priory, and their Angevin courtiers scattered across the Channel to France. As for the King of Rome, he took refuge in a windmill just by St Anne's Hill, from which he shortly after had to surrender

Keere Street, Lewes

ignominiously – a Quixotic episode that gave satirists great play. I
retain an early text but must explain that 'wende' here means
'thought', 'stel' is the mill-stone, and 'mangonel' were military
engines for casting stones:

> The kyng of Alemaigne wende do ful wel,
> He saisede the mulne for a castel,
> With hare sharpe swerdes he grounde the stel,
> He wende that the sayles were mangonel.

Just as we came upon Lewes suddenly from Cliffe Hill, so now we
leave it suddenly, for after the prison it passes out of sight. Although
still at low altitude, we are already in downland, and the sense of
isolation is increased by the abandoned aspect of the racecourse,
still traceable around the declivity of Cuckoo Bottom. The
dilapidated racecourse buildings look really rather romantic, and
the viewing platform from a distance resembles a Florentine
watch-tower. But impending housing development around the
equestrian centre, now in the former racing complex, will soon alter
the look of this place. After the racecourse it is gently up the flanks
of Mount Harry and Blackcap, passing areas of thorn-scrub. Mount
Harry is not named after Henry III but probably derives from the
Old English *haerg*, a shrine. Blackcap's name comes from the group
of pines that formerly crowned it: after they were destroyed during
the last war, more were planted, though the plaque recording this
has been stolen. In this way we come to the point where we rejoin
the South Downs Way, just where it takes its right-angle turn.

Stage 17
Arundel loop 11 miles

SPECIFICS

The first half is near or beside the Arun, to the edge of Arundel
Park. The second half is through forestry, and then up between
fields to rejoin the ridge. There are $1\frac{1}{2}$ miles on surfaced roads
(some on pavements through Arundel), and virtually all the rest is
on earth or grass paths, not hard, with a boggy patch in both halves.
It is all beside or through woodland, except for 3 miles through
arable. About twelve gates to open. Westbound cumulative ascent
344 m, descent 140 m. Bridle-route throughout. Together with the
main route of $3\frac{1}{2}$ miles, produces a circle of $14\frac{1}{2}$ miles. See maps 12
and 11.

Route westbound

From Houghton to **Bignor Hill road** 11 miles (17.5 km)

(a) *From Houghton to Arundel High Street* 4 miles (6.5 km)
From Stage 8 turn left off the B2139 in Houghton into South Lane.
At the bottom of the lane turn right along a track near the right
bank of the Arun. Later this track reduces to a path, at first beside
the river, then mounting slightly through woods outside the
crumbling walls of Arundel Park. At a gate go to the lower corner of
a field, then on as a track to South Stoke. Turn right at a barn and
cross an access road into a confined bridleway. This leads ahead to
water-meadows, which we cross, maintaining direction to find,
through gates, a confined path up past Foxes Oven cottage. At a
road turn left for 80 m, then right down the road which leads past
the Black Rabbit, then Swanbourne Lake, and around to Arundel
(from the Black Rabbit there is an alternative footpath in the
hanging woods to the right of the road). At Arundel turn right into
the High Street.

(b) *From Arundel High Street to Bignor Hill road* 7 miles (11 km)
From the High Street go along Tarrant Street and to the bypass
roundabout. Just by the A27 go right between twin houses, and
immediately after, take a bridleway half left up into woods. The
bridleway later continues along the upper edge of woods, with fields
to the left, passing a cottage on the way. Where a gate and *'Private'*
notice bar the way, the route is through a gate half left across a field,
and then through gates along the edge of fields to enter Rewell
Wood, passing to the right of the cottage at Rewell Barn. Then
along a straight ride within the forestry plantation to where the path
forks at the end of the ride. Here bear left and downhill. More than
half a mile on, at a bridleway crossing, turn right on a track which
leads further downhill, then up to the A29. Cross onto an access
road, then left for 50 m. Turn right on to a bridleway path through
Baycombe Wood for nearly half a mile. At a point where several
bridleways converge, take the path half right through a bridle-gate
(signed *'Bridle Road to Bignor'*). The path goes straight through the
middle of the large fields on Little Down and Great Down,
mounting steadily. Then ahead through a wood, becoming a
confined track with a field to the right. At the end turn right for
200 m, then half left, and so up to the Latin signpost on Bignor Hill
on Stage 8.

Route eastbound

From Bignor Hill road to **Houghton** 11 miles (17.5 km)

(a) *From Bignor Hill road to Arundel High Street* 7 miles (11 km)
At the Latin signpost on Stage 8 take the direction *'Noviomagus'*,
then veer slightly leftward downhill. At a fence turn half right for
200 m, then left. The confined track, with a field to its left, leads
down and then through a wood, to emerge as a path going straight
down through the middle of the large fields of Great Down and
Little Down. It comes to a bridle-gate where several bridleways
converge: go half left along the bridleway path through Baycombe
Wood for nearly half a mile, to a road. Here turn left for 50 m, then

right by an access road to cross the A29, and ahead down a track
through woods. This track soon starts to rise: more than half a mile
from the A29 it comes to a bridleway crossing. Turn left up the path
above a bank and continue ahead for half a mile in Rewell Wood.
The path veers to the right and then enters a straight forest ride.
Continue to the end of the ride and then leave Rewell Wood,
maintaining direction along a track which goes at the edge of fields
and through gates, and ahead across a field to the line of a wood.
Here find a track leading half right along the upper edge of woods
with fields to the right, passing a cottage on the way. Where the
fields end, the bridleway goes ahead down through wood to arrive
between twin houses at the Arundel bypass roundabout. Then up
into the town, into Tarrent Street to the High Street.

(b) *From Arundel High Street to Houghton* 4 miles (6.5 km)
From the High Street go down towards the bridge, then left along
the avenue beneath the castle walls past Swanbourne Lake and to
the Black Rabbit (from the lake there is an alternative footpath in
the hanging woods to the left of the road). The small road continues
between cliffs; then turn left for 80 m, and right through a
bridle-gate into a confined path which leads down to
water-meadows through more gates. The route is then across the
pasture, picking up the track of a confined bridleway to South
Stoke. Cross a small access road: beyond a brick barn find the
bridleway up and left as a track beside a field, and then down to a
gate. Then up into another field to a gate. Here a path leads into
woods and soon runs along the right bank (left as you look
upstream) of the Arun. Later the path graduates to a track; at the
end, turn up into South Lane in Houghton, to join Stage 8.

Approach by car

At start: Houghton is on the B2139, between Storrington and
Whiteways Corner (park off the main road). *At end*: up the very
small road from Bignor up Bignor Hill. *Also*: at Arundel, on the
A27 and A284 (car-parks); and by the A29 near Slindon.

Approach by other transport

Train: British Rail at Amberley and Arundel (both ½ mile off route).
Local buses: Southdown services at Arundel to Worthing (hourly,
two-hourly on Sundays); also possibility of Southdowns Ramblers
bus on summer Sundays. *Taxi*: Arundel Taxi (0903–882418).

Refreshment

Pubs: Houghton, George and Dragon (real ale, meals); Offham,
Black Rabbit (real ale, meals); Arundel, Bridge Hotel (real ale,
meals); Slindon, Newburgh Arms (real ale, meals). *Restaurants and
snacks*: several in Arundel.

Accommodation

Hotels or guest houses: Norfolk Arms Hotel, High Street, Arundel
BN18 9AD (Cat 5/4/5; 0903–882101); Arundel House Hotel, 11
High Street, Arundel BN18 9AD (Cat 3/3/2; 0903–882136).
Other: Arundel Youth Hostel, Warningcamp, Arundel BN18 9QY
(0903–882204).

Admission

Arundel Castle (Arundel Trust), April to October, daily except
Saturdays, afternoons. Arundel Wildfowl Trust, daily.

Stage 17
Arundel loop

DESCRIPTION

In South Lane at Houghton there are pretty old cottages, notably
Mousehall which is one of the best in Sussex with flint panels set in
regular timber frames and windows of the original size. The lane
ends by the rushes of the Arun. Like the Ouse and Adur, the Arun
is now embanked and its level often higher than the meadows
around it. As a result it is strongly tidal in these reaches, although
here still ten miles from its mouth. Formerly it spilt around on its
alluvial flats, and this is why there are no houses in the
water-meadows. Our route to Arundel is throughout at the base of
the chalk, just where it meets the silts and gravels through which the
river winds. Arun, incidentally, is a back-formation of Arundel,
which in its turn means horehound valley: horehounds are types of
deadnettles, and had added significance in old days as homeopathic
medicine, the white horehound for bronchial and digestive
complaints and the black horehound for the bite of a mad dog or to
relieve convulsions. Formerly the river was called the Tarente. To
our left the reeds and wild irises (or flags) with large yellow flowers
eventually give way to the river itself. To our right are the hanging
woods of ash and beech, much covered with ivy and clematis, the
ground carpeted with spurge-laurel and wild garlic: and later come
alder and a colony of hellebore, a tall clumpy evergreen with
beautiful fingered leaves. The crumbling wall of Arundel Park and
the sinister creepers give this stretch a wild abandoned appearance
accentuated by the cliffs of the old chalk quarries, which were
largely used for building the river and railway embankments.

Across the river are the church and houses of North Stoke on
their chalk promontory, and we go around them in a semi-circle
from Houghton to South Stoke. Stoke drives from *stoces*, a place,
and relates probably to the significance of these two points as
guarding the river gap. From our route it is obvious that before

there was any bridge the valley could equally well have been
traversed to North Stoke, as between Houghton and Amberley
Station: indeed it would be the more natural route. This
geographical fact is the key to the immense earthwork nearly a mile
long, which starts just to our right (by a quarry where we come close
to the river and look along the straight stretch) and goes up the hill
and over to Fairmile Bottom. It is up to 30 m wide, the ditch alone
18 m, and it is clearly prehistoric. Because it is a 'covered way' (i.e.,
dug out from the ditch on either side) it doesn't look like a
fortification, though it may well have been used as such at times.
What is evident is that the ditch provided the line of the ancient
ridgeway as it crossed the valley – when not flooded – from here to
North Stoke. Here is where the tribesmen would have driven their
herds or flocks, the ford always a hazardous place not only because
of the water but because of unseen predators – human or otherwise
– in the thick vegetation. The War Dyke testifies to intense concern
for this place by these prehistoric people, who also formed
settlements in the area of the present park.

   South Stoke is hardly more than a farm, but has its church – St
Leonards, Early English at the west end, though much restored and
with a slender shingled spire. It also has a roost of cormorants
which make an impressive sight as they fly along the river in a huge
V formation. The bridleway from here to Offham encounters its
boggy patch below Foxes Oven wood, where we briefly leave the
chalk. Offham is another little settlement on a promontory, as
indeed its name denotes – Offa's *hamm* – *hamm* being the Old
English word for dry land at the bend of a river: a word once so
important, but now needing eight words to give its meaning. After
the cutting through it we come again to the Arun by the cheerful
Black Rabbit, and see the battlements and chimneystacks of the
Castle, now a mile away. Between us and the Castle is the Arundel
Wildfowl Trust Centre.

   In an area of only 60 acres, the Wildfowl Trust undertakes a
concentration of activity involving conservation, research,
education and recreation. Here is a collection of tame birds from all

over the world, such as the Carolinas and Goldeneyes from North
America, the Mandarins from China, the Hawaiian Goose, and the
Australian Black Swan. Some are in side-pens for protection, others
are sharing communal pens with different species. Most are
pinioned, some are full-winged. When the Canada geese circle the
area with noisy honks, the grounded swans flap their useless wings
in impotent imitation. Besides these tame or semi-wild birds, the
area is designed to attract British wild fowl, especially the winter
migrants. Winter is the best time to view the birds in their bright
plumage, gathered for the food and water. Here are the mallard and
the wigeon, and the geese who have come from Greenland or
Siberia: it is hoped that Bewick's Swans will also flight into
Arundel. All these migratory birds, large and small, are a source of
wonder. The fact that they variously have the ability to sense the
earth's magnetic field, to steer by the sun and the stars, to recognise
landmarks and to memorise nesting-places, is amazing enough. But
when one considers the distances they travel and the sheer
performance of the heavy geese who, for example, fly non-stop the
600 miles from Iceland to Scotland in fifteen hours or so, one feels
not only clumsy but timid – even if one is a long-distance walker!

Swanbourne Lake is artificial, originally made for a water-mill
but now used for rowing-boat trips. There are swans on it, which is
just as well as it means swan-stream. Incidentally, the pinioning and
ringing of birds of all sorts by the conservationists had an early
equivalent with swans, who were protected for the benefit of the
local magnates; and the instructions to the water-bailiff at Arundel
included the marking of swans: 'Earl of Arundel, butted on the right
wing, and their heels both cut off. Bishop of Chichester, on the left
wing, and three notches on the right side of the beak.' Behind
Swanbourne lake is Arundel Park, 1,200 acres. Some parts of the
landscaping have been spoilt by conifer plantations, but it still
contains fine vistas, and besides the usual oaks and beeches there
are good examples of the evergreen holm oak, or ilex. Then it is
over the stone bridge, past the former dairy house, and along a
splendid four-lined avenue of limes, their sweetly-scented flowers
hanging in clusters in July.

Lime avenue at Arundel

Eighty years ago E.V. Lucas, in his guidebook *Highways and Byways in Sussex*, with staunch democratic Protestantism described Arundel as languishing 'under the shadow of Rome and the Duke'. But I doubt if many of the citizens of Arundel feel oppressed by these shadows nowadays, and one of the great attractions of the place is its tradition of independence from the nationalistic trends of recent centuries. The family of Howard has held the Dukedom of Norfolk for 500 years, during which time the English monarchy has passed from Plantagenets to Tudors to Stuarts to Hanoverians, and then to the Houses of Saxe-Coburg-Gotha, and now to Windsor. And apart from one lapse in the last century, these dukes have remained Roman Catholic: one of their heirs (Philip Howard, Earl of Arundel) has even been sanctified. So it is with a feeling of historical continuity that we pass by the castellated masonry of Arundel Castle, with its keep, barbican, curtain wall, tilting yard, chapel, and baron's hall – even though most of what we see is hardly more than 100 years old and was built from the profits of the family's coal-mines around Sheffield. The medieval castle was largely destroyed in the Civil War, mostly during the seventeen-day siege when it fell to the Parliamentarians on 6 January 1644. Originally it had been the castle of Roger de Montgomery, awarded the Rape of Arundel by William I in 1067: the castle and estates passed to the d'Aubignys, then Fitzalans, and so to the Howards.

Higher even than the banner from the top of the Castle keep is the slender *flèche* of the Roman Catholic cathedral, built 1868–73 in a French Gothic style (for finer architecture of the same period the private chapel in the Castle gives a more exquisite impression). The tall pinnacles and buttresses of the cathedral have the effect of hiding the historic parish church of Arundel just across the road, of which the most remarkable thing is that it is divided into two. To the west of a glass-plated iron grille is the Anglican parish church of St Nicholas: a gilded reredos, a centrally placed altar, some fourteenth-century murals. To the east of the grille is the Roman Catholic Fitzalan chapel, with the tombs and monuments of the Earls of Arundel and Dukes of Norfolk. The bitternesses of the past

Arundel Castle

– the persecutions, the smashing of statues and windows, the
stabling of horses in the church, the firing of cannon from the tower,
and the building of a brick wall to ensure ultimate segregation – all
these painful memories are faintly stirred by this graceful though
emphatic grille. But the wounds of past controversy are now healing
and ecumenical services are sometimes held through the grille,
re-establishing the spiritual unity of this lovely 600-year-old church,
whose peal of eight bells floats above the town on Sundays.

At Arundel Bridge one can see the old wharfs where ships and
barges used to come up from the sea. By the Bridge are also the
ruins of the medieval hospice, or Maison Dieu. In the High Street,
the central open space was originally a cluster of buildings, then a
town hall, then a cattle-market, and now is a memorial garden.
Until early in this century it was also the site of the town
water-pump. Looking up the High Street, one notices Georgian
frontages, including the Norfolk Hotel with arched coach entry.
In Tarrant Street there are shops which retain their old windows and
one of them has an overhang, revealing it to be Tudor in origin.
There is also a Victorian furniture depository with an arcaded front.
All these old buildings recall the time when Arundel was a largely
self-sufficient county town with a strict class structure, trades and
services, very few visitors, and no tourists.

Re-entering the countryside after Arundel, we soon come to our
second boggy patch, in the copse just past the back of the hospital:
again, this is due to straying fractionally off the chalk, here on to the
mottled clay of Reading beds. We are soon back on firmer ground
and can admire the beechwoods to our right before going across the
arable towards Rewell Wood. To our left the coastline is only five
miles away, across the loams and clays of the coastal plain
traditionally known as the Champion (*campagne*). As it happens,
the name Rewell is also from the French: the circular path that
skirted the foot of the hill on the far side of the wood was called
roelle, Old French for a little wheel. Rewell Wood is now mainly
Forestry Commission. We pass Corsican pine on our right and
coppices of sweet chestnut on our left. This is a tempting place for
deer, as evidenced by the tall wooden hides from which they are
observed and shot. Then come plantations of beech and more

Corsican pine. The rides and firebreaks in Rewell Wood are well
endowed with thick margins of native scrub such as pussy willow,
which help preserve insect life. There is also much silver birch, used
to provide light shading and good fir protection. At the edge of the
plantations we pass the original wood with mature oaks and yews.
Then it is the coppices of Madehurst Wood to the main road.

Just over a quarter-mile away (along the road we use for only 50
m) is Slindon. Here is another unspoilt downland village, with the
usual mixture of flint and brick, and individual houses set at angles
between gardens: a tree with a bench around it provides a focal
point. The church of St Mary is mainly Victorian Early English
outside, but thanks to the flint this stylistic derivation is a successful
one. Inside, the genuine features are more apparent, and the church
contains the only medieval wooden effigy, in Sussex, that of Sir
Anthony St Leger. There is also a plaque commemorating that
Stephen Langton, the powerful Archbishop of Canterbury who was
a participant in the signing of Magna Carta, died at Slindon in 1228,
it being a manor belonging to the see of Canterbury. For cricketers
it must be recorded that Slindon was the home of Richard Newland,
one of the originators of the game (Slindon played London in 1744
and suffered only their second defeat in forty-four matches); for
walkers, that Hilaire Belloc lived here on three occasions: as a boy
with his mother, first at Slindon Cottage, then at the Grange, and
later as a newly-wed at Court Hill Farm. As so often, the large house
here, Slindon Park (Elizabethan but much restored), is now a
school.

Slindon means hill-slope; and this is appropriate, because it is the
site of a fascinating geological feature – a raised beach. Hundreds of
thousands of years ago a sea wore away at the rocks here, a sea 60 m
higher than the present one: raised beaches are detectable also at
Arundel and Goodwood. Slindon is of special interest because large
flint implements were discovered here in what are known as 'combe
deposits'. These are debris of disintegrated chalk with nodules of
flint, boulders, sandstone, etc, and also occasional bones and
implements, which were washed down by summer streams over the
frozen chalk during the ice ages. The stratification of these
implements makes it clear that they belonged to Early Man. So far

no bones of Early Man have been found in Sussex (although some fraudulent archaeologists for a while nearly fooled the world that they had discovered the skull of an early hominoid at Piltdown, eight miles north of Lewes).

After the road it is through the hazels, cypresses, and sycamores of Baycombe Wood, and on to Little Down. Here begins our two-mile progression up the dip slope of the downs, towards the ridge and the radio masts on Burton Down. Going through the middle of the wide expanse of cornland gives a fine sensation of space, as the sky gradually broadens as we gain height. To our right is Dale Park House, a modern residence in a superb position on the site of a former mansion. It is in the parish of Madehurst, whose houses are out of our sight beyond. Madehurst means a wooded hill where speeches are made, and this derivation is endorsed by an area in it called 'No Man's Land', where moots or local meetings were held. Here we can picture the Saxon tribesmen sitting in a circle and hearing arguments for and against some important communal issue, a primitive form of decision-making antedating the establishment of feudal authority or legal practices. To our left is the small cone of Nore Wood, lined with traces of lynchets. Then we come into the highwoods of Great Down, and the distant views are lost. Invisibly Stane Street is converging with us from the left, revealing itself dramatically at the crest, as described in Stage 8.

Stage 18
Petworth spur 7 miles

This spur goes north to Petworth. The first half is on the chalk ridge, and a mixture of arable and wood. The second half is on wealden clays and across the Rother, basically agricultural land but ending through Petworth Park. There is a quarter-mile of surfaced road, about 3 miles of track, and the rest paths. About eight gates to open. Outbound, cumulative ascent 142 m, descent 305 m. Although the first half is a bridleway, the second half is only so in parts, and so this stage is not a bridle-route. Petworth Park is closed from 9 pm (or dusk, if earlier) to 9 a.m. See maps 11 and 10.

Route outbound

From Bignor Hill road to **Petworth Market Square** 7 miles (11.5 km)

(a) *From Bignor Hill road to Barlavington Lane* 3 miles (4.5 km)
From the Latin signpost go along the South Downs Way 200 m to the Stane Street bank, then leave the Way to go ahead uphill on a track leading just to the right of the radio masts on Burton Down. The chalk track continues ahead downhill. Just before it comes to a field in the saddle of the ridge and bears left, leave the main track for a path to the right, then almost immediately at a fork bear left along a confined bridlepath across the saddle. At a gate the route continues gently uphill as a grass track through wood. Where it emerges on to grass, leave the evident track which bears right and go ahead to a gate, then down by a path through arable to another gate in another saddle. Here continue uphill, rejecting bridleways to the right, on a confined path around the upper edge of a wood. Soon after the path starts its descent, keep to the right at forks downhill: at a gate go down through a field to Barlavington Lane.

(b) *From Barlavington Lane to Petworth Market Square* 4 miles (7 km)

Across the road at a gate take the bridleway leading left: then shortly after, at a bridleway junction, turn right and downhill with a wood to the left, and between fields to cross between two levels of water at Burton Lake, then ahead on grass up to a surfaced driveway. Go along the drive as far as Burton church. Here the bridleway leaves the drive and goes slightly left along a track through Burton Farm. Cross a road and go straight ahead into wood, bearing left a few metres on: the path leads to the A285. Turn right along the pavement; then, less than a quarter-mile on, turn left on to the small surfaced road towards Kilsham Farm. Where this road turns left, continue ahead along a confined track which leads on past cottages to a footbridge over the Rother. Follow a lane around to the right for nearly a quarter-mile. At a cottage, turn left on a path through fields: this later bears right towards a copse, then left to maintain direction. Cross the A272: a few metres right, at a lodge, enter Petworth Park by a cricket ground. Go ahead into the park by a further gate and pass in front of Petworth House. Beyond the house and gardens find the pedestrian tunnel, and exit to the right into North Street, then up past the church and down Lombard Street to Market Square.

Route inbound

From Petworth Market Square to **Bignor Hill road** 7 miles (11.5 km)

(a) *From Petworth Market Square to Barlavington Lane* 4 miles (7 km)

From Market Square go up Lombard Street then past the church and along North Street. Turn left into the yard of Petworth House, then by a pedestrian tunnel into the park. Go left in front of the house across a drive towards railings: then by a gate through a cricket ground to a lodge and park gate. Turn right on to the A272 for a few metres, then left on a footpath across arable. At a copse the path turns right, then left to maintain direction. At a cottage, turn right on to an unsurfaced lane: this leads to a footbridge over the Rother. Continue ahead on a confined track past cottages, later joined by a small road from Kilsham Farm. At the A285, turn right uphill for less than a quarter-mile, then left on to a path between bushes. This emerges at a road: cross the road and go ahead along the farm-road through Burton Park Farm. This leads on as a track and joins a surfaced drive to the right of Burton church. Go along the drive: where it turns right, go ahead on grass down between two levels of water in Burton Lake, then ahead up between fields with wood on the right. At a bridleway junction, turn left to a gate at Barlavington Lane.

(b) *From Barlavington Lane to Bignor Hill road* 3 miles (4.5 km)
Across the road at a gate, up through a field to a gate into a wood. Up into the wood, then keeping to the bridleway leading left at a fork and continuing uphill to emerge at the top of the wood. Then up and around to the left, as a confined path at the edge of the wood. The path leads down to a saddle: then across a confined track by a gate, uphill between arable to a further gate. Here maintain direction on grass for a few metres to pick up a track from the left, and go ahead gently downhill by the track between bushes. After a gate the route reduces to a confined path across a further saddle, and later comes to a pronounced chalk track. Follow this track leftwards and uphill, to pass just to the left of the radio masts on Burton Down, then ahead gently downhill to the bank of Stane Street and pick up the South Downs way to the Latin signpost.

Approach by car

At start: up very small road at Bignor, up Bignor Hill. *At end*: Petworth is on the A283, A272, and A285 (car-park near the centre). *Also*: at Barlavington at a point ½ mile off the A285, just south of Duncton, where the lane turns by gates with bridleway signs.

Approach by other transport

Local buses: Southdown services at Petworth. *Taxi*: Petworth Taxi
(0798–42691).

Refreshment

Pubs: Duncton, Cricketers Arms (meals); Petworth, Petworth Park
Hotel (real ale, meals). *Restaurants and snacks*: several in Petworth.

Accommodation

Hotels or guest houses: Angel Hotel, Petworth GU28 0BG (Cat
3/3/5; 0798–42153); Osiers Farm, London Road, Petworth GU28
9LX (Cat 1/2/2; 0798–42528).

Admission

Petworth House (National Trust), April to October, Wednesday,
Thursday, Saturday and Sunday afternoons. Duncton Chalk Pit
(Sussex Trust for Nature Conservation), open access.

Stage 18
Petworth spur

DESCRIPTION

Stage 18 differs from all the others because it strikes a line away from the chalk and goes through other geological structures so as to give a route to Petworth. Although topsoil and vegetation usually disguise the difference, the chalk on Bignor Hill is Upper Chalk: then along the northerly ridge it is Middle Chalk, changing to Lower Chalk as we come down Duncton Down to the road at Barlavington. After the road, a few hundred metres on Upper Greensand bring us to the marly clay of the Gault: after Burton Lake this soon yields to the sands and ferruginous rocks of the Folkstone beds. Once across the A285 we are on the sand-rocks and clay of the Sandgate beds, and then come the valley gravels and alluvia of the Rother. Beyond the river the remainder of the route is on the sand, loam, and chert of the Hyde beds, whose formation can be well seen in the entrance to the sunken lane just past Rotherbridge. These are all successive layers of the Cretaceous period, deposited in an order the reverse of this summary, with the Hyde beds the oldest and the Upper Chalk the youngest. The reason why we encounter such a large number of layers in such a short distance is that not only has the central chalk been washed away but also all these strata are gently tilted in an upward northerly slant.

The first half of the stage is memorably beautiful, with a touch of wildness that is lacking on the main South Downs Way. In a matter of only three miles we go up or around three little hills, each time with charming and changing perspectives of the adjoining hills and valleys, which reveal themselves so well from this short northerly ridge. Pure chalk track, narrow earth path, grassy track, open field, wooded way – all these follow in quick succession, for the most part bounded by thick bushes of every variety that border broad slopes of arable or disguise a dew-pond or a round barrow. On Farm Hill

we emerge from their protective embrace and get a really
magnificent view – arguably the best in the entire South Downs.
From this vantage-point of 185 m we look eastwards. Stretching
away is the ridge of the downs back to Wolstonbury Hill twenty
miles off. Its gentle undulations give the appearance of a mighty
wave sliding in over the weald, with Chanctonbury Ring perched
like a surf rider on its crest. The distant scene is unchanged from
thousands of years ago, the light greens of the downs and the dark
greens of the weald apparently devoid of habitation. But closer in,
although the wooded flank of Bignor Hill and the expanse of
Amberley Wildbrooks maintain the theme, the housing around
Storrington and Pulborough destroys the illusion. And below us are
the cultivated fields of the villages described in Stage 8 – Bignor,
Sutton and Barlavington.

  After Farm Hill comes Barlavington Down, and then Duncton
Down which stands on the corner: on the northern side of it is the
disused chalk pit owned by the Sussex Trust for Nature
Conservation, and the paths through the woods are bordered with
Common Spotted Orchids. Once across the road by Barlavington,
the scene changes as we proceed through the fields below the scarp
with an ash wood to our side. Next we cross between upper and
lower levels of a lake. Burton Lake is in fact composed of three
ponds. There is the small upper pond which we see; this flows into
Gilford Pond which in its turn flows into Hammer Pond, each of
around 30 acres. Gilford Pond was dammed to look decorative from
Burton House, and what remained of the old village of Burton
(farmstead by a stronghold) was flooded. Hammer Pond is of an
earlier date, for it provided a head of water for an iron forge in the
seventeenth century. Pig iron (in sows) was brought here, reheated,
and hammered to reduce the carbon content. Malleable
wrought-iron which could be made into weapons or tools was
produced with water-wheels powering the hammers and bellows for
the fires. A visitor to Burton in 1635 saw 'hot swarthy Vulcans,
sweating, puffing, hammering, drawing out those rusty sows into
barrs by rumbling, noysing, Bedlam water mills'.

Burton church

Burton House is now a girls' school of the Woodard Foundation, called St Michael's Burton Park. The main house is a heavy neo-classical structure of 1831, with massive columns, and is now joined by a complex of new school buildings. Built on the site of one of the houses of the Gorings, the present house belonged to the Roman Catholic Biddulph family. As a boy, Hilaire Belloc was befriended by the Wright-Biddulphs. It was from here that he first walked up Duncton Hill, here also that in a chalet in the grounds he wrote *The Four Men*. And on Sundays they would walk to Mass at the Catholic church of St Anthony and St George a quarter-mile to our left, which the Biddulphs had founded together with a village school. Duncton itself (Dunneca's farmstead) is a small scattered village on the A285 also just to our left. The church of Holy Trinity was built (one imagines in rivalry) in the same year as the Roman Catholic church – 1866. Duncton is known as the home of James and William Broadbridge, farmers who introduced 'round-arm bowling' (as opposed to under-arm bowling) into cricket in the 1820s, and the pub is called the Cricketers Arms. The Cricketers Arms at Duncton is the scene of the magisterial oration by Mr Justice Honeybubble to the quarrelling yokels as described in *The Four Men*.

The two Victorian churches at Duncton are by the busy road, but right beside our bridleway and far from the roads, tucked away in the park and framed by trees, sits the exquisite mellow little church of Burton. Its dedication is unknown, but it dates from the eleventh century, with Norman nave and chancel. The interior retains the flavour of Jacobean times, since wholesale repair was made to it on the orders of Archbishop Juxon in 1636. It retains a rood screen, a large family tomb and brasses of the Goring family, and a painted coat of arms. In such surroundings one can glimpse the setting of worship in the seventeenth century, and hear echoes of that rich and robust language which formed the English prayer-book.

The park at Burton is now mostly under plough, though groups of beech and sycamore are preserved in it. Burton Park Farm is mixed, with corn, root vegetables and a herd of Friesians. At a road, a

detour three-quarters of a mile to the right would bring us to Burton Mill. This water-mill is on the site of the former iron forge. It had fallen into disuse by the beginning of this century, but is now one of those which have happily been restored to working order by local benefactors and volunteers. After a short section, past larch and by bay and laurel, we come to the main road and go along the verge for nearly a quarter-mile. Where we turn off it, we cross the line of the former railway between Pulborough and Midhurst, and around to the right is the former station, a wooden building now a dwelling and brightly painted, looking strangely like a scene set for Anna Karenina or some other Russian period piece. We approach the Rother between fields lined with poplars, and are now on the rich arable land of the Petworth estate. This little river, a tributary of the Arun, is not to be confused with the larger Rother which 'crawls to find the fickle tide' around the border of Sussex and Kent. It rises on sandstone near Liss and comes around by Petersfield and Midhurst, a delightful fast-flowing stream. Its name is a back-formation from Rotherbridge (cattle bridge) – the very place where we cross it, though now on a fine wooden foot- and bridle-bridge. Originally the river was called the Scir, that being Old English for bright or clear. Then it is by lane and between fields to the gate of Petworth Park.

Although our route is only across a corner, Petworth Park now unfolds for our delight. We can appreciate it all the more than those who arrive by car because on our walk over the hills and through the fields we have intimately experienced both natural landscape and practical man-made landscape. Here in the park is a brilliant simulation of natural landscape by practical man-made devices. This was the great achievement of the English eighteenth-century style, a development which rejected the rigid formalism of the past – a formalism which continued in the rest of Europe – and whose aim is best expressed in the lines of Alexander Pope:

He gains all points, who pleasingly confounds,
Surprizes, varies, and conceals the bounds.

Deer in Petworth Park

Petworth Park as we see it was first created to the plans of Lancelot ('Capability') Brown in 1754, and made even more 'natural' a few decades later. The stream is dammed to make a serpentine lake, the trees are in clumps and copses which accentuate the humps and hollows of the ground, and lodges, temples, urns, a folly, and an ornamental boat-house provide focal points in a flow of perspectives which stretches for fully $1\frac{1}{2}$ miles north-westward. The mature beeches, oaks, limes, planes, and sweet chestnuts perfect the scene in a way which Brown and his patron did not live to see, and represent their organic legacy for future generations. A herd of some 400 fallow deer browse in the park. Fawns are born in June and early July, and the mother gives birth away from the rest of the herd in bracken or nettles. During the spring the males' antlers fall off and new ones form, covered with velvet. As the rutting season looms in September the males become restless and rub their antlers violently to remove the velvet and prepare for battle. The season lasts for six weeks, with much roaring, fighting, and mating.

The grass sward comes right up to the long façade of Petworth House: nature here encounters art. But nature also permeates the interior of this palace of art in the canvases of the famous artists who have sought to recapture it. We see a romantic landscape by Claude Lorraine, and Richard Wilson's depiction of the valley of the Arno. The forest of Fontainebleau provides a scene from France, and the countryside of the Netherlands is shown in the paintings of Hobbema, Cuyp and Teniers. But nearer at home the English landscape is seen through the eyes of Gainsborough and Turner – Turner, who was a constant visitor to Petworth and used the old library above the chapel as his studio. He interprets for us scenes in the Thames valley and at Brighton and Chichester: and best of all to those who have walked Stage 18, the park at Petworth. His two oils of it in the Turner Room both diffuse the colours of the setting sun, gazing where the eye cannot gaze, and penetrate the spectrum reflected in the lake and the effect of the light upon the deer and the trees. Always facing the sun, his canvas 'Petworth House from the Lake; Dewy Morning' hangs in the White Library.

Turner was a protégé of George Wyndham, third Earl of Egremont, who as much as any other represents what was best in the old aristocratic landowning tradition. That he was kindly and hospitable was good in itself, cultured and knowledgeable, commendable. But the really significant thing is that from when he succeeded in 1763 to when he died in 1837 he lived for most of the year at Petworth and was a keen agriculturalist who was particularly concerned to improve the lot of the small tenant. We have an account in Charles Greville's diaries of his giving a fête in the park to the local people at the time of the agricultural depression of the 1830s. Fifty-four tables, each fifty feet long, were placed in a vast semi-circle on the lawn before the house, with two great tents in the middle, and plum puddings, loaves, and innumerable joints catered for at least 4,000. But the old peer 'could not endure that there should be anybody hungering outside his gates, and he went out himself and ordered the barriers to be taken down and admittance given to all. They think 6,000 were fed.' The other principal benefactor of Petworth was Charles Seymour, sixth Duke of Somerset who, with the fortune of his wife (heiress of the great northern family of Percy) ordered the building of the house in 1688. However, he was a fractious bully, pathologically imprisoned in his pride; and although we may admire his munificence we must surely deplore the system that upheld such so-called aristocrats. These two very different men were largely responsible for Petworth House, particularly the Marble Hall and Grand Staircase dating from the era of the Duke, and the Carved Room and the North Gallery from that of the Earl: and for the accumulation between them of paintings, furniture, and sculpture that would have been the envy of many a Continental ruling prince. And monarchs came to admire – Charles III of Spain, Frederick William IV of Prussia, and Alexander I of Russia.

   Clustering close behind the great house, and in complete contrast to the park on the other side, is the town of Petworth (Peota's enclosure). One can understand the pressure for a bypass, whilst at the same time strongly resisting the proposal that one should be made through the park. The town is a compact mass of narrow streets, courtyards, and alleyways. The church of St Mary the Virgin is virtually all restored, though the walls are basically fifteenth-century. It has a painted barrel-roof in the nave and a chapel with a fine tomb and bronze coffin-plates of the Percy family. Lombard Street is cobbled and traffic-free, the houses of bricks, slats, or tiles. In Market Square stands the imposing stone town hall (1793). The square is the scene of the annual November fair, held here for at least 700 years though now a shadow of its former self. Reflecting a changed society, a bright new Petworth Festival has arisen, with music and drama and events which include ballooning in the park.

Stage 19
Lavant loop 11 miles

SPECIFICS

This loop is around the Lavant valley, and both halves have similar characteristics. In all, some $3\frac{1}{2}$ miles are through wood, $1\frac{1}{2}$ by copses, 2 on or beside pasture, and the rest basically on arable. There are $2\frac{1}{2}$ miles on surfaced roads, 2 on hard flinty track, and the rest on grass or earth, with a soft section on Bow Hill. About twelve gates to open, most of them in a half-mile stretch over the Lavant. Westbound, cumulative ascent 432 m, descent 442 m. Bridle-route throughout. Together with the main route of $6\frac{1}{2}$ miles, produces a circle of $17\frac{1}{2}$ miles. See maps 9, 8, and 7.

Route westbound

From Heyshott Down to **Telegraph House** 11 miles (18 km)

(a) *From Heyshott Down to Binderton House* $5\frac{1}{2}$ miles (9 km)
On Heyshott Down on Stage 9 the route passes a crossing fence and a group of trees (grid reference 894165). Just to the east of these, a bridleway leads southwards down through Charlton Forest for 1 mile, crossing on the way a footpath, and later veering slightly left. At Burntoak Gate, continue on a confined track to a large wooden signpost. Take the direction for Singleton through a gate, and over the right flank of Levin Down. Later pick up the line of a fence to a gate, then go down on the faint line of a track across grass to a further gate into a sunken lane. Left on to the A286 and through Singleton. Just beyond the village, turn left up the road marked for Goodwood for nearly 1 mile (using the verge where possible). Fork right by St Roche's Lodge on to a small unmarked road. Where the surfacing ends, turn half right on to a bridleway signed for Binderton. The path leads between fields through three gates, then across the meadows and the Lavant through several more, to the A286 at Binderton.

(b) *From Binderton House to Telegraph House* 5½ miles (9 km)

Go up Binderton Lane: where the surfaced lane turns left, continue ahead along a track which reaches the B2141 by Deans Cottages. Right along the road for 200 m, then left on to a path leading up into the yew forest. At the top of the hill, by a house, take the track rightwards along the ridge: later the track descends by the edge of the wood to Chilgrove by the White Horse. Turn left up the B2141 for nearly half a mile (using the verge where possible), rejecting the drive forking right to Upton Farm, but taking the second track forking right. This leads to Phillis Wood, and then ahead as a path at the lower edge of the wood up to the Royal Oak at Hooksway. Sharp left up the surfaced lane, then sharp right on to a confined track. This leads through gates to a surfaced drive past Telegraph House, to join Stage 10 (grid reference 808176).

Route eastbound

From Telegraph House to **Heyshott Down** 11 miles (18 km)

(a) *From Telegraph House to Binderton House* 5½ miles (9 km)

At the sharp turning on the flank of Beacon Hill on Stage 10 (grid reference 808176), go through the gate past Telegraph House and along the surfaced drive for more than a quarter-mile to where it turns right. Here maintain direction through gates on to a confined track. At a small surfaced road, turn sharp left down to Hooksway. By the Royal Oak, turn right on to a path at the base of a combe along the lower edge of Phillis Wood. After the wood a farm-lane curves left to the B2141. Go left down the road for nearly half a mile (using the verge where possible). Just past the White Horse turn right up a track: a quarter-mile on, take the bridleway half left into the wood, keeping up the ridge. Later, by a house, turn half left down a bridleway which leads out of the yew forest to the B2141. Right along the road for 200 m, then left on to a track which is later joined by a surfaced lane, and so to Binderton House and the A286.

(b) *From Binderton House to Heyshott Down* 5½ miles (9 km)
Cross the Lavant by the bridleway through several gates, then up to
the line of a hedge. The route then goes ahead as a track between
fields, through three gates. At a car-park by St Roche's Hill go
along the small road, then join a larger road downhill for nearly 1
mile (the verge can be used for some of it). Right on to the A286,
and through Singleton. Shortly after the village, find a bridleway up
to the right. In the pasture beyond, go uphill to the left of Levin
down to find a gate; then on, keeping above the line of a wood, to a
large wooden signpost. Take the confined track to Burntoak Gate,
then up into Charlton Forest, ahead at an intersection, and later
bear right, to join Stage 9 on Heyshott Down.

Approach by car

At start: nearest point is 1 mile from the start, at the junction of
Stages 9 and 10; then by Stage 9 to the start. *At end*: nearest point is
at the car-park on Harting Down off the B2141, 1 mile south of
South Harting, then by Stage 10. *Also*: at Singleton on the A286;
and at Binderton on the A286; and at Chilgrove on the B2141.

Approach by other transport

Local buses: Southdown services at Singleton and Lavant to Bognor
Regis, Chichester and Midhurst (hourly). *Taxi*: Chichester, Starline
(0243–784927).

Refreshment

Pubs: Singleton, Horse and Groom (real ale, meals); Chilgrove,
White Horse; Hooksway, Royal Oak (real ale, meals). *Restaurants*:
Chilgrove, White Horse.

Accommodation

Hotels or guest houses: Woodstock House Hotel, Charlton PO18
0HU (Cat 4/4/2; 024363–666); Richmond Arms Hotel,
Goodwood, Chichester PO18 0QB (Cat 5/4/5; 0243–775537).
Other: Woodlands Hall of Residence, Chichester PO19 3PA
(0243–786321); stabling at Goodwood Stables, Chichester
(0243–774107).

Admission

Chilsdown Vineyard, May to September, daily; Weald and
Downland Open Air Museum, April to October, daily except
Monday; West Dean Gardens (Edward James Foundation), April
to September, daily; Goodwood House (Goodwood Estates),
Easter to October, Sunday and Monday afternoons, also Tuesdays,
Wednesdays and Thursdays in August; Kingly Vale (Nature
Conservancy), partially open daily.

DESCRIPTION

The Lavant rises south of the ridge, so has no channel cutting through the line of the downs. It flows to the sea through Chichester Harbour, whose mud-flats have discouraged seaside housing development. In consequence the Lavant valley remains comparatively isolated and unspoilt, and we can still see why it has been a favourite place for princely seclusion, not merely for the Dukes of Richmond but long before their ownership. The village of West Dean (which means valley) is probably where Alfred held court; and a charter of Ethelred refers to Edelingedene, meaning the valley of the princes. The Earls of Arundel owned estates here, and one of them lived for most of his life at Downley Lodge just above Singleton. The Lavant is now hardly more than a stream, as we can see when we cross it twice, but formerly it was larger, when the water levels on the downs were higher. Its name is Romano–British, deriving from the Latin *labor*, to glide.

Easing down through Charlton Forest between hazel bordering the path, we pass plantations of beech, larch, thuja, and then Douglas firs and beeches together. The firs will be felled first, enabling the longer living and slower growing beeches to expand. In among the higher plantations are a few older trees which break the monotony. The mossy verges are hosts to woodland wildflowers, with primrose and violet prominent in spring. Once out of the forest, a lonely corner of countryside brings us towards Levin Down, and a notice '*Boundary of open country*' brings short relief from enclosures as we cross this small hump, usually with sheep on it.

Despite the main road through it, Singleton is an attractive village with quiet lanes. The name means farmstead by the thickets, which implies that then, as now, there was a lot of woodland here. In fact the Domesday Book entry for Singleton, at that time quite a large

place with two water-mills, mentions the '150 hogs that come in
from the wood'. There are many eighteenth-century cottages, of
flints with red-brick dressings, and a few earlier ones with timber
frames. One of the first houses we pass is Little Drove House, with a
pediment and a doorway with Doric columns. The last house is the
Post Office Shop, built on to the former toll-house. The church of the
Virgin Mary has a Saxon tower and nave walls, and an Early English
interior with aisles. There are Tudor pews, and also a monument to
Tom Johnson, huntsman of the Old Charlton Hunt (Charlton itself
is only half a mile away, and in it is Fox Hall, a former hunting-lodge
now available for short leases from the Landmark Trust): his
aristocratic patrons have here commemorated his sporting life.

> Here Johnson lies. What hunter can deny
> Old honest Tom the tribute of a sigh.
> Deaf is the ear, which caught the opening sound,
> Dumb is the tongue, which chear'd the hills around.
> Unpleasing truth, death haunts us from our birth
> In view; and men, like foxes, take to earth.

Half a mile off route, after leaving Singleton, is the Chilsdown
Vineyard at West Dean. Thirty years ago there were no vineyards in
England, but now there are about fifteen in Sussex alone, including
ones at Alfriston and Lewes: Chilsdown can best serve as an
example. It covers thirteen acres of land facing southeast and at
around 70 m altitude. The soil is a clay silt-loam overlying the chalk.
The vines are mostly of German stock and planted at about 2,000
plants to the acre. Great care has to be given to tending the vines –
pruning, wiring, weedkilling, spraying, and topping. The harvest is
about mid-October, and about 24 tonnes of grapes are picked in a
week. The grapes are made into wine by crushing and then inducing
fermentation by processes involving the introduction of sulphur,
sugar, and yeast. Bottling takes place in April. The result is
Chilsdown wine, 'a crisp, clear, fruity and dry white wine that is best
served lightly chilled'. Let us hope that Chilsdown and other
English vineyards flourish and overcome the formidable difficulties

of a highly labour-intensive operation conducted on the northern fringe of viniculture.

We next pass the entrance to the Weald and Downland Open Air Museum. This is a most excellent project in which a growing number of old buildings, rescued from decay or destruction in various places in southern England, have been dismantled and re-erected in the lovely parkland of West Dean. A visit adds a dimension to one's appreciation of the downland villages, for here are buildings that were at one time common but now are very rare. There are reconstructions of a Saxon sunken hut and a charcoal-burner's camp; medieval farmhouses and cottages; a Tudor market hall; cattle-sheds, barns, a treadmill, and a water-mill which is grinding corn. Here one can study the technical aspects of traditional buildings, particularly the development of timber-framing, best seen in the complex roof structures. In fact, the saw-pit shed contains a range of tools used for the handling and conversion of timber, whereby we can learn about the tree fellers and sawyers who produced posts and beams from the fallen oaks of the weald.

After a dull mile up a broad road (use the verge for the second half) we come to St Roche's Lodge of West Dean Park. West Dean Park is a large country mansion faced with flint, built in the Gothic style in 1804 by James Wyatt and considerably renovated in 1893. The estate passed from the Earls of Selsey to Mr William James, heir to an American timber fortune, and is now held by a trust. At present it comprises some 6,500 acres of which about a third is woodland, a third is farmed directly and a third by tenants. We go right round it in Stages 19 and 10. As to the house, it is now used as a college which specialises in teaching crafts to adults, with courses ranging from cane-seating to calligraphy and from pottery to wrought-iron work.

Had we been standing at St Roche's Lodge one morning in late July in the first few years of this century we might have seen an immaculate carriage drawn by two horses emerging from the drive, carrying a fat, bearded, elderly gentleman and a young doll-like lady. This would have been Edward VII and his hostess, Mrs Willie James, on their way to the Goodwood racecourse up the hill, whose

modern grandstand we can see. The King's presence put the
ultimate seal on what was already a great social event and a
highlight of the flat-racing season. Perched up on the downs, and
with the course splendidly visible from the spectators' stands,
Goodwood is by common consent the most attractive race course in
England. It is owned by the Goodwood Estate and is the successor
to the equestrian tradition of the old Charlton Hunt – the first
race-meeting there was in 1801. Famous horses such as St Simon,
Bayardo, and Kincsem have raced here in the main events, the
Goodwood Cup, or the Stewards Cup (a six-furlong handicap).
Goodwood House is only a mile and a half beyond the race course,
but because there is no entry to the park on this side we are faced
with a three-mile diversion from St Roche's Lodge, going up past
the race course on the road signposted for Goodwood.

   Goodwood is the seat of the Dukes of Richmond, descended
from Charles II and Louise de Kerouailles and hence head of
the semi-royal first family of Sussex. Their record in terms of estate
management and nature conservation is impressive, and includes
the planting of over a thousand cedars in the park: they also
advocated Parliamentary reform at an early stage, and acted against
the local smuggling Mafia when it was strongest. Their house is
packed with treasures – Van Dycks, Lelys, Knellers, Canalettos,
Reynoldses; also French works of art (acquired by the third duke
when ambassador to the court of Louis XV) – Sèvres porcelain,
Gobelin tapestries and suites of furniture. The unusual shape of the
house (built by Wyatt in an uncompleted form) suggests the
unostentatious easy way of living that so characterises the English
'stately homes'. Hidden away in the park are gems such as
Molecomb, Carne's Seat, the Shell House grotto and, nearer at
hand, the stables, still used for their original purpose. In the park,
besides the many cedars, there are tulip trees, cork oaks, California
redwoods, swamp cypresses and Chilean beeches. The Goodwood
Estate at present consists of about 12,000 acres, including large
sections of the Lavant valley.

   After passing around the top of West Dean Park, and the

Houses and haystacks at West Dean

larchwoods and arboretum within it, we come to the point where the road ends at a small car-park. Here a path leads up St Roche's Hill, with two radio masts atop and named after a former chapel to St Roch. St Roch was a wealthy young man who, like St Francis, rejected his privileged life to help the poor and sick. When on pilgrimage to Rome he caught the plague and went off to die in the woods, but a dog daily brought him bread and he recovered, only to be arrested as a vagrant and to die in prison .He became a tremendously popular saint in France and Spain, was an intercessor against the plague, and was usually depicted showing the plague sores on his leg and accompanied by a little dog. On the summit of the hill is the Trundle (meaning a circle) which is the rampart and ditch of an Iron Age fort. This fort evidently controlled the land between the Arun and Harting Down. But what was only recently discovered (from air photographs) is that within the central area are traces of a far older encampment, of the late Stone Age. The very faint lines of two ditches, maybe for a camp, maybe for burials, have been established; also pottery, and a skeleton and a phallic bone-carving. From another Neolithic camp (at Whitehawk, near Brighton) there is evidence that ritual cannibalism was practised by these people, rather deflating to those idealists who like to think that prehistoric societies lived in a sort of Golden Age. The Trundle provides a panorama of the Lavant valley, and in summer its slopes give a fine display of the lesser centaury, whose dense clusters of unstalked pink flowers lie within rosettes of leaves; also here is the Frog orchid, with inconspicuous flowers slightly scented.

From the car-park, a broad earth track descends south to Chichester and it is possible to reach the city by bridleway. This route is down the earth track for a mile and a half to East Lavant: then by the church (St Mary's) turn on to the road towards Boxgrove: less than half a mile later, turn right on to a path which skirts the perimeter of Goodwood airfield: at the end of this, turn right into Chichester. From our route on Stage 19 towards Binderton, the most conspicuous object is the spire of Chichester Cathedral. This elegant spire rises 84 m from the ground and was

The track to Chichester

built (Giles Gilbert Scott) to replace the previous spire which one night, in 1861, collapsed in on itself; that is to say, it suddenly disappeared into the tower which supported it. Apparently the sacristan who went to open the Cathedral next day noticed nothing amiss until he beheld the pile of rubble lying on the floor. Chichester is the ancient capital of Sussex, but is rather far off-course for a detailed description here. Suffice it to say that it is on the site of the Roman city of Noviomagus Regnentium, of which the amphitheatre is now covered by housing. On the evidence of an inscription it is supposed to have been the capital of Cogidubnus, a client king of Rome referred to by Tacitus. (Cogidubnus is certainly a good name for a client king, suggestive of cogitation or dubiousness, rather than the heroic virtues of a Cassevelaunus or a Boadicea.) Defences were built in the third century against the Saxon marauders, but in time the ruins of Noviomagus became a Saxon town (Cissa's Castra). At the Norman conquest, the Rape of Chichester went to Roger de Montgomery, together with that of Arundel; and later the city became the episcopal seat of government, notably under St Richard. It was spared industrialisation and so has become, like Lewes, a pleasant county town.

We cross the Lavant, gliding unembanked through fields with cattle grazing; just before it is the line of the former railway. At Binderton (Beornoryo's farm) there is a fine eighteenth-century house with bold orange paintwork. It is now divided into flats, and at one time was let to Sir Anthony Eden. Near it is the ruin of Binderton chapel, which the bishop refused to consecrate as he thought it was superfluous. After the beeches and ilexes of Binderton House come cornfields, looking not so different from when William Cobbett rode by 160 years ago: 'The corn all fine; all good; fine crops, and no appearance of blight.' That great radical also gave good marks to the enlightened estate of Goodwood and noted 'a pig at almost every labourer's door'. Deans Cottages, by the next road, provide an example of present estate-housing; and then it is up a path on to Bow Hill.

From the Trundle we have seen across the valley the dark, almost black, aspect of Bow Hill, a long north–south ridge and an outlier of the main chalk block of the South Downs. We have been looking at one of the largest concentrations of yews in Europe, and our route now goes through the northern part of it. Of all the main forest-formers of downland, the yew has suffered most from man's activity and has been least replanted because of its uncommercial characteristics – slow growing, small size, and foliage poisonous to animals, particularly when cut or wilted. This is despite the great virtues of its hard, elastic, close-grained wood which is used for furniture, flooring, panelling, mallets and small tool handles; also for long-bows in the past. We pass yews of around seventy years old, but in Kingly Vale itself, a mile to our left, there is a grove of very old trees, some at least 500 years old, making the yews the oldest plants on the downs. Walking around and under the yews, one can understand the sense of mystery, even fear, that they have evoked, with tales of spells and witchcraft. Through their canopy of needle-leaves and long labyrinthine branches the sun permeates weakly, to add a yellowy tinge to their dark-red barks and to the earth below, covered with the tiny cones of the male or the red arils of the female. Where we go along the ridges, the yews have suffered heavy damage from westerly gales, recalling Francis Thompson's lines in 'A Fallen Yew':

> For this firm yew did from the vassal leas
>   And rain and air, its tributaries,
>   Its revenue increase,
> And levy impost on the golden sun,
>   Take the blind years as they might run,
>   And no fate seek or shun.

On Bow Hill, besides the yews, are ash, oak, privet, holly, and also whitebeam, whose light, dream-like colouring contrasts dramatically with the dark yews. On the summit (a mile along the ridge leftwards) are four Bronze Age burial mounds known as the Devil's Humps, and a series of defensive earthworks. Nearer to our route (down to our right) is Goosehill Camp, a double-bank circular enclosure. The ridge walk can be heavy going in wet weather because it is on clay, overlying the chalk. We get views westwards

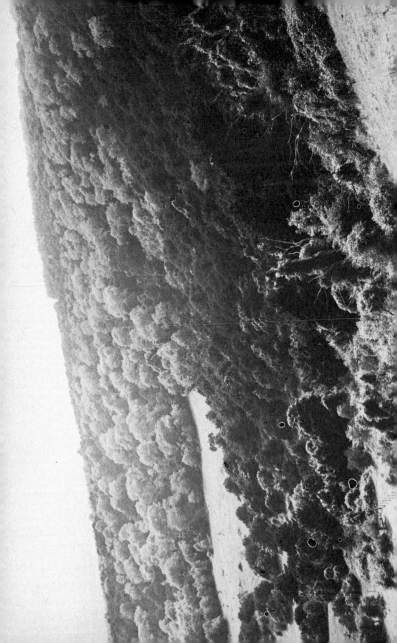

across Stoughton Down: Stoughton means the farm by the place, the place probably being where the South Saxons were beaten by the West Saxons in a bloody battle in 685. At Chilgrove (the grove in the gorge) there are a few cottages and the White Horse restaurant, and then we enter Phillis Wood, a large beechwood of the West Dean estate. Batten Hanger to our left has recently been felled and is bright with oak carpeters. We come to Hooksway and the Royal Oak, a pub much patronised by South Downs walkers, in an isolated spot in the wooded valley, slightly spoilt by the new building opposite. From here it is up the lane (stinking hellebore in the hedge) and then by bridleway up past Telegraph House to rejoin the South Downs Way.

Yew and ash in Kingly Vale

Stage 20
Stansted spur 8½ miles

SPECIFICS

This stage leads generally down the dip slope, crossing a combe on
the way, with a steep descent. More than 4 miles are in woods,
including 2½ miles through Stansted Forest: the rest is through
arable. One mile is on small surfaced road, half a mile on hard track,
nearly 2 miles on grass, and the rest on earth path. About eight
gates to open. Outbound, cumulative ascent 140 m, descent 260 m.
A bridle-route except for the Stansted avenue (riders for Rowlands
Castle must go via Holme Farm bridleway, then right along the
road). See maps 5, 6, and 7.

Route outbound

From Coulters Dean to **Rowlands Castle** 8¼ miles (13.5 km)

(a) *From Coulters Dean to West Marden* 5 miles (8 km)
Just before Coulters Dean, going westwards on Stage 11 (grid
reference 748195), at the final turn of the road take the path left
inside the edge of a wood, which shortly afterwards inclines up to a
bridle-gate. From here the route through Ditcham Wood is marked
with '*Bridlepath*' signs. We leave the wood, turning left at a
bridle-gate along a belt of trees to a drive. Right along the drive,
then just short of Ditcham House go half left down an unsurfaced
road: where this turns, take to the path leading towards forestry,
and then steeply down into Downley Bottom. Turn right and go
along the ride at the base of the combe through the woods, till it
veers right a quarter-mile on. Here take a gate on the left, to incline
up the bank to Ladyholt. Just before the cottage, turn sharp left
along the upper edge of the wood and then to the crest of a hill.
Then turn right along the crest. Half a mile on, at a gate, the route
leads confusingly half left through a grass field to a bridle-gate in a

belt of trees. From here follow the track straight ahead, down across
three fields to a surfaced road. A few metres to the right, find the
bridleway left through a gate up into the yew wood, and under
electricity wires up to the corner. Then left, along a confined track,
keeping to the bridleway past Horsley Farm and to a road.

(b) *From West Marden to Rowlands Castle* 3½ miles (5.5 km)
Turn right along the road, then first left on to a small road. 200 m
on turn right along a track through Lodge Farm, and then between
fields into Stansted Forest, maintaining direction. The bridleway
comes to the edge of the forest with fields to the left, and continues
down the edge as far as a surfaced drive. Turn right on the drive to a
lodge at a road: (this is the end of the bridleway). Then ahead along
the grass of the avenue. At the end the path leads down, slightly
rightwards, across a drive to a road, and so left and under the
railway into Rowlands Castle.

Route inbound

From Rowlands Castle to **Coulters Dean** 8½ miles (13.5 km)

(a) *From Rowlands Castle to West Marden* 3½ miles (5.5 km)
Leave Rowlands Castle under the railway arch, taking the left-hand
fork. Where the road turns, take a footpath right into Stansted Park.
The path crosses a drive and goes up through trees to the avenue.
Go along the grass of the avenue to where a road crosses it (from
here the route is bridle). Go past a lodge on to a surfaced drive.
Where the woods on the left fall away, turn left up a path on the
edge of the forest, with a field to the right. Later the bridleway
penetrates into the forest, maintaining the same general direction. It
emerges between fields, then goes past Lodge Farm and along a
track to a road. Then left, then right at a junction. Shortly
afterwards, before the road descends, a confined track leads left.

(b) *From West Marden to Coulters Dean* 5 miles (8 km)
The confined track leads, as a bridleway, past Horsley Farm and on

to the yew trees of Robin Wood. Turn right along the top of the wood under electricity wires, then veer left obliquely downhill through the wood and across a field to a road. A few metres right, then left on a track straight across three fields. Then, at a belt of trees and a bridle-gate, the route leads confusingly half left through a grass field to a bridle-gate at a fence. The path is now along a small crest at the edge of fields to a crossing track. Then left down, to join the upper edge of a wood. Just before Ladyholt cottage turn sharp right down a track. This brings us to the ride at the bottom of an afforested combe, which we follow along to the right. Keep to the lowest ground to the very edge of the forest, then go steeply left uphill by a path which leads around to an unsurfaced road going up towards Ditcham House. Here take the drive away from the house for a quarter-mile, then a path left along a belt of trees to a wood. Now turn right along a ride: the route through Ditcham Wood is now marked with '*Bridlepath*' signs. We come to a bridle-gate, and shortly afterwards arrive on Stage 11, just by Coulters Dean.

Approach by car

At start: on the B2146 between South Harting and Nursted, take the very small road to Sunwood Farm and Coulters Dean. *At end*: Rowlands Castle is 2 miles off the A3 at Horndean. *Also*: at West Marden on the B2146.

Approach by other transport

Train: British Rail at Rowlands Castle (at end of stage), and also at Petersfield (3 miles from start of stage). *Taxis*: Petersfield, Clarkes Taxi (0730–62364); Havant, Borough Cars (0705–477970.

Refreshment

Pubs: Compton, Coach and Horses (real ale); West Marden, Victoria Inn; Rowlands Castle, Castle Inn (real ale).

Accommodation

Hotels or guest houses: Bear Hotel, Havant PO9 1AA (Cat 5/4/5; 0705–486501).

Stage 20
Stansted spur

DESCRIPTION

The main block of the Forestry Commission's Queen Elizabeth
Forest comprises 2,430 acres, and this stage goes through two
sections of it. We start in Ditcham Woods, mainly beech with
low-grade broad-leaved trees: the railway roars by in a cutting to
the right. Then comes an interval along the drive to Ditcham Park
School and down the side of Downley Bottom. Here we enter the
West Harting Woods. There are large plantations of Norway spruce
(*Picea abies*) and Western red cedar (*Thuja plicata*), and the
bridleway along Downley Bottom also has cypresses lining it. A
number of yews which predate the plantations (of 1960 to the left
and 1966 to the right) are preserved, nice round blobs among the
mass of points. By now we are back in Sussex, from Hampshire. We
touch the county boundary again at Robin Wood, and then at the
end of the stage at Rowlands Castle, making this a border route
between Sussex and Wessex.

The large parish of Harting (see Stage 10) was, from medieval
times, divided into two estates – East and West. West Harting was
owned by the Fortescues and then Carylls. In the seventeenth
century the Carylls, like their counterparts, the Fords of East
Harting, built a house for themselves up on the downs – the Fords at
Uppark and the Carylls at Ladyholt. Water was a problem for both
these houses (before the present Uppark House was built and
supplied with piped water) but could be got expensively and
inconveniently from deep wells, with donkeys turning a hoist to
raise the buckets. The Fords thrived throughout the period and had
close connections with Cromwell, and later William III. The Carylls
unfortunately backed the losing side, retaining their Roman
Catholic allegiance, and John Caryll went into exile in France as
confidential secretary to James II. His nephew, also John Caryll,
had to endure a set of petty restrictions when he became squire of

Ladyholt: but being a warm-hearted and gregarious man, he welcomed a group of his intelligent friends for long summer visits. These included John Gay and Alexander Pope, whose letters to John Caryll were discovered much later in a farmhouse on the Ladyholt property, and give a delightful impression of the conversations that must have occurred when they were together with Caryll's family here. It was Caryll who suggested to Pope the theme of 'The Rape of the Lock', based on a petty quarrel between their young friends Miss Fermor ('Belinda') and Lord Petrie ('The Baron'), and so Caryll gets his honoured mention in line 3 of the poem. Although Pope does not record in verse or prose any description of the Ladyholt estate, it must have impressed him by its Elysian beauty, the solitude of the sheep-filled combes and the new belts of trees and avenues across West Harting Down and Foxcombe being such an absolute contrast to the cramped and hectic life of London – 'Dear, damn'd, distracting town, farewell!' An amusing insight into their relationship comes from a letter of Pope's, 1717: 'When a hogshead of good French wine falls into Ladyholt Park, whether out of the skies or whatever element that pays no customs, you would favour me with about twelve dozen of it at the price you give.'

This connivance in smuggling turned to tragedy at Ladyholt some years later. In February 1748 a gang led by William Carter captured, tortured, and murdered a revenue officer, William Galley, and his informer, David Chater, here on the estate, and threw Chater's body down the Harris well, some 200 m from the house. The local authorities, led by the Duke of Richmond, set up a full-scale manhunt, and Carter and others were found, tried at Chichester, and hanged. The butler at Ladyholt was suspected as an accomplice but was released. The house itself later became abandoned and was destroyed. It stood in the first field we come to, on emerging from the woods. A lonely cottage is now the only habitation here, and some of its building materials probably come from the old house.

Now follows a section through arable, at first to the side of fields, then through them, leading up along a spur and then gradually down to a road. Ahead is the line of Compton Down with the yews

of Robin Wood along it. The village of Compton (valley farmstead)
is 1½ miles off, left along the road, then right. A large tree adds
character to the group of houses at the centre, and at the end of the
village is St Mary's church, mostly 1849 though with a
twelfth-century chancel arch, and a pretty timber bell-turret with
shingled spire. The yews of Robin Wood yield in impressiveness
only to those on Bow Hill and Old Winchester Hill (Stages 19 and
12) on our route. As cypresses are to the country houses and farms
of Italy, so the yew is the chief ornamental tree of the gardens of
England. But since it is usually trimmed into topiary, the sight of it
standing as a wide-spreading tree is always exciting. In its native
environment here on the chalk downs it looks best when massed in a
wood with bare pasture or fields around, its humpy outline
complementing, rather than harshly breaking, the line of the hill.

After Robin Wood comes a track between hazel hedges, the very
best way to observe the fields of Horsley (horse clearing) Farm,
with its flint farm-buildings. At a road we are only a quarter-mile
from West Marden, down to the left. This is one of a group of
Marden settlements, the others being East, North, and Up. West
Marden is in the parish of Up Marden, and so does not have its own
church. The word means boundary hill and is pronounced 'Marn'.
Then once through Lodge Farm, we come into Stansted Forest.

Stansted Forest owes its origin to the forest of Bere, a hunting
ground of the medieval kings. Henry II had a manor (or
hunting-lodge) at Stansted, and falconers were established to look
after the 'king's birds' in the park. Richard I hunted deer and wild
boar here. The countryside that they saw was utterly different to
what we see – no enclosures, a few hut-like buildings, large areas of
scrub – but at least certain spots in Stansted forest are so little
changed that it would not seem out of place if through the trees
there sped a stag, pursued by men on horseback armed with
swords and spears, and with great deerhounds bounding towards
their quarry by sight. Where we enter the forest (between Batty's
Park and Wythy Piece) we pass oaks whose age ranges from 120 to
250 years. These early plantations have produced great trees with

Middle Lodge, Stansted

tall straight trunks, the earliest ones planted before the Industrial Revolution, when wood was the material for so many things, including the ships, made of 'heart of oak'. Then on Rosamond's Hill, where we have a field to our left, we pass hybrid larch (a cross between the European and Japanese larches) and some Scots pines, as well as a continuation of oaks and beeches which culminate in an area which is thought to be primeval in that it has never been cleared for agriculture or for systematic plantation. Across the field is Lumley Wood, originally a beech hanger but now filled up with pine. Then along the drive where new trees have been planted – ash and beech. Such are the pressures of the modern ecological system that even in a large forest like this, natural regeneration is hardly possible: pheasants and rabbits in particular obstruct it. It is good to see tall young ashes, since they do not transplant as easily as other trees.

An ornamental lodge, with a portico and a plaque commemorating a plantation of trees and the death of George III in 1820, reminds us that we are in the grounds of a great house, Stansted (stony place), which we can now look back to from the road. This estate was owned by the d'Aubignys, Fitzalans, and then Lumleys (Earls of Scarborough): and in recent times by Ponsonbys (Earls of Bessborough). The Lumleys were a powerful new family of Tudor times, and to their house came Edward VI and Elizabeth I; George I and William IV also paid visits to Stansted. The original house was destroyed by Parliamentarian forces in 1644 and a new house built in the 1690s, later enlarged by Wyatt. This in its turn was destroyed by fire in 1900, though the grey-faced service block remains. The red-brick mansion that we see is to the design of Reginald Blomfield, in the seventeenth-century style. It looks magnificent from the road and avenue, and of course the avenue and countryside look magnificent from it. The effect is the same as when Daniel Defoe came here in the 1720s and wrote: 'The Earl of Scarborough's fine seat at Stansted, a House surrounded with thick Woods, thro' which there are the most agreeable Vista's cut, that are to be seen anywhere in England; and particularly at the West

Stansted avenue

Opening, which is from the front of the house, they sit in the dining room, and see the Town and Harbour of Portsmouth, the Ships at Spithead, and also at St Helen's; which, when the Royal Navy happens to be there, is a most glorious sight.' In the trees to the right of the house is the chapel, visited by Keats in January 1819 and thought to have inspired passages from 'The Eve of St Mark' and 'The Eve of St Agnes'.

Now we turn and walk down the vast avenue, the vista from the house to the end being fully $1\frac{1}{2}$ miles. It was formerly lined with beeches all the way, but those in the first half had to be felled when they succumbed to beech disease (*Nectia ditissima*) following the parching summer of 1976. The effect of it is that the cell-wall structures break down, and the sap comes out through the bark as fungus. To our right are plantations of Spanish chestnut, and further on are Norway spruce and Douglas fir among the older oak. On the other side is Lyels Wood, with oak and hazel coppices. In the trees we will probably see grey squirrels, whose population has to be kept under control because of the damage they do to the trees – stripping off the barks of beeches to get at the sap: also possibly we may see fallow deer, who like to come to Stansted Forest, especially during the breeding season in June. And pheasants, bred for the organised shoots. At the end of the avenue is a grove of large beeches in the Sling, taking full advantage of the exposed chalk, which in most of the forest lies under a layer of clay with flints. Then it is across the Hampshire border and into Rowlands Castle, under the railway to where the village green curves around. The place of honour is occupied by a church, not Anglican but Congregationalist, and so not dedicated to any saint, of sturdy flint and brick.

Key to maps

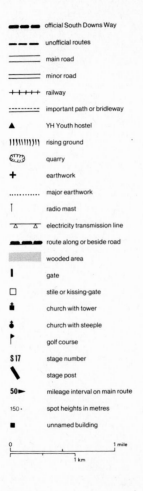

━ ━ ━	official South Downs Way
‒ ‒ ‒	unofficial routes
═══	main road
═══	minor road
++++	railway
‒‒‒‒‒	important path or bridleway
▲	YH Youth hostel
)))\\\\))))\\	rising ground
⬬	quarry
✛	earthwork
·········	major earthwork
⊤	radio mast
△ ── △	electricity transmission line
━ ━ ━	route along or beside road
	wooded area
❙	gate
☐	stile or kissing-gate
♦	church with tower
♠	church with steeple
⚑	golf course
S 17	stage number
╲	stage post
50►	mileage interval on main route
150 ·	spot heights in metres
■	unnamed building

```
0                                    1 mile
├──────────┬──────────┤
        1 km
```

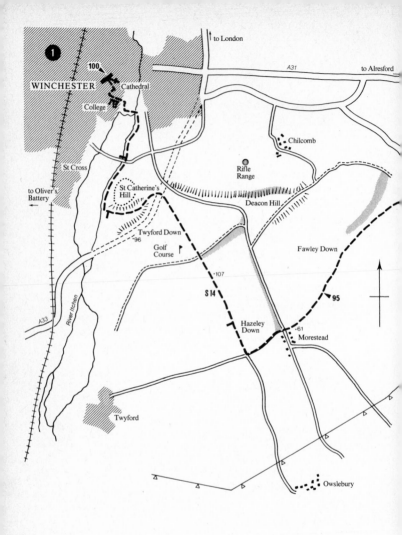

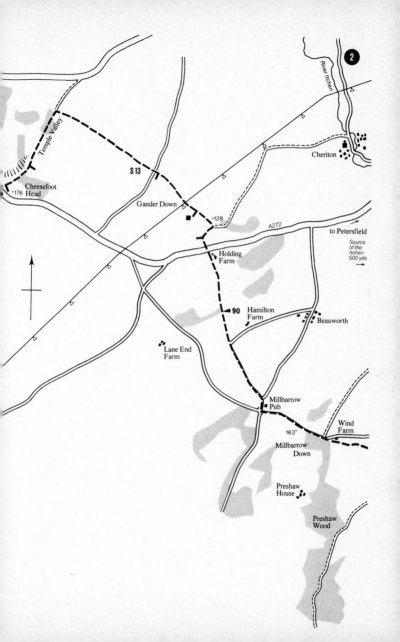

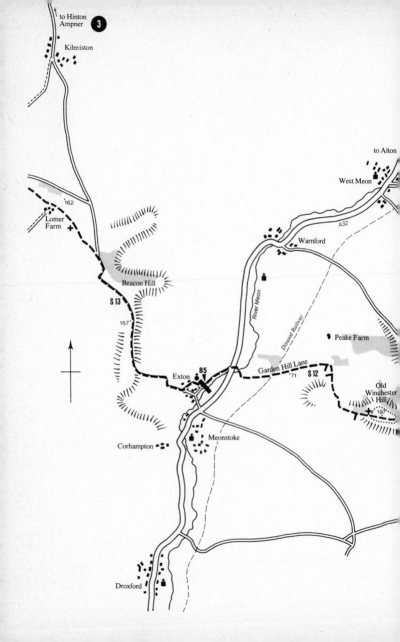

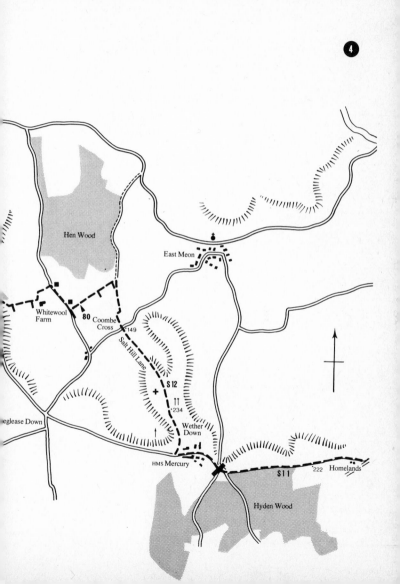

4

Hen Wood

East Meon

Whitewool
Farm

80 Coombe
Cross

·149

Salt Hill Lane

S 12

·234

eglease Down

Wether
Down

HMS Mercury

S 11

·222 Homelands

Hyden Wood

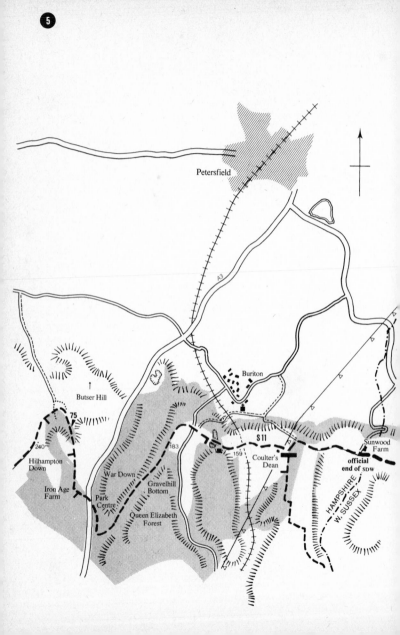

5

Petersfield

A3

Buriton

Butser Hill

↑

75

240

Hilhampton
Down

Iron Age
Farm

Park
Centre

War Down

Gravelhill
Bottom

Queen Elizabeth
Forest

183

159

S 11

Coulter's
Dean

official
end of SDW

Sunwood
Farm

HAMPSHIRE

W. SUSSEX

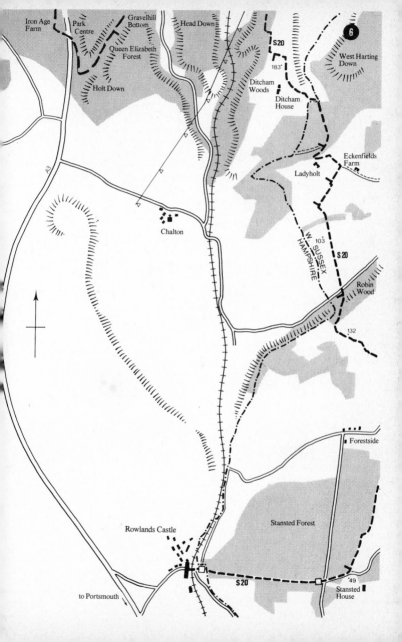

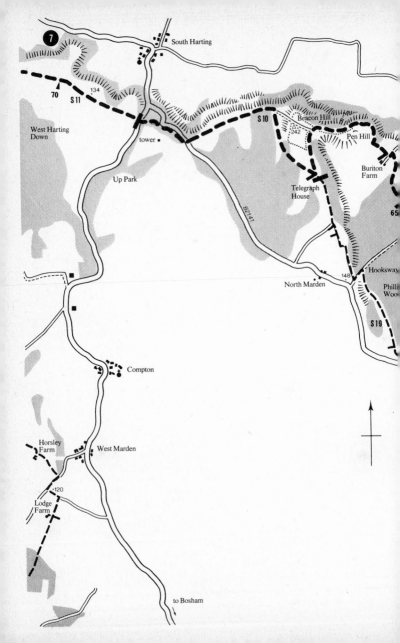

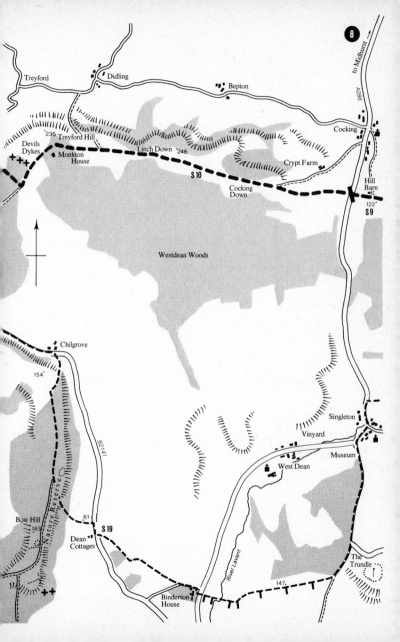

to Midhurst

A286

Treyford Didling Bepton

Cocking

Devils Dykes 235 Treyford Hill Linch Down 248

Monkton House

Crypt Farm

S 10

Cocking Down

Hill Barn

122

S 9

Westdean Woods

Chilgrove

154

B2141

Singleton

Vinyard

Museum

West Dean

Nature Reserve

Bow Hill 183

61

S 19

Dean Cottages

River Lavant

147

Binderton House

The Trundle

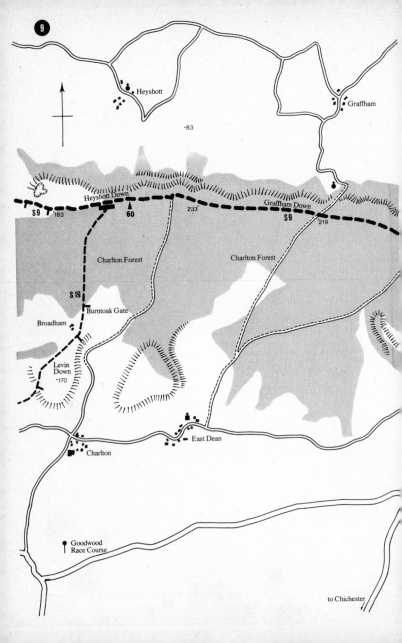

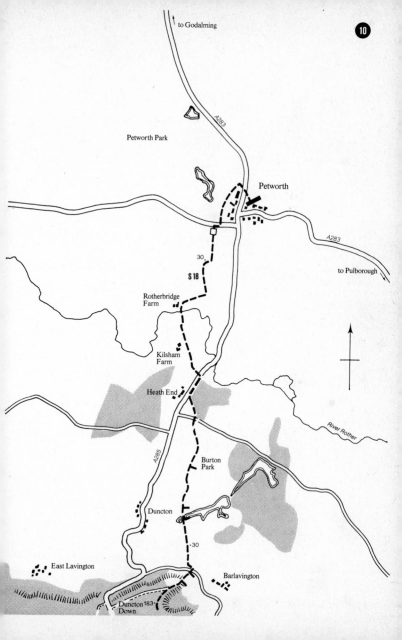

to Godalming

A283

Petworth Park

Petworth

A283

to Pulborough

30

S 18

Rotherbridge
Farm

Kilsham
Farm

Heath End

River Rother

A285

Burton
Park

Duncton

30

East Lavington

Barlavington

Duncton Down 183

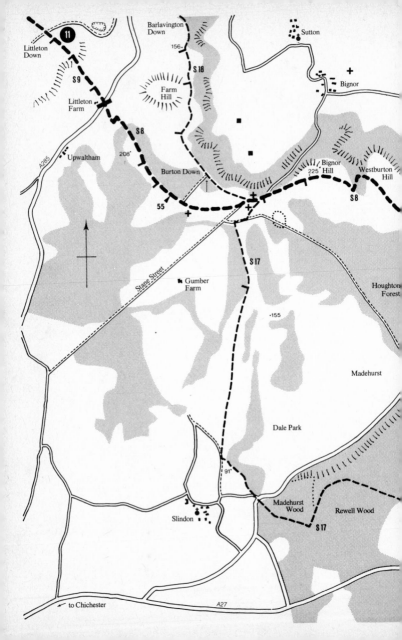

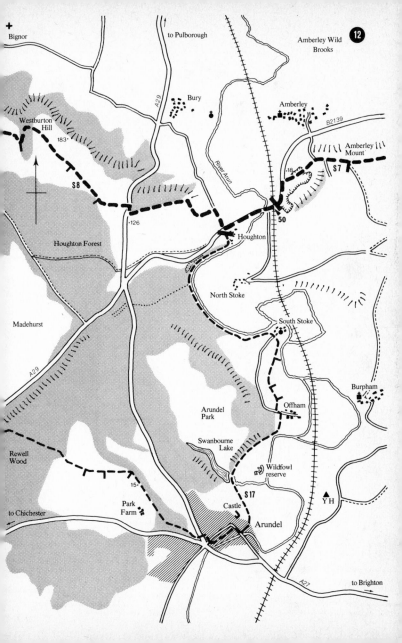

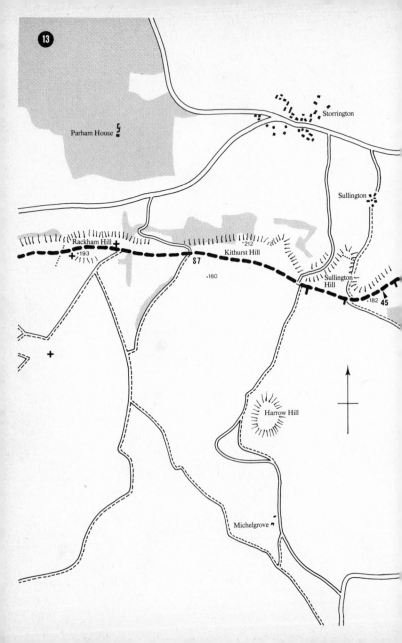

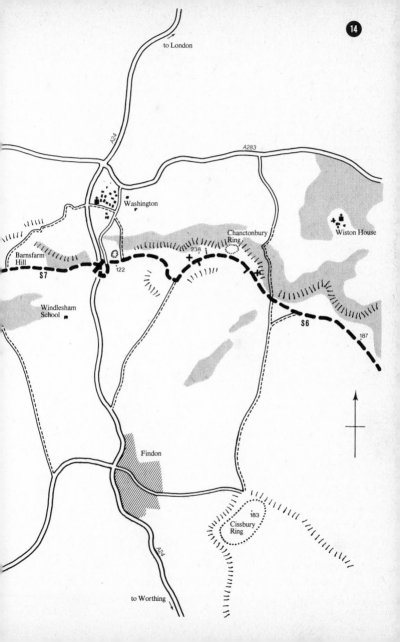

to London

A283

Washington

Wiston House

Chanctonbury
Ring

Barnsfarm
Hill

S7

238

122

Windlesham
School

S6

187

Findon

183
Cissbury
Ring

A24

to Worthing

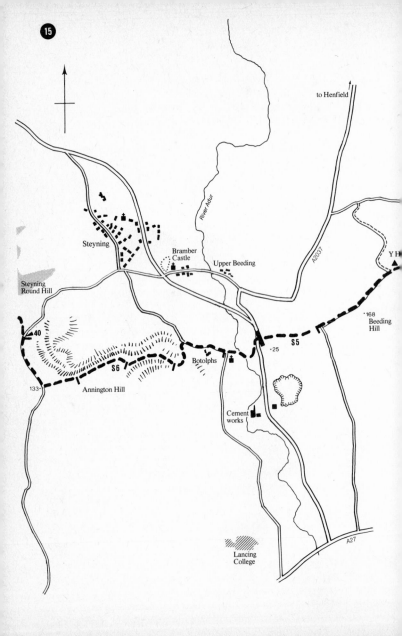

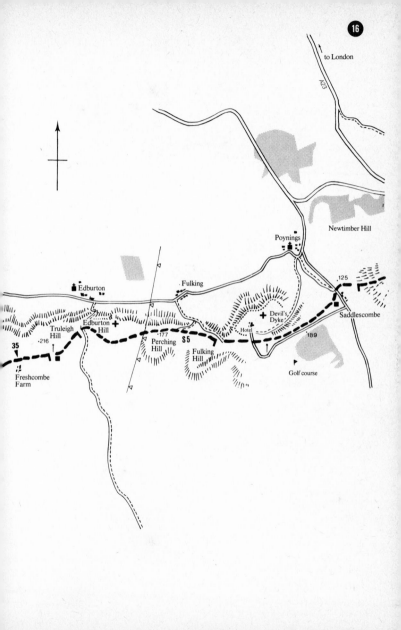

to London

A23

Newtimber Hill

Poynings

Fulking

Edburton

Devil's
Dyke

125

Saddlescombe

Truleigh
Hill

Edburton
Hill

Hotel

·216

Perching
Hill

·177

S5

189

35

Fulking
Hill

Golf course

Freshcombe
Farm

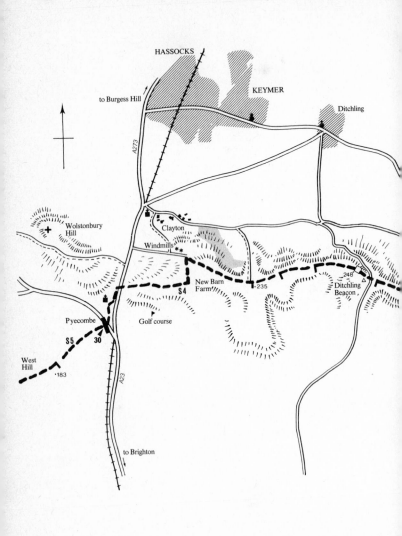

17

HASSOCKS

KEYMER

Ditchling

to Burgess Hill

A273

Wolstonbury
Hill

Clayton

Windmills

New Barn
Farm

·235

·246

Ditchling
Beacon

S4

Golf course

Pyecombe

S5   30

West
Hill

·183

A23

to Brighton

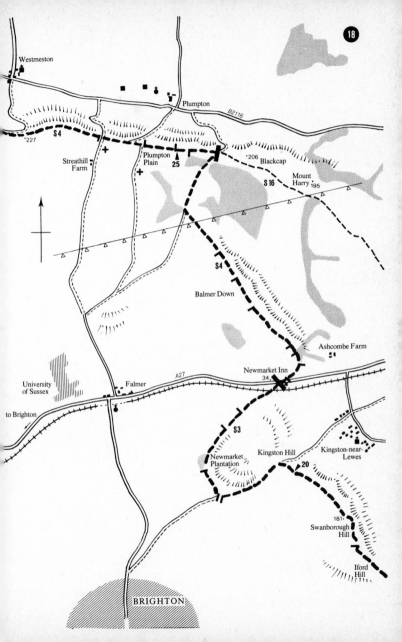

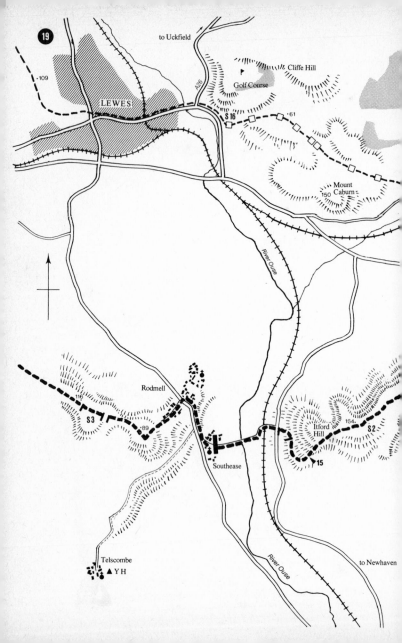

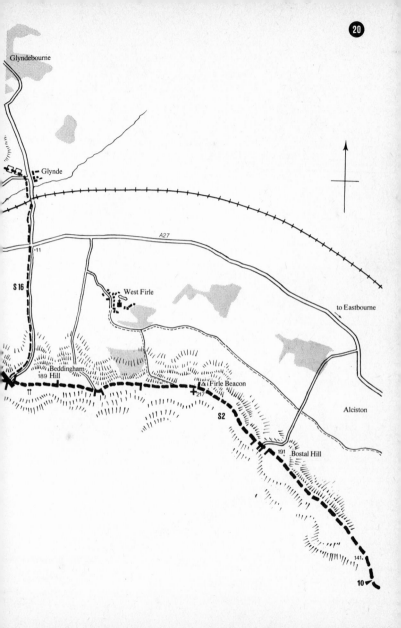

Glyndebourne

Glynde

A27

·11

S 16

West Firle

to Eastbourne

Beddingham
189 Hill

TT

▲ Firle Beacon
·217

S2

Alciston

191 Bostal Hill

141·

10

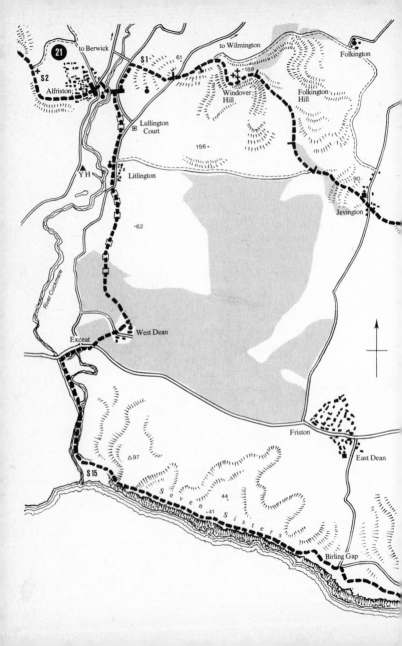

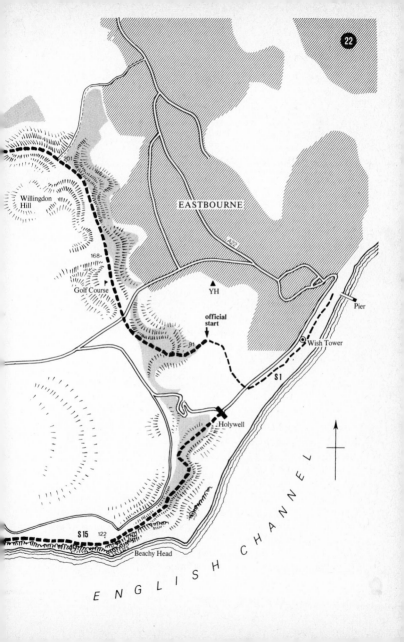

Appendix 1
Useful facts

USEFUL ORGANISATIONS

British Rail travel enquiries (01–928 5100). *Bus travel enquiries*:
Southdown (0273–606600), Hampshire Bus (0962–52352). *East
Sussex County Council*, Southover House, Lewes BN7 1YA
(07916–5400). *Long Distance Walker's Association*, 29 Appledown
Close, Alresford, Hampshire SO24 9ND (096273–4939).
Ramblers' Association, 1 Wandsworth Road, London SW8 2LJ
(01–582 6826).   *Society of Sussex Downsmen*, 93 Church Road,
Hove BN3 2BA (0273–771906). *South-East England Tourist
Board*, 1 Warwick Park, Tunbridge Wells TN2 5TA (0892–40766).
Southern England Tourist Board, Town Centre, Leigh Park,
Eastleigh SO5 4DE (1703–616027). *Weather forecasts*: Brighton
(0273–8091), Portsmouth (0705–8091). *West Sussex County
Council*, County Hall, Chichester PO19 1RQ (0243–777100).
Youth Hostels' Association, Trevelyan House, 8 St Stephen's Hill,
St Albans, AL1 2DY (56–55215).

POINTS OF INTEREST

(1) Two unofficial long-distance paths link to our main route. At
Stage 1, the Wealdway, an 80-mile route from Eastbourne to
Gravesend; at Stage 13, the Wayfarers' Walk, a 70-mile route from
Emsworth to Ingpen Beacon. (2) Pub opening-times on weekdays
are sometimes from 10.30 (or often 11 or 11.30)–14.30 and
18.00–22.30 or 23.00, and Sundays 12.00–14.00 and 19.00–22.30.
Your welcome will be greater if you take off your muddy boots
before being asked. (3) Churches are generally open in daytime,
especially at weekends: of those that are closed, the key is often
obtainable. They rely on your generosity. (4) Only very occasionally
will cattle be encountered actually on the route. But if they are,

keep an eye out for bulls, since the present law is unsatisfactory for walkers on public rights of way (confining total exclusion only to dairy-breed bulls of over ten months old). (5) Sussex has probably been more written about than any other English county, but the two general guides to the area which provide the best introduction are David Harrison's *Along the South Downs* (Cassell) and Ben Darby's *The South Downs* (Robert Hale).

COUNTRY CODE

All users of the countryside should observe the Country Code which is: (1) Guard against all risks of fire (2) Fasten all gates (3) Keep dogs under close control (4) Keep to public paths across farmland (5) Use gates and stiles to cross fences, hedges and walls (6) Leave livestock, crops and machinery alone (7) Take your litter home (8) Help to keep all water clean (9) Take special care on country roads (10) Make no unnecessary noise.

Appendix 2
The formation of the downs

In the Cretaceous period (c.135–65 million years ago) the whole of
what is now south-east England was covered by a shallow
fresh-water lake. Into this lake flowed great rivers which deposited
sands and clays. Later the lake became part of a tropical sea, of
increasing depth. During the millenia the shells of innumerable
marine organisms, mostly the minute foraminifera, drifted on to the
sea-bed as sediment. These shells were rich in calcium and other
minerals. Together with these, purely chemical precipitates
augmented the process whereby imperceptibly, at a rate of only
about 1 cm every thousand years, a great flat layer of pure white
limestone, 250 m or more deep, had formed below the sea,
stretching from Dorset and the Thames valley over into the Pas de
Calais. Later, within this chalk, a solution deriving from sponge
spicules and the remains of other siliceous matter became
re-deposited into horizontal seams, where they were formed into
flint.

In time the buckling of the surface of the earth caused this chalk
layer to contract into a shallow dome, still below the sea, with its
highest part over the centre of Sussex and its lowest in the area of
the Channel. Still later, the dome, now mostly covered by tertiary
deposits, emerged from the sea, and then began the process of
erosion. First the action of the waves, then of the rain and wind,
wore away the chalk and ground down flint nodules into pebbles.
Water flowed from the surface of the chalk because it could not
penetrate into it, due either to a high water-table level or to its
becoming frozen in glacial periods. The streams and rivers formed
great furrows over the dome and eventually the central part of the
chalk-bed entirely drained away, so that only the fringes – such as
the North and South Downs – remained. We still see the ends of the
furrows in the valleys of the Cuckmere, Ouse, Adur and Arun; and
the dry remnants of subsequent streams in the combes that shape
the hills.

Trundle, Old Winchester Hill, and St Catherine's Hill. The Belgii had wheel-turned pottery, gold coinage, and heavy ploughs. At the time of the Roman invasions they were polarised into two powerful groups, the Atrebates and the Catuvellauni.

Burial methods. In Neolithic times a few funerary mounds were erected for the burial of exceptionally important chiefs. The body was placed inside a wooden mortuary chamber and this was then covered by an enormous elongated mound of earth, up to 60 m long and usually facing east. In Sussex there are twelve long barrows, all on the downs. In the Bronze Age barrows became round, generally smaller, and more numerous. Of about 1,000 in Sussex, nearly all are on the downs, and about 400 of them line the South Downs Way, though most are now either ploughed over or scarcely visible. The great majority are 'bowl barrows' (like an inverted bowl, and with a ditch), but some are 'platform barrows' (flat topped), 'bell barrows' (a ledge between mound and ditch), or 'ring barrows' (a ditch but no mound). In the early Bronze Age the bodies were buried, but over a period the practice of cremation was substituted for inhumation. Cremation meant putting the ashes in or under an urn. Although the mound was usually made for only one burial, subsequent burials were often made in it. Personal weapons and possessions were placed in the grave. These have attracted grave robbers through the ages, so that practically all the barrows had been dug into before the advent of modern archaeology. For the mass of ordinary people, burial in the Stone or Bronze Ages meant having one's body dumped, or summarily buried in the earth, or perhaps flung down a redundant flint mine, until cremation later became more usual.

Appendix 4

Downland Farming

Land use. The land is enclosed into large fields of up to 60 acres or more, which are usually cultivated by rotation. For instance, a field might have three years of grass followed by five years of corn. In winter or spring the corn can be distinguished from the grass by its broader blades – the wheat broader than the barley. The first year of the grass is sometimes drilled with the last year of the corn, producing an undergrowth. The ley grasses used are generally more productive than the downland turf. The grass is used for different purposes; for instance, one year for lambs, the next for silage and hay, and the next for cattle. All except the very highest points are served by water from the mains pumped up to reservoirs.

Corn. The seed is drilled either in autumn or spring: this spreads the working time-scale and takes full advantage of the soil. The crop is barley or wheat: in summer, barley is recognisable by its beard and by its ear bending over on ripening. In spring, the crops are sprayed with insecticides and other chemicals from machinery that moves along 'tram-lines'. In a five-year cycle of corn, a field might be drilled with spring barley, then winter wheat, then winter barley, then spring wheat, etc. The harvest is from late July. Generally the downland chalk is less productive in yield than the greensands or clays, but is more economical to farm because the fields are larger and dryer.

Sheep. The classic South Downs sheep has been replaced by new cross-breeds which are larger and leaner (e.g., 'South Half Breed cross Suffolk' or 'Blue-faced Leicester cross Scottish black-face'). The sheep are reared for meat, their fleece being sold off cheaply. Five hundred ewes will produce at least 750 lambs, which are usually born in the barn in March and then released into the fields. By July, these are sold for slaughter except for 50 or so which are kept for breeding. The ewes can lamb for around six years.

Cattle. The most usual cattle are Friesians or Canadian Holsteins, both black-and-white (the Holsteins with larger legs). These are milking cows. Herds can be up to 250 head, but are usually around 100. Calves are usually born in autumn. Bullocks are sold off for fattening, and are slaughtered at 1–1½ years for beef. Cows produce their first calf at 2–3 years old, and one a year thereafter. The birth induces lactation, which lasts for 305 days, gradually declining in productivity. Milking is done twice daily, and the milk is sent to the farmers' co-operative Milk Marketing Board.

Appendix 5

Heights of the principal downs

		metres			metres
S1	Beachy Head	163		Rackham Hill	193
	Willingdon Hill	201	S8	Westburton Hill	184
	Wilmington Hill	214		Bignor Hill	225
S2	Bostal Hill	191		Burton Down	245
	Firle Beacon	217	S9	Littleton Down	255
	Beddingham Hill	189		Graffham Down	230
S3	Swanborough Hill	192		Heyshott Down	233
	Newmarket Hill	197	S10	Linch Down	248
S4	Blackcap	206		Treyford Hill	235
	Ditchling Beacon	248		Beacon Hill	242
S5	West Hill	211		Harting Down	227
	Devil's Dyke Hill	217	S11	Holt Down	200
	Edburton Hill	192		Butser Hill	270
	Truleigh Hill	216	S12	Wether Down	234
S6	Steyning Round Hill	189		Old Winchester Hill	212
	Chanctonbury Hill	238	S13	Beacon Hill	201
S7	Barnsfarm Hill	206	S14	Cheesefoot Head	176
	Kithurst Hill	213			

Appendix 6

Principal downland wildflowers

English name	Scientific name	Family	Flowering
Basil (Wild)	*Clinopodium vulgare*	Deadnettle	July/Sept.
Bluebell	*Endymion nonscriptus*	Lily	April/June
Burnet Saxifrage	*Pimpinella saxifraga*	Parsley	July/Sept
Campion (Red)	*Melandrium rubrum*	Pink	April/August
Celandine (Lesser)	*Ranunculus ficaria*	Buttercup	March/May
Centaury (Common)	*Centaurium minus*	Gentian	July/Sept
Cowslip	*Primula veris*	Primrose	April/May
Daisy	*Bellis perennis*	Daisy	March/Oct
Dandelion	*Taraxacum officinale*	Daisy	March/Oct
Dropwort	*Filipendula vulgaris*	Rose	May/August
Flax (Fairy)	*Linum catharticum*	Linaceae	May/Oct
Fleawort (Field)	*Senecio intergrifolius*	Daisy	May/June
Harebell	*Campanula rotundifolia*	Bellflower	July/Sept
Hawkweed (Mouse-eared)	*Pilosella officinarum*	Daisy	May/August
Horseshoe Vetch	*Hippocrepis comosa*	Pea	May/July
Kidney Vetch	*Anthyllis vulneraria*	Pea	May/August
Knapweed (Greater)	*Centaurea scabiosa*	Daisy	July/Sept
Lady's Bedstraw	*Galium verum*	Bedstraw	July/August
Marjoram	*Origanum vulgare*	Deadnettle	July/Sept
Milkwort (Common)	*Polygala vulgaris*	Milkwort	May/Sept
Nettle (Stinging)	*Urtica dioica*	Nettle	June/Sept
Orchid (Common Spotted)	*Orchis fuchsii*	Orchid	May/August
Orchid (Early Purple)	*Orchis mascula*	Orchid	April/June

Parsley (Cow)	*Anthriscus sylvestris*	Parsley	April/June
Poppy (Field)	*Papaver rhoeas*	Poppy	June/August
Primrose	*Primula vulgaris*	Primrose	March/May
Ragwort (Hoary)	*Senecio erucifolius*	Daisy	July/Sept
Rampion (Round Headed)	*Phyteuma tenerum*	Bellflower	July/August
Rockrose	*Helianthemum chamaecistus*	Cistaceae	May/Sept
St John's Wort (Common)	*Hypericum perforatum*	St John's Wort	July/Sept
Scabious (Small)	*Scabiosa columbaria*	Scabious	July/Sept
Speedwell (Germander)	*Veronica chamaedrys*	Snap-dragon	March/July
Thistle (Carline)	*Carlina vulgaris*	Daisy	July/Sept
Thistle (Stemless)	*Cirsium acaule*	Daisy	July/Sept
Thyme (Wild)	*Thymus drucei*	Deadnettle	June/Sept
Violet (Hairy)	*Viola hirta*	Violet	March/May
Vipers Bugloss	*Echium vulgare*	Forget-me-not	June/Sept
Willowherb (Rosebay)	*Chamaenerion augustifolium*	Willow-herb	July/Sept

Index of places and people

(Route specifics in **bold** type)